PHILADELPHIA
READS
Raising a City of Readers

This Book is
Brought to You by
The Tom and Adrienne Jacoby
Book Bank at
Philadelphia READS

Andrew Podnieks is the author of more than sixty books on hockey.
The following is a select list:

Hockey Superstitions

Honoured Canadiens

Players: The Ultimate A–Z Guide of Everyone Who Has Ever Played in the NHL

The Complete Hockey Dictionary

World of Hockey: Celebrating a Century of the IIHF

A Day in the Life of the Maple Leafs

Canada's Olympic Hockey History, 1920–2010

A Canadian Saturday Night

*Portraits of the Game: Classic Photographs from the Turofsky Collection
at the Hockey Hall of Fame*

ANDREW PODNIEKS

SID VS OVI

CROSBY AND OVECHKIN - NATURAL-BORN RIVALS

McClelland & Stewart

Library and Archives Canada Cataloguing in Publication

Podnieks, Andrew
Sid vs. Ovi : Crosby and Ovechkin, natural-born rivals / Andrew Podnieks.

ISBN 978-0-7710-7116-4

. 1. Crosby, Sidney, 1987–. 2. Ovechkin, Alexander, 1985–. 3. Hockey players – Biography. 4. National Hockey League – Biography. I. Title.

GV848.5.A1P643 2011   796.962092'2   C2011-902198-6

We acknowledge the financial support of the Government of Canada through the Book Publishing Industry Development Program and that of the Government of Ontario through the Ontario Media Development Corporation's Ontario Book Initiative. We further acknowledge the support of the Canada Council for the Arts and the Ontario Arts Council for our publishing program.

Published simultaneously in the United States of America by McClelland & Stewart Ltd., P.O. Box 1030, Plattsburgh, New York 12901

Library of Congress Control Number: 2011925614

Cover art: © NHLI via Getty Images

Typeset in Palatino by M&S, Toronto
Printed and bound in Canada

This book was produced using recycled materials.

McClelland & Stewart Ltd.
75 Sherbourne Street
Toronto, Ontario
M5A 2P9
www.mcclelland.com

1   2   3   4   5   15   14   13   12   11

CONTENTS

3. OVECHKIN TAKES CONTROL

4. CROSBY GETS TO THE CUP FIRST

5. FULL-ON RIVALRY

6. CROSBY DOES IT ALL

7. THE RIVALRY DAMAGED

EPILOGUE

PITTSBURGH AND WASHINGTON:

A HOCKEY PRIMER

Like a boxer who is repeatedly knocked to the canvas only to get up in the final round and win the fight, the Pittsburgh Penguins are the most survival-tested organization in sports. The team was one of six granted a spot in the NHL in 1967 as part of the doubling of the league from six teams to twelve. Other new franchises included state rivals Philadelphia, St. Louis, Oakland, Los Angeles, and Minnesota.

Yet, in each of the three distinct periods of the Penguins, the team faced the very real threat of relocation, such was the sorry state of its on-ice performance and off-ice finances. The first chapter in the team's history started in 1967 and continued to 1983. The Penguins missed the playoffs in eight of those seventeen seasons and did little damage in the years they did qualify. The lowest point came in 1975, when the Penguins, ahead in the quarter-finals against the Islanders, having won the first three games of the best-of-seven, lost the next four and were eliminated, the first time a team had blown a 3–0 lead since 1942.

At the same time, the team declared bankruptcy, when creditors lined up demanding to be repaid on their investment. It seemed almost certain that the Pens would move to Denver. However, another group of investors stepped in and saved the day, keeping the Pens in Pittsburgh.

The next low point came in 1983–84 when the Penguins had a record of 16–58–6, their 38 points putting them dead last in the league. They were averaging fewer than seven thousand fans a game and again were in financial difficulty, but finishing last, which they later admitted they did intentionally, entitled them to the first overall draft choice in June 1984. They selected Mario Lemieux, but even this simple announcement turned into an embarrassing moment.

The whole hockey world knew well in advance that Lemieux was in a class by himself, but in the days leading up to the draft his agent and the team's general manager, Eddie Johnston, couldn't agree on a contract. So, when Lemieux's name was called on draft day at the Montreal Forum, Mario remained in his seat, neither shaking the GM's hand nor coming to the stage for the traditional donning of the team sweater.

Soon enough, though, Lemieux signed with the Penguins, changing the course of the franchise – though not right away. As the team was slowly constructed around their star player, it missed the playoffs for the next five of six seasons.

Lemieux developed into the game's greatest player not named Gretzky, and the Penguins went on to win the Stanley Cup in 1991 and '92. But by 1997, Lemieux was fed up with the league's refusal to crack down on defensive tactics such as hooking, holding, and interference, and he retired. Much of his salary had been in the form of deferred payments, and soon after he hung up his skates, the team went into bankruptcy again, Lemieux's millions seemingly lost. He decided to buy the team using this money as equity, both saving the team, again, and recouping his money (sort of).

In order to maximize his investment, as it were, he returned to the ice and played successfully for several more years. All along, he had one interest off-ice – to build a new arena.

Nicknamed The Igloo, the Civic Auditorium and Mellon Arena was old and without luxury boxes, had few revenue streams beyond ticket sales, and would be the ruin of the team if it wasn't replaced. Years of frustration forced Lemieux to put the team up for sale early in the 2005–06 season, this despite the fact the team had just won the right to draft Sidney Crosby. Research In Motion's co-CEO, billionaire Jim Balsillie, bought the team, but as soon as Balsillie made it clear his intention was to move the Penguins, NHL commissioner Gary Bettman stepped in and disallowed the sale.

Eventually, Lemieux got the City of Pittsburgh on board for a new facility. He retired because of heart palpitations in early 2006, and Crosby became the focus of the franchise, taking the team to a Cup win in 2009. The Consol Energy Center opened soon after, and the Penguins are now a thriving franchise in a league awash with financially unstable teams.

Although the Washington Capitals have never had the financial troubles of the Penguins, they, too, have had a history clearly divided. Washington was granted a team in 1974, along with Kansas City (the ill-fated Scouts), which promptly went out and had the worst season in the history of sports, the Caps winning only eight of eighty games in the first year, scoring just 181 goals and surrendering 446. They won only one of forty road games, losing a record thirty-seven in a row. They missed the playoffs each of their first eight years in the league, but in 1982 the team turned a corner when incoming GM David Poile engineered a blockbuster deal with Montreal that got them Rod Langway, Doug Jarvis, Brian Engblom, and Craig Laughlin.

The Caps then made the playoffs for fourteen straight years but never went far until 1998, when they made their first and only trip to the Stanley Cup finals. They were swept in four games by the vastly superior Detroit Red Wings, and a year later Ted Leonsis took control of the team. A more aggressive owner, Leonsis made a huge splash in 2001 when he lured Jaromir Jagr away from the Penguins, signing the scoring champion and MVP to a seven-year contract worth $77 million, the largest in league history.

While it was a noble attempt to bring success and celebrity to the team, the results were disastrous, and Jagr was traded three years later. Undaunted, Leonsis later signed Alex Ovechkin, to the new biggest contract in NHL history, midway through the 2007–08 season, a thirteen-year deal worth $124 million. Ovechkin had been selected by the Caps first overall at the 2004 Entry Draft and after only two and a half years established himself as one of the most dynamic goalscorers in the game. Ovechkin has proved popular, later becoming captain, but he has yet to deliver playoff success. His presence, though, has ensured sellouts at the Verizon Center (formerly the MCI Center) and financial stability for the team, and, in turn, he has been given a contract of value commensurate to his star value.

And so, as the second decade of the twenty-first century unfolds, Pittsburgh and Washington have the two best players in the game on their respective rosters and have created a rivalry around these stars. They are both captains of their teams and have won several individual awards, but so far only Crosby has won the Stanley Cup. Ovechkin still has plenty of time to win his own, as both are only now reaching their prime. The rivalry is young and the Cup old. Who will get there next?

1

FROM THE CRADLE TO THE NHL

GENESIS

1987

To understand the genesis of the Crosby-Ovechkin rivalry, one needs to go back to the year 1987, a momentous year in the history of hockey, and a key date in the origins of hockey's greatest rivalry of the twenty-first century.

Troy Crosby, Sidney's father, was drafted 240th overall by the Montreal Canadiens at the 1984 NHL Entry Draft. The seventeen-year-old goalie, who turned eighteen September 11 that year, was a huge Habs fan and realized a dream just by being selected by the *bleu, blanc, et rouge*. That was as far as his dream would go, however. In today's game, a 240th draft choice has a chance, though very small, of making it to the NHL, but thirty years ago, the chance was virtually nil.

Troy had no illusions. He didn't go to the minors and try to work his way up. He wasn't interested in being a career minor leaguer, and he had no desire to pursue a career in Europe. Instead, Troy soon got married and settled in Cole Harbour, Nova Scotia, a suburban community just a half hour's drive from Halifax, where he'd been born. Indeed, he was still only twenty years old when, on August 7, 1987, his wife, Trina, gave birth to a healthy boy they named Sidney Patrick.

The front-page headline in the *Globe and Mail* that day read: "Marathon swimmer nearing her goal," in reference to

Vicki Keith's attempt to swim a double crossing of Lake Ontario non-stop.

Several days later, an announcement in the *Halifax Mail Star* read: "CROSBY – Troy and Trina (nee Forbes) are pleased to announce the birth of their son, Sidney Patrick Crosby, born 10:25 am, August 7, 1987, at the Grace Maternity Hospital. Weight: 8 lbs., 2 ozs." Close, but, no, the newborn did not weigh 8 pounds, 7 ounces – that would have been too "87 freaky," even by Crosby's standards.

A simple announcement, it marked the arrival of the boy who would become the world's greatest hockey player.

At about the same time, Mario Lemieux, Wayne Gretzky, and Canada's other greatest hockey players were gathering in Toronto for training camp in preparation for the 1987 Canada Cup. What *is* freaky is that Lemieux was drafted first overall in 1984, when Troy Crosby was selected 239 names later. The two played junior against each other, Mario for Laval Voisins (1981–84), and Troy for Verdun (1983–84). "I've been told he's got a photo in his den where he's looking back into the net . . . I was on a breakaway, and I roofed it," Mario revealed of his playing career against Troy. "He was a little late on it."

In all, ten players from Canada's 1987 Canada Cup team went on to be inducted into the Hockey Hall of Fame, but the names of Lemieux and Gretzky tower over all others from that tournament. For starters, training camp was the final and defining moment of Lemieux's maturation. Dogging it one day during practice, he was excoriated by Gretzky for wasting his talent by settling for mediocre greatness instead of pushing his boundaries every day. Gretzky said flat-out that Mario was a more talented player than he, and capable of so much more than what he'd already accomplished – a remarkable reprimand, given Lemieux's incredible career to date.

The public dressing-down inspired Lemieux, who raised his game during the Canada Cup, and then throughout the rest of his career, a career that ended with the veteran Lemieux playing alongside the rookie Crosby, eighteen years old in January 2006 when Mario retired.

Lemieux later credited Gretzky with taking his game one level higher, and the two were regular linemates at the 1987 Canada Cup, notably during the crucial finals games, thanks to coach Glen Sather. Lemieux led all scorers with eleven goals in the tournament, and Gretzky assisted on nine of them.

Canada and the Soviet Union disposed of their semi-finals opponents, Czechoslovakia and Sweden, respectively, to set up a dream finals, a best-of-three between hockey's two supreme powers. While Canada's roster was deep in talent, the Soviets were no less talented. The KLM troika of Vladimir Krutov-Igor Larionov-Sergei Makarov were in the primes of their career, and the rest of the roster was a who's who of great Soviets – Fetisov, Kasatonov, Kamensky, Kravchuk, Nemchinov, and Svetlov. Of course, behind the bench was Viktor Tikhonov, a legend in his own right.

Hockey may have been more politically charged during the 1972 Summit Series, which ended with Paul Henderson's heroic goal in the final minute of the final game, but never before or since has hockey been witness to a three-game series as in 1987, a set that Tikhonov – the losing coach, no less – later called the best three hockey games ever played. No one could provide a contradictory example.

Game one was back and forth. The Soviets built a commanding 4–1 lead midway through the game, only to see Canada chip away and finally take the lead on a Gretzky goal with just 2:59 left in regulation. Victory was now in sight. But the goal had barely been announced over the PA system when

Andrei Khomutov tied the game, just 32 seconds later, to send the game to overtime. Just 5:33 into the fourth period, Alexander Semak scored the winner to send the Montreal Forum fans into the street in dismay.

Game two was even more dramatic, given the must-win situation for Canada. Incredibly, Canada could not protect a lead and the relentless Soviets rallied not once, not twice, but three times. Canada built a solid 3–1 lead in the first period, only to allow the Soviets to tie the game. The home side went ahead 4–3 and 5–4, but Kamensky was the hero, scoring with just 64 seconds left in the third to force the game to overtime again in a 5–5 game.

This game wasn't decided in the first period of the unlimited sudden-death overtime. It wasn't until 10:07 of the second overtime that Mario Lemieux banged in a loose puck past goalie Evgeni Belosheikin to give Canada a 6–5 win and force a deciding third game. Upon retiring in 1999, Gretzky cited this second game as the finest of his international career. He played some forty-five minutes of the game and registered assists on five of Canada's six goals.

Game three in Hamilton was the ultimate showdown of skill and tension-filled excitement ever played. The Soviets had leads of 3–0 and 4–2 in the first period and looked to have Canada down and out, but then the home side scored the only three goals of the second to take a 5–4 lead. Again the Canadians couldn't hold a third-period lead, however, and Semak tied the game midway through the third to suggest a third overtime game was imminent.

But with less than two minutes to go and a faceoff deep in Canada's end, Sather noticed his counterpart had made a tactical error. Star defenceman Vyacheslav Fetisov was not on the ice. Sather sent his best players out, and soon enough

Gretzky was carrying the puck into the Soviet end with Lemieux trailing over Gretzky's right shoulder and defenceman Larry Murphy racing to the goal. Gretzky made a drop pass, and Mario buried a wrist shot over Belosheikin's glove. This time, Canada held the fort and won, 6–5, capping the greatest games in international hockey history.

But while these games were being played out on ice before millions of hockey-mad fans in Canada and the Soviet Union, something as incredible occurred far away from the television cameras. Gretzky invited the entire Green Unit, which included the KLM line plus defencemen Fetisov and Alexei Kasatonov, to his house in nearby Brantford, Ontario, accompanied, of course, by coach Tikhonov. (In the Soviet days of Communism, no player could be trusted.)

Larionov and Fetisov in particular spoke English conversationally, and for the first time Gretzky learned of their desire to play in the NHL. Indeed, he learned, this was the aspiration of most world-class Soviets, but under the Iron Curtain regime it was not likely to happen.

Who could have known that thanks to perestroika just a few years later, every Soviet guest at this barbeque in Brantford would be playing in the NHL? And who could have known that a two-year-old boy in Moscow, one Alexander Mikhailovich Ovechkin, would grow up to usher in a new wave of modern Russians who could play where they wanted, when they wanted, and for however much they wanted, in large part because of events in 1987? Even more ironic, Ovechkin's first NHL hero was none other than Mario Lemieux.

The 1987 Canada Cup was never to have an equal. Perestroika eroded the developmental system for hockey in the new Russia for many years, and the United States, with its burgeoning and flourishing programs, quickly supplanted

Russia as the main rivals to Canada, as indicated by the 1991 Canada Cup and the 1996 World Cup of Hockey.

Perhaps the lone significant game between Canada and Russia in the 1990s was the 1992 Olympic gold-medal game when the Soviets/Russians were in a transition phase. Called the CIS (Commonwealth of Independent States), the team covered over the "CCCP" on its sweaters and listened to the Olympic anthem, not the Soviet anthem, after victories. In that Olympics' finals, they beat Canada, 3–1, and since 1992, the Russians have yet to even appear in another Olympic gold-medal game. Further, they didn't win World Championship gold again until 2008, a drought of fifteen years after they won in 1993, in Munich.

After 1987, international hockey was never the same, and neither was the Canada-Russia rivalry – until Crosby and Ovechkin burst onto the hockey scene.

CLOSE, BUT NO FACEOFF

2004 WORLD U20 (JUNIOR) CHAMPIONSHIP

There is a small detail associated with the NHL Entry Draft that is rarely significant but that had a major impact on the Crosby-Ovechkin rivalry. The draft is held annually towards the end of June, after the Stanley Cup is won and the NHL Awards Ceremony has taken place. However, to be eligible, players must be eighteen years old by September 15 of their draft year. In other words, if one player is born on September 14 and another on September 16, the former is eligible for the draft a year earlier than the latter.

Take the case of John Tavares, for instance. He was born on September 20, 1991, but such was the frenzy around his imminent position as a first-overall draft choice that teams wanted him to be eligible for 2008 instead of 2009. Rumours circulated that he might even sign a pro contract on his eighteenth birthday – fully a year before being draft-eligible – in order to start his pro career sooner and to be a free agent after one year, so that he could then sign with whatever NHL team he so desired. In the end, Tavares and his family decided not to challenge the legality of the NHL's draft regulations. He played a fourth year of junior and was selected first overall by the New York Islanders in 2009.

This birthdate rule had major and opposite implications for Crosby and Ovechkin.

Crosby was born on August 7, 1987, and Ovechkin was born on September 17, 1985. As a result, Crosby was drafted when he was seventeen years old, in July 2005, while Ovechkin was drafted just one year earlier, despite being nearly two years older. Had Ovechkin been born just two days earlier on the calendar, he would have been draft-eligible for 2003, not 2004. Guess what team had the first overall selection in 2003? The Pittsburgh Penguins! Two days' difference prevented the two best players in the game from being teammates, not adversaries.

As well, other circumstances prevented the two stars from facing each other on ice earlier in their careers. The natural starting point for a matchup would have been the World U18 Championship, but the calendar was again the culprit. This tournament is held towards the end of the season. For Ovechkin, who started playing in the Russian senior pro league as a sixteen-year-old, playing in the U18 was a natural conclusion to the year. But for Crosby, who skated for Rimouski Oceanic in the Quebec Major Junior Hockey League (QMJHL), playing in the U18 was impossible because he was deep into playoffs and Memorial Cup games and was unavailable to Team Canada.

Despite being only sixteen years old, Ovechkin played at the 2002 U18 World Championship in Slovakia. He led all players with 14 goals and 18 points in only eight games, but his Russians lost to the United States, 3–1, on the final day of the round-robin medal group and had to settle for a silver medal. Nonetheless, he had already made his mark. His trademark shot, his bull-in-a-China-shop hitting, and his tremendous competitive desire were already in evidence,

Canada led 2–1 after forty minutes, the Russians rallied for two goals in the third period to win, 3–2. A further irony is that one of Canada's goalies was Marc-Andre Fleury, the player selected first overall in the 2003 draft by the Penguins in place of Ovechkin.

During this same 2002–03 season, Sidney Crosby was a fifteen-year-old playing for Shattuck-St. Mary's, a prep high school in Faribault, Minnesota, renowned for its sports programs. Many well-known players before and since attended "SSM," including Jonathan Toews, Zach Parise, Ty Conklin, Angelo Esposito, and Ty Gretzky, one of Wayne's sons, who was drafted by the Chicago Cubs in 2011.

Jack Johnson, selected third overall by Carolina, two spots behind Crosby in the 2005 NHL Entry Draft, was a teammate at Shattuck and the two have remained friends ever since (indeed, they hung out together during the week of the 2005 Entry Draft). The next year, Crosby was selected by Rimouski first overall in the midget draft, and he returned to Canada to begin his major junior career after leading SSM to a national championship.

The Shattuck connections run much deeper than just a list of notable alumni, however. In the fall of 2010, Taylor Crosby, Sidney's fifteen-year-old sister, enrolled at SSM to join the school's U16 girls' team. But she decided to follow her father, rather than her older brother, by strapping on the pads and playing goal. Troy, the family's patriarch, was drafted by the Montreal Canadiens in 1987, just months before Sidney was born. Across the hall, Anthony Brodeur, sixteen-year-old son of legendary goalie Martin, played for the U16 boys' team, and the previous year Stephanie Lemieux, daughter of Mario, attended Shattuck.

It wasn't until the summer of 2010, when Taylor was old enough, that the siblings played seriously together. Sidney took shots on Taylor at the family house, and his sister fared pretty well. "I was so nervous," she said. "We didn't keep count, but I did stop a couple. I was happy with that."

The Crosby-Ovechkin excitement started to gain a little momentum during the 2003–04 season. Ovechkin was in his third year of pro hockey with Dynamo Moscow, and Crosby was tearing apart the QMJHL with his scoring exploits. At training camp in December 2003 for the upcoming World U20 event, Crosby made Team Canada as a sixteen-year-old, only the sixth player so honoured (after Bill Campbell, Jay Bouwmeester, Eric Lindros, Wayne Gretzky, and Jason Spezza).

Ovechkin, of course, who had played the previous year, was on the Russian roster, but the two nations played in opposite groups during the preliminary round robin, meaning they would face each other only in the playoff elimination round, if at all. Ovechkin's teammates that year in Finland were a fairly anonymous lot with two notable exceptions, Evgeni Malkin and Alexander Semin. Ovechkin and Malkin became good friends off the ice but loyalties were soon to be divided during the NHL season when Malkin and Crosby became teammates. Malkin was drafted second behind Ovechkin in 2003. Semin, meanwhile, joined Ovechkin in Washington after the Capitals had drafted him thirteenth overall in 2002.

future NHL stars, notably Ryan Getzlaf, Jeff Carter, Dion Phaneuf, Mike Richards, Brent Seabrook, Brent Burns, and Fleury. Canada rolled over the opposition to reach the gold-medal game, outscoring the competition by a 32–5 aggregate in five games. Crosby-Ovechkin history would have to wait, however, because the Russians lost to Finland 4–3 in the quarter-finals and the players never faced off against each other.

Russia had defeated Canada in the two previous gold-medal games, and Finland's win over the Russians in 2004 was nothing short of shocking. Ovechkin scored a go-ahead goal midway through the third period to make it a 3–2 score for Russia, but the Finns rallied to tie the game two and a half minutes later. Valtteri Filppula sent the 5,720 fans in Helsinki into a state of frenzy by scoring the winner with just thirteen seconds left in regulation time. Ovechkin went home, and Canada faced the United States for gold.

That game was not without its drama. Canada was in control, leading 3–1 after two periods, but a colossal gaffe by Fleury gave the Americans a 4–3 win. The goalie whiffed on a Patrick O'Sullivan shot early in the final period and didn't look particularly solid on the tying goal, off the stick of Ryan Kesler. But the winning goal came without the Americans touching the puck. Fleury played the puck in front of his own goal, but his clearing attempt hit his defenceman Braydon Coburn and bounced past him into the net. Stunned, the Canadians could not recover and had to settle for a third straight silver.

Crosby finished his first important international tournament with two goals and five points in six games. His first goal, late in a 7–2 win over Switzerland on December 28, 2004, made him the youngest player to score a goal in U20 history. He started the tournament as a fourth-line player, but with every game he was given a bit more responsibility, playing on the power play, getting more ice time, and responding in kind with better play. Midway through the tourney, Crosby even betrayed a bit of confidence: "I've been happy with the way the tournament has gone for me," he said on New Year's Day. "I'm getting more and more comfortable, and I think the coaching staff has shown more and more confidence in me as the tournament has gone on."

But when he arrived back in Canada after the tournament, he talked only of the bitterness of the gold-medal loss and his promise to make sure that would never happen again.

In the end, Crosby and Ovechkin were in the same city playing the same event, but they didn't skate against each other in the same game. That momentous occasion would have to wait another 364 days.

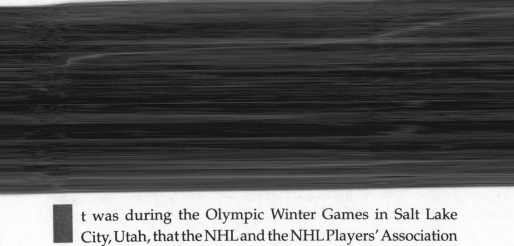

t was during the Olympic Winter Games in Salt Lake City, Utah, that the NHL and the NHL Players' Association (NHLPA) jointly announced that the next edition of the World Cup of Hockey would be played two and a half years later. Like all other Canada Cups/World Cups, it would be played before the start of the NHL season. There was one fact about the event that stood out, however. The championship game was to be played at the Air Canada Centre (ACC), in Toronto, on September 14, 2004. This ominous date marked the last day of the Collective Bargaining Agreement, or CBA, between players and league, and even in 2002 it was clear its expiration at midnight on September 14, 2004, was to become hockey's Armageddon.

The World Cup was a huge success with fans in Canada and produced excellent television ratings thanks to a dramatic 2–1 win by Canada over Finland in the climactic game. The postgame celebration started awkwardly as captain Mario Lemieux looked as if he weren't exactly sure what to do with Frank Gehry's trophy, perhaps not the ugliest prize ever created but a perplexing one all the same. Opaque and two-tiered, it was intended to remind one of ice, but its wavy and boxed shape, with a small dish atop onto which the winners' names were to be engraved, was out of the ordinary, to be sure.

Once the ACC fans went home and the players dispersed, the hockey world came to a standstill. The World Cup excitement reached its climax mere hours before the lockout began, a lockout that had "months and months" written all over its pockmarked forehead. In truth, the NHL and the Players' Association had barely begun serious discussions prior to the expiration of the old Collective Bargaining Agreement, league commissioner Gary Bettman steadfastly refusing to allow the league to play games until a salary cap was in place to control expenses while NHLPA Executive Director Bob Goodenow was equally stubborn in promising that the players would never sign a new agreement that included said salary cap. Almost a year later, salary cap in place, the two sides signed a new deal, but both leaders will go down in history as the men who prevented the Stanley Cup from being contested for the first time in the trophy's glorious history (the 1919 finals were cancelled after five games because of the influenza pandemic).

Players had already started making contingency plans of one sort or another. Many Europeans simply returned home to play. Some North Americans also went overseas. Many big-name players stayed at home, not wanting to risk injury. Young players returned to junior or played a year in the AHL. Some hosted charity games or elaborate pickup games.

In Toronto, the World Hockey Association tried to re-form. In April 2004, it had announced the interests of four teams – Toronto, Hamilton, Quebec, and an unnamed U.S. city. That number increased to seven over the summer, the last being Detroit, which promised to play out of the Pontiac Silverdome. Bobby Hull, the man who established the credibility of the original WHA in 1972 by leaving the NHL to play for a million dollars, became WHA2's commissioner.

By fall 2004, details started to fall into place and new teams emerged. The Toronto Toros would play at the Skydome; the Halifax IceBreakers, at the Metro Centre; the Quebec Nordiks (with the old nickname but radically altered spelling), at Le Colisée. Other teams included Hamilton, Detroit, Miami, Vancouver, and Dallas.

The league held its first Entry Draft on July 17–18, 2004, at the Fallsview Casino Resort in Niagara Falls, Ontario, even before the World Cup and the inevitable lockout. It declared intentions, as had been done in 1972, to draft seventeen-year-old players, so that Sidney Crosby would be eligible. In its press release, WHA2 noted that both Wayne Gretzky and Mark Messier were seventeen when they were drafted by the WHA.

There was great irony in the new league's attempted launch, however. Whereas the original in 1972 based its existence on greatly increased salaries, the new version implemented a $15 million salary cap plus a $5 million salary for a "marquee player." Instead of revolutionizing player salaries again, it established the cap that the players were at the same time fighting with the NHL about in CBA negotiations.

Day one of the draft was reserved for amateur players and day two for professionals. Crosby was selected first overall by the Toronto Toros, followed by Thomas Vanek (Halifax), André Benoît (Detroit), Corey Locke (Hamilton), Dion Phaneuf (Toronto, acquired from Dallas), Steve Bernier (Quebec), and Brent Seabrooke (Founders' franchise). In all, there were thirty rounds of drafting, a total of 240 amateur players being named to the eight teams. Amazingly, Alex Ovechkin wasn't selected until 52nd overall when Hamilton chose the Russian teen.

As telling was the pro draft the next day. Quebec had the first overall choice and selected Simon Gagne. Travis Green (Halifax) went second, followed by Dany Heatley (Detroit), Michael Ryder (Hamilton), Joe Thornton (Toronto), Todd Bertuzzi (Vancouver), Eric Lindros (Dallas), and Brad Richards (Florida). These names represented some of the best players in the NHL in 2004. Of course, all of these players had their star qualities, but what this list made clear was the total absence of a star power, a void left by Wayne Gretzky when he retired in 1999 and not filled until Crosby and Ovechkin started playing in 2005. To say these two brought the league out of obscurity is not overstating things.

But there it was. On a warm summer's day in Niagara Falls, Sidney Crosby was presented with an opportunity to turn pro and start making millions of dollars. He was sixteen that day, turning seventeen three weeks later, and he had a decision to make à la Bobby Hull, Gretzky, and Messier. The politics of the moment were far different, however, for Sid the Really Young Kid. If he were to sign, he would be endorsing a salary cap, a financial structure NHLPA Executive Director Bob Goodenow was willing to fight to the death to avoid. Did Crosby want this tablet around his neck when the NHL finally came back to life? Hardly.

And so it was that in late August 2004, Crosby officially turned down a three-year, $7.5 million offer from Hamilton of the new WHA. Hamilton had secured Crosby's rights because the Toronto franchise was having trouble finding a suitable arena in which to play, the ACC obviously not an option and the Skydome proving impracticable. Crosby consulted with his agent, Pat Brisson of IMG, and his father, and decided junior was the best place to be, for several reasons, first among which was tending to unfinished business at the World U20

(Junior) Championship where he vowed to win gold and avenge the loss in the final game of the previous season.

"It wasn't an easy decision and the offer was very flattering," Troy Crosby said gracefully and respectfully of an offer that the family surely never took seriously in light of the onion-thin basis upon which the WHA2 was trying to start up in the first place. "It was a lot of money. I realize some people might not understand why Sidney turned down the offer" – which included a guaranteed $2 million even if the WHA2 didn't play a single game. "He has his mind made up right now about where he wants to play. He wants to stick to his plan of playing another year in Rimouski. He's 17, and he's not playing for money right now. He feels playing junior is the best way to continue to develop."

While the WHA2 was wooing Crosby on one side of the hockey world, Lugano, a club in Switzerland's top league, was trying to get him to Europe by dangling a three-year, $10 million contract under his nose. The appeal to this option was that the team and league were well established (unlike the attempted revival of the WHA, which seemed to be depending on Crosby's signing for its start-up) and the possibility to dictate his own future. If he were drafted in the NHL lottery by a team that didn't appeal to him, he could play in Switzerland for a hat trick of years and return home a free agent.

There was nothing about the WHA2 or Europe to tempt Alexander Ovechkin. His future was decided on April 6, 2004, in another twist of fate. That day, the NHL held its draft lottery to determine the order of the first five selections. Incredibly, Pittsburgh finished 30th overall in the standings, meaning that in the old days the Penguins would have automatically earned the first selection. But to prevent teams from intentionally playing poorly for an entire season to obtain that first pick, the NHL instituted a lottery in 1995 much like the NBA's, in which that first overall selection could be awarded to any one of the five worst teams.

The lottery is based on mathematics and probability. It involves the fourteen teams that don't make the playoffs, but no team can move up more than four places, so that coveted first overall selection is available only to the bottom five teams. As well, no team can move down more than one position. The process sees fourteen balls numbered 1–14 put into a lottery machine. Four are drawn, and the resulting combination favours the 30th team with a 48.2 per cent chance of winning first overall draft. The 29th team has an 18.8 per cent chance; the 28th team, a 14.2 per cent chance; the 27th, a 10.7 per cent chance; and the 26th, an 8.1 per cent chance.

In fact, in the fifteen years of NHL lotteries to date, only five times has the last-place team retained its status to draft first overall. In 2003, the Florida Panthers should have been first to choose, but the Penguins moved from fourth spot to top to choose goalie Marc-Andre Fleury. In 2002, the Panthers lost to Columbus, and the Blue Jackets selected Rick Nash. The previous year, Atlanta moved up two spots and took Ilya Kovalchuk. The lottery has been very successful in disturbing the plans of the 30th-place team more often than not.

In 2004, Washington finished ahead of the Penguins and Chicago in the final regular-season standings, 28th overall, but the Capitals won the lottery and the right to draft Ovechkin. Pittsburgh chose second and called the name Evgeni Malkin, but the rest of the top ten were as obscure as the first two were revelatory.

Chicago, picking third, took Cam Barker. Andrew Ladd (Carolina) was fourth, followed by Blake Wheeler (Phoenix),

Al Montoya (NY Rangers), Rostislav Olesz (Florida), Alexandre Picard (Columbus), Ladislav Smid (Anaheim), and Boris Valabik (Atlanta).

For the second straight year, Pittsburgh missed an opportunity to make Ovechkin a teammate, rather than an adversary, of Crosby's. But then again, the 2005 draft lottery was also weighted based on performance, so one would think a team other than the Penguins would have won the rights to Crosby.

The WHA2 never got off the ground. Crosby returned to the Q for another season, and Ovechkin remained in Russia with Dynamo Moscow. But midway through this 2004–05 season, the two best teens in the world would finally meet in a winner-take-all game in their first on-ice clash that would come to define the greatest rivalry of their generation.

TWO KIDS PLAY FOR GOLD

JANUARY 4, 2005: CANADA 6–RUSSIA 1

In hockey, more than any other team sport, family matters. Basketball is a game best learned on the street or a cement schoolyard. Baseball and football require only the grassy fields of the local park. But hockey needs the single-minded dedication of parents who will buy the equipment and do the driving from game to game, arena to arena, often at ridiculously early hours.

And in both Crosby's and Ovechkin's cases, family played particular and, in many ways, similar roles. First, there was the class factor. Ovechkin lived in a two-bedroom apartment shared by three families, twelve people in all, on the tenth floor of a depressing old building constructed in the days of the Soviet Union. Crosby's family had to live with Troy's mom when Sidney was young and later moved into a small house in small-town Nova Scotia. The means to hockey success, in other words, was internal fortitude rather than financial clout. Both kids were well grounded by their modest upbringing and close relationships with their parents.

Ovechkin's mother, Tatiana, was one of the best female basketball players of her generation, a two-time Olympic gold medalist who wore number 8, the number Alex later adopted as his own. His father, Mikhail, was a top soccer prospect until he suffered a serious groin injury late in his teens, wiping out any dreams of a pro career in Europe.

Sidney had his father, Troy, a draft choice by the Montreal Canadiens. Sidney was also, in terms of companionship, an only child, in that his sister, Taylor, was eight years younger. They never played hockey together or took shots with each other or played road hockey together. The age gap was always so great that Sidney was simply way too developed to play as an equal with her. Instead, Sidney started in his grandmother's basement, firing pucks at the poor grandmother, without a care in the world. "She wasn't easy to beat," he said years later, recalling his first target. This was at a time when the entire family, down on its luck, was living under one roof.

Soon after, Sidney started taking shots on his dad in their own basement in their own house, in a small rink Troy had designed, but Sidney quickly developed too hard a shot in such a small space for Troy to be of any use. "He was killing me," Crosby Sr. said later. "I told him, 'You don't need a goaltender; just shoot at the net.'" Soon enough, Sidney was practising on his own, using the family's clothes dryer as a target, scuffing it black like Gerry Cheevers had done with his mask three decades earlier. This quirky biographical fact was played up in 2005 when Sidney appeared on *The Tonight Show* with Jay Leno, who promptly brought out a dryer and asked him to fire away.

Ovechkin was one of three children. The eldest, Sergei, was fourteen years older than Alex, the youngest. Mikhail, the middle child and three years older than Alex, never played hockey or skated with any of the passion of Alex, and as such wasn't much of an influence on the youngest of the Ovechkins. And so, for both Sidney and Alex, they were blessed with athletic parents but then had to discover and nurture their love of hockey on their own.

The apocryphal beginnings for Alex came at a local Moscow sports store when the two-year-old picked up a little stick and puck and helmet and refused to part with these treasures when his parents wanted to leave the store.

Alex didn't join his first organized team until age seven, with Dynamo, an organization with which his mother had been associated for years through her basketball career. That is how he got access to ice time day and night.

But Alex's first memories on ice were not pleasant. "After four months, I'd had enough," he revealed years later. "I decided I didn't like it."

While his dad wanted Alex to play soccer and his mom wanted him to play basketball, it was his big brother Sergei who drew Alex back to the hockey rink, for reasons that can only be described as prescient.

It was Sergei who saw Alex's love of the game at a young age and insisted he continue to play, even when their parents were unable to take Alex to the arena. Sergei filled the breach and took him to the Dynamo sports complex, an environment in which his skills could be nurtured and developed to a level that matched his desire to play.

By the time he was eight, Alex was back with Dynamo, no better a player but much stronger of mind and more determined. He discovered just how weak his skating was compared to the other boys who had been on ice for years. Alex couldn't even skate backwards properly. "I was mad," Alex said. "I tell my dad we must practise and get stronger."

And so he did. The two would go to the arena at six in the morning, and Alex would skate for a couple of hours before school. After classes, he was back on the ice with his team, and then he'd skate some more at an outdoor rink near his apartment. In all, he'd be on the ice six or seven hours a day, every day, practising with a drive that displayed his competitive streak and would not be satisfied until he had realized his dream – to play in the NHL.

Alex drew inspiration from Sergei every minute of every day, an inspiration that became life-altering just a short time later. On September 17, 1995, Alex's tenth birthday, Sergei was in a car accident and hospitalized with a broken leg. Alex had a game the night of the accident and visited Sergei the next day. The day after his visit, Sergei died due to a blood clot that had developed in the broken leg.

The very next night, Alex was back on ice. "His brother wasn't even in the ground, but we decided he shouldn't skip the game," father Mikhail said. "He played while tears were flowing down his cheeks. He cried the entire game, but he played. He wanted to play. We were obviously not thinking about hockey that day. We didn't want him to sit at home and dwell."

Tatiana had an incredible childhood in her own right. Struck by a car at age seven, she almost lost her badly damaged right leg to amputation. It was a miracle she could walk again, let alone play basketball at a world-class level, and when a Russian newspaper chose its greatest women basketball players of all time, she headed the list as point guard.

When Ovechkin accepted the Ted Lindsay Award in 2010, he held the trophy, looked up to the heavens, and said, "I want to share this with my brother who passed away, and I just want to say, it's all about him." He kissed his index finger and pointed heavenward in a gesture of love. Indeed, he said he thought of Sergei every day, every game. "He put me back on the ice," Alex said.

In boyhood, both Crosby and Ovechkin loved hockey. They loved skating, loved the speed and skill required to play the game, loved the ice and arena and stick and puck. That love, first and foremost, helped develop their skills. In Sidney's case, he advanced through the ranks by playing with older kids in a series of leagues with a series of evermore challenging teams – and always proving to be the best no matter what level or how challenging. At twelve, he was playing bantam AAA with the Cole Harbour Red Wings; at fourteen, he was playing midget AAA with the Dartmouth Subways, leading them to the provincial championship.

The development of young athletes in Canada and Russia could not be more different. While Crosby moved around to get the best possible experience from year to year, Ovechkin belonged to a system in which a team took a player in childhood and nurtured him through the ranks of development. Alex stayed with Dynamo until he left to play in the NHL. So, while Crosby was moving from Cole Harbour to Dartmouth to Shattuck and on to Rimouski, Ovechkin stayed with Dynamo. By the time he was sixteen, he was playing on the organization's professional team, playing against the best adult players in the country. It was here he skated for four years until his first NHL game, in what was called the Russian Super League (precursor to the KHL – Kontinental Hockey League).

The NHL lockout of 2004–05 had a positive effect for both players. For Crosby, the huge pressure to turn pro at some crazy age or to leave junior for a new challenge was put on hold, and for Ovechkin another year in Moscow could only prepare him better for the NHL a year later. Both players, though, were expected to be stars for their respective nations at the 2005 World U20 (Junior) Championship in North Dakota, and both players had something to prove.

Crosby was a sixteen-year-old the previous year when Canada was upset by the United States in the gold-medal game, and Ovechkin's team finished a disappointing fifth after winning gold in 2003.

So, here were these two players leading their teams into the 2005 U20 championship, both with their pride on the line, both with plenty to prove and high ambitions. Yet, as much as their situations were similar, Ovechkin had two significant advantages. First, he was nineteen years old, while Crosby was only seventeen. As well, he had already been drafted first overall. He exuded confidence based on his place in draft history and the inevitability of his playing in the NHL. Crosby was still only a prospect, a mere "might be" alongside a first overall draft choice.

"I've watched world juniors ever since I knew what was going on in hockey, and you see the pride that Canada has, so when you get a chance to represent your country you want to try and do that," Crosby said. He was a grudge-holder, though, and he vowed for a full year to avenge that gold-medal defeat from 2004.

Even before the playoff round began, the Crosby-Ovechkin comparisons were being stretched every day by media, but what could the players say? Ovechkin was honest but could provide little solid copy. "I've never even seen him play," he said of his hypothetical nemesis. "Of course, I have heard lots of good things about him. If the draw of the tournament makes us play against him and Canada, I will be ready."

Alas, Canada and Russia played in different groups, though on the same days, throughout the Preliminary Round. But whereas Christmas Day started with a resounding 7–3 win over Slovakia for Canada, the Russians were stunned, 5–4, by the 2004 gold medalists from the United States, playing before a home crowd in the gorgeous Ralph Engelstad Arena in Grand Forks, North Dakota. Ovechkin did his part,

ring once and adding an assist, and not surprisingly he led
ıl skaters with six shots on goal. Crosby, wearing number 9
because Hockey Canada doesn't permit high numbers, scored
twice and added a helper in leading his team to victory.

Both players were blessed with talented sidekicks in their
unfolding drama. Ovechkin had Evgeni Malkin who, many
scouts believed, was perhaps not as gritty but more talented
with the puck and more dangerous one-on-one than Ovechkin.
Crosby had Patrice Bergeron as a roommate off ice and the two
played on a line with Corey Perry. Bergeron was with the team
only because of the lockout. The nineteen-year-old had made
the Boston Bruins the previous year and had an excellent
rookie year in the NHL at age eighteen, finishing the season
by helping Canada win gold at the 2004 World Championship.
But with the NHL stoppage and being U20-eligible, Bergeron
happily returned to the junior ranks and took Crosby under
his wing off ice. On ice, the two had what they call chemistry,
and, with Perry, they formed one of the best lines in U20 history. In Canada's first game, the first four goals were all produced by a Crosby-Bergeron combination. "We played well,
but we can play better, I think," Crosby said after the game.
"We'll kind of set our standard there [the Slovakia game] and
get better as the tournament goes on."

Crosby played right wing on the line to accommodate
Bergeron at centre, but it was the veteran of the NHL, three
years older than number 87, who was effusive after the game.
"It's amazing to get a chance to play with Sidney," he said. "He
has such great vision. He sees things happening a second or
two before they do. When he's crossing the blue line, he has an
idea of what's going to happen two passes ahead at the net."

Two days later, both teams played afternoon games.
Crosby scored two more goals to lead Canada to an 8–1

demolition of Sweden, early signs that this team could score at will against all comers. At the same time, Russia was skating to an impressive 4–1 win over the Czechs, but Ovechkin was held to a single assist. Malkin led the way with two goals.

Some twenty-four hours later, Crosby and Canada did it again. He scored two more times and the team pummelled the Germans to a 9–0 count. As if watching this game with one eye, Ovechkin also scored twice and Russia hammered Belarus, 7–2. On the final day of the round robin, Crosby had a quiet and pointless game in an 8–1 defeat of Finland, but Ovechkin stepped up with two goals and an assist as Russia took down the Swiss, 6–1.

Both Canada and Russia finished in first place of their respective groups and advanced directly to the semi-finals. Canada then booked a date in the gold-medal game with a 3–1 win over the Czechs. Although Crosby was limited to a single assist, he was a dominant factor in the game, a game much more lopsided in Canada's favour than the score might indicate. Shots were 42–11 for Canada, Crosby counting seven of that number. The team held a 1–0 lead after the first period and made it 3–0 midway through the game. Canada was never really in danger of losing.

The Russians were out for vengeance, facing the Americans again in the other semi-finals. It wasn't much of a fight. Ovechkin had two more goals and an assist, and the Russians broke open a close game with four unanswered goals in the third period to win, 7–2.

Just about every time the United States hosts the U20, it holds the tournament near the border to allow the rabid Canadian fans easy access to games. Grand Forks was no different, and thousands of fans poured over the Manitoba border to watch their Canadians play. But this being a wintry climate and the games in December and January, nasty weather reared its ugly head. Such were the storms that many Canadians were stranded in Grand Forks, one night having to sleep (or, at least, stay) in the arena. The U.S. might have been the hosting country, but Canada's fans made this a Canadian event. And what better way to end the tournament than with a Canada-Russia game for gold. Crosby vs. Ovechkin. One game. One player would wear the golden laurels; the other would have to wear a silver anvil around his neck.

Although this was a game very much about the Canada-Russia rivalry – and Russia's 3–0 record against Canada in gold-medal games at U20 – it was also clear that a close second for fan interest was game one of the emerging rivalry, Sid the Kid versus Alexander the Great. "He is the first overall pick, so for sure it is going to be a big deal," Crosby said, diplomatically. "But I just want to come out with a win. I'm not trying to turn this into me versus him. It's not that at all. This is more of a team thing for me."

Never one to tip his hand, Crosby wasn't about to give Ovechkin or the Russians any chalkboard motivation. "I think we are looked upon as being offensive players and that we come to play in games like these. We are both going to be ready."

Ready, for sure. Canada's coach, Brent Sutter, was the most successful in U20 history. He coached only two years – 2005 and 2006 – but won two gold medals and didn't lose a game, his record a perfect 12–0–0. He knew how to handle kids, and he knew how to change his approach for each game, based on his opponent. For Russia, he had one simple strategy – give Ovechkin everything he could handle, and see what was left.

The answer – not much.

Ryan Getzlaf scored just fifty-one seconds after the opening faceoff to stake Canada to the early lead, a lead the team doubled about seven minutes later. Although Alexei Emelin got one back before the first intermission, Canada's strategy of hitting Ovechkin every time he had the puck paid off. Early in the second, worn down, he suffered a shoulder injury that kept him out of the rest of the game. It came as a result of a crushing Crosby bodycheck at a moment Ovechkin had left himself vulnerable.

Even today, one of Ovechkin's favourite moves is to skate down the left wing with the puck and then cut to the middle to release a quick shot. This was always an effective play because the defenceman would usually back up to the top of the faceoff circle out of respect for what else he might do with the puck. From there, and using the defenceman as a screen, the right-shooting Ovechkin could beat any goalie any time with his bullet drive and quick release.

But on this day, Crosby was waiting. He nailed him with a clean but devastating hit that altered the tenor of the game. "I knew it was him," Crosby later admitted. "And really it was a situation we knew to look for. From watching him, and from the scouting reports, we knew that Ovechkin liked to pull up at the blue line and skate towards the middle."

The hit also took its toll on Crosby. He was, after all, hitting a freight train. But the kid from Cole Harbour wouldn't let the pain show. He wasn't dominant in the game, but the hit – clean, devastating, perfectly timed – was the play of the game, the turning point.

Ever the competitor, Ovechkin sat at the end of the bench exhorting his teammates, but Canada scored four times in the second period and cruised to a 6–1 win for gold. At the conclusion of the game, Ovechkin's right arm under his sweater and taped, he shook hands awkwardly with Crosby, the left hand of the injured Russian grasping in twisted fashion the right of the victorious Crosby. Crosby's line had a quiet game, but Bergeron was named tournament MVP. Ovechkin was named Directorate Award–winner as Best Forward.

As confrontations go, this turned out to be more symbolic than classic. The two super teens didn't go one-on-one all game, and Canada was so dominating that the game was, alas, a mismatch. Crosby did not dominate and Ovechkin was a spectator for nearly two-thirds of it, but at the end of the day number 9 took home gold and number 8 had the silver. Round one to Crosby.

WELCOME TO THE BIG TENT

NOVEMBER 22, 2005: WASHINGTON 4 AT PITTSBURGH 5

Two players could not have more different off-ice personalities than Crosby and Ovechkin. In the days leading up to the 2004 NHL Entry Draft, Ovechkin happily admitted he wanted to be the first overall selection. "I want to be number one because I always want to be number one," he boasted. "If I play, I want to be number one. If I'm drafted, I want to be number one. Always number one."

Crosby, on the other hand, deflected the surety of his being first overall by remarking on the lottery used to determine the draft order coming out of the lockout. "There's a little bit of an excitement factor, a surprise factor, not knowing exactly where I'm going to end up. It'll be fun to see how the lottery works out."

Ovechkin's attitude made sense in some ways, recalling the famous words of Alexandre Daigle in 1993 after being selected first overall by Ottawa, one of the biggest busts in draft history. "Nobody remembers number two," he noted, with what turned out to be pathetic prescience for his own failed future.

Brashness in a hockey player was not common, but it wasn't an entirely unfamiliar land, either. But when that brashness came from a Russian, it was not only extraordinary but groundbreaking. Think of the 1972 Summit Series, which concluded with four games at Luzhniki Arena in Moscow. Fans sat on their hands, contemplatively appreciating the game action. Communist Soviets were not allowed to show their emotion, but when CCCP fell, a new Russia, an emotive one, awakened. Ovechkin's English wasn't polished or pure, but its succinctness captured his heart through the few words he could speak.

"He does not look like the Soviet hockey-school player," said legendary goalie Vladislav Tretiak, who would know better than anyone. "From a side, it seems that he is half Canadian."

Everyone who was anyone was asked to weigh in on Crosby. Hockey Canada scout Blair Mackasey compared Crosby to two Hall of Famers: "He is built similarly to Marcel Dionne, with a big rear end and thighs. He wins one-on-one battles and has a bit of a mean streak, and with his speed, he also reminds me of Pat LaFontaine."

Scotty Bowman said that "Crosby makes a lot of plays, plus he can score. He is a lot like Lemieux that way."

Indeed, Crosby never shone the light on his own head. He didn't have to. Although a child prodigy with a hockey stick, he started to come into clear focus in July 2002 when he attended an IMG summer camp for top prospects. The camp, held in Los Angeles, was a way for IMG to curry favour to top would-be clients or young clients newly drafted but not yet at the top of their game. As such, most were eighteen years of age. The agency also brought in big-name NHLers to make the experience a memorable one for the youngsters, and on this day Wayne Gretzky stepped on the ice to see what the fuss was about with the fourteen-year-old Crosby, by far the youngest player out there.

Gretzky was impressed by Crosby's vision on the ice, his passion for playing, and his dedication to fitness and conditioning. "He's dynamite," number 99 said, his opinion immediately exploding virally throughout the hockey world. More impressive, forgetting everything else, Crosby was simply the best player on the ice that day, despite being a veritable child playing alongside young men.

Less than a year later, in May 2003, Gretzky declared that the best prospect in the world was Crosby after a reporter had asked whether any of 99's records could be beaten. "Wow. I hadn't heard that," Crosby remarked at the time. "That's something else. That's pretty special for Wayne Gretzky to say that. I don't think his records will ever be broken. That's a compliment for him to say that, for sure."

For as long as the NHL existed, it had one player who towered above all others, the player who literally represented the league and game for his skills, domination, toughness, and ferocious competitive spirit. It was Gretzky until he retired in 1999. He came into the league in 1979, a year after Bobby Orr played his final game. Before Orr, Gordie Howe carried the league's reputation on his shoulders. Before him, Maurice Richard, and between the wars a series of great players, from Howie Morenz to Aurèle Joliat, Ace Bailey to Hap Day and Syl Apps.

Furthermore, the great star of the league always had a foil, a specific adversary or opposite, someone who made the star look even better by challenging him, by providing a contrasting character, by being almost as good. Gretzky had Mario Lemieux, who might well have had more natural talent but who lacked the tenacious drive. Orr had Denis Potvin, who considered himself better than Orr, or Brad Park, who played like Orr but not quite as well. Howe was to the NHL what Maurice Richard was to French Canadians, and before these two icons it was any opposing pair of top players for Toronto and Montreal who created a rivalry that drove the game.

And so Crosby had Ovechkin, and both players arrived in 2005 to re-ignite interest in a league that had lost a year to a lockout of unparalleled duration and damage. The league had a new logo, a shootout, two-line passing, and other rules intended to dramatically alter the presentation of games. But nothing could match the energizing impact of simply releasing the Crosby and Ovi opiate into the veins of the league's nearly bloodless body. They revitalized interest in the game and brought fans back to the arenas. Their natural rivalry (Canadian versus Russian) was extended by the NHL to include Pittsburgh and Washington. The league needed them in 2005 more than at any other time in its existence.

Even though he was still only fifteen years old when Gretzky praised him, it was clear all signs pointed, Dalai Lama-like, to Crosby's being anointed the next spiritual leader of the league, the good-looking, polite, sportsmanlike, and supremely talented player who would define the league and game. Finally, a player who could take Gretzky's mantle and wear it gracefully under pressure. And a worthy opponent, who could challenge him and say, "I'm better," and sometimes be right.

The way the two players were drafted couldn't be more night versus day. Ovechkin was the first player chosen, in 2004. That draft, in Raleigh, North Carolina, was yet another day in 2004 that was overshadowed by one topic – the imminent expiration of the CBA and the even more imminent lockout that would follow on September 15.

Ovechkin stood on the podium beside Capitals' owner Ted Leonsis, who saw the prospects of his team's success skyrocket with the choice. "When he stood next to me [on stage]," Leonsis later recounted, "I honestly could feel his heart pumping, which is what everyone has been saying about him – his engine runs at higher RPMs."

Pittsburgh selected second and took Ovechkin's friend and countryman, Evgeni Malkin, but there was never any discussion, à la Taylor (Hall)-Tyler (Seguin) in 2010, about who might go first overall. Ovechkin was miles ahead in the ratings.

But Caps fans hoping to see the eighteen-year-old Russian phenom in the lineup any time soon would have to take cold comfort in the World Cup two months later, the only North American action Ovechkin would be able to play at the highest level prior to the lockout. To further complicate matters, the International Ice Hockey Federation (IIHF) had tried unsuccessfully to broker a new Player Transfer Agreement between European club teams and the NHL, leaving the movement of players from the Continent to the NHL in limbo.

European teams were tired of receiving a pittance as compensation for their best players, and Russia was adamant that stars like Ovechkin should command millions of dollars in transfer fees, not a standard $200,000 as had been the case. Ovechkin still had one year left on his contract with Dynamo, so if there was going to be hockey in the fall of 2004, and if the Caps wanted Ovechkin in their lineup, they were going to have to pay large dollars to Dynamo to make this happen. In fact, Dynamo pegged the price at exactly $2 million, a sum the Capitals had no intention of paying, of course.

What fans also couldn't know was that two other first-round choices by the Caps in 2004 – Jeff Schultz and Mike Green – would also prove to be invaluable to the team's success. But the Ovechkin selection was as unsatisfactory as it was celebratory, like seeing the *Mona Lisa*, but behind glass.

Ovechkin's situation remained unresolved for a year because of the lockout. He stayed in Russia and played for Dynamo, and he even went so far as to sign another contract, with the KHL's Avangard Omsk, in the summer of 2005 for the next season. This time, though, he had an out clause that expired July 20, 2005. That is, he could opt out of his Omsk contract without penalty before that date. Complicating matters further, Dynamo had matched Omsk's offer (in the $3 million-a-year range) and it believed that by doing so Ovechkin was still Dynamo property. The two teams were headed to court in Russia to resolve the dispute. When Ovechkin signed on for another year in the KHL, the lockout was still very much in play, but on July 13, the NHL and NHLPA resolved their differences.

Caps GM George McPhee was confident the contractual problems in Russia would not hinder Ovechkin from playing right away in the NHL. "He's not driven by the money," McPhee suggested. "He wants to prove himself in the NHL."

Ovechkin arrived in Washington for the first time on September 1, 2005. He immediately signed a three-year, entry-level contract paying him the rookie maximum of $984,200, but the deal included bonuses that could drive that salary closer to $4 million each year. Steve Eminger, the incumbent number 8 on the team, surrendered Ovi's favourite digit and took 44, and Ovi settled in to Washington, D.C.

The player contract is a tangled web of bonuses and extras based on what seems to be an endless succession of numbers. Ovechkin's incentives included an additional $212,500 for several achievements, notably scoring 20 goals, recording 35 assists or 60 points, averaging .73 points per game (not .72 or .71), winning the Calder Trophy, being one of the top three players on the Capitals in the year-end ranking of plus-minus leaders, and being named to the NHL's all-rookie team.

And that's just Schedule A. Schedule B offered more perks. If he finished first in the league in goals, assists, or points, he'd get $150,000. If he were second, he'd get $140,000, and so on, as long as he finished in the top ten. If he were tops in points-per-game average, he'd get $100,000, down to $10,000 for tenth.

"If I win the bonus, I'm glad," he commented. "If I didn't win the bonus, it's okay. I came here for my dream. If I want money, I could stay in Russia and make three million bucks. Money is always money. It's good. So you go to restaurant, you don't have to think about it."

Crosby ended up with a similar contract laden with bonuses, but his situation entering the league was so much different. When the 2005 draft took place at the Westin Hotel in Ottawa on July 22, the league was abuzz with great news. The lockout was over. A salary cap was in place to help even the financial playing field among the 30 NHL teams. And the game had undergone revolutionary change. The two-line pass was allowed; obstruction would be dealt with stringently by the incoming director of officiating, Stephen Walkom; goalie equipment was going to shrink; a shootout would ensure no game ended in a tie. Offence and skill were going to be promoted whenever and however possible.

And then came the Sidney Crosby Sweepstakes, as the 2005 Entry Draft came to be known. All thirty teams would have a chance at winning the right to select him first overall. The lottery was again a matter of probability, this time based on performance by each team in the last several years. All teams started with three balls, but lost one for each time they'd made the playoffs in the past three seasons or had had a first overall selection in the last four years. When the math had been done, four teams had all three of its balls in the mix – Buffalo, Columbus, the Rangers, and Pittsburgh, all with an equal 6.3 per cent chance of getting the top pick. Ten teams had two balls (4.2 per cent), and the remaining sixteen teams had but one ball (2.1 per cent).

The lottery started in reverse order, to create some drama at the televised event. The first ball out belonged to Tampa Bay, representing the 30th selection, and most Canadian teams were eliminated in the middle of the pack. But Montreal, Crosby's boyhood team, was still in the mix late in the game, before earning the fifth selection. After that came Minnesota and Carolina, leaving two teams wondering who would choose second, and who would get first – Pittsburgh or Anaheim. Mario Lemieux versus Ducks GM Brian Burke!

With only two teams remaining, the league switched the order. Next ball out would belong to the number-one team. Gary Bettman opened the envelope with Academy Award-like drama, revealing the logo of . . . the Pittsburgh Penguins! Mario's franchise was saved. Anaheim had the second choice (and, when the time came, selected Bobby Ryan).

The "new NHL" got off to a great start. The best teen in the game, a Canadian, would be playing in an American city. The owner and best player, Lemieux, who had been trying for years to build a new arena, would have a much easier time of it, and a franchise once headed to Hamilton, if RIM owner Jim Balsillie's ambitions had been realized, was now among the most stable of teams in the bulky thirty-team loop.

"He's going to have a major impact," Lemieux acknowledged soon after selecting Crosby. "It's really going to help us bring back our fans and grow the game and make it better for everybody involved," he continued. "He's going to be a big part of the puzzle going forward. He has all the tools to be a great, great player in this league and have a great career. To be able to get him here for hopefully his whole career will certainly help us get a new building. This is something special."

Tom McMillan, the Penguins' vice-president of communications, put it more succinctly. "The phone started ringing at

4:31 p.m. that day," he explained, since Pittsburgh had named Crosby at 4:30 p.m. "Our staff said they would stay until the phones stopped ringing. They stayed until midnight. Think about it. It's a Friday in July in Pittsburgh and it's 4:30. You don't sell season's tickets on Friday evenings in July."

The team that had finished thirtieth among thirty teams in average attendance in 2003–04, the last year of play before the lockout (fewer than 12,000 a game), was certain never to have such woes for the next two decades or so of Crosby's career.

By the time Pittsburgh played Washington for the first time of the season, at the Igloo, both Crosby and Ovechkin had had numerous games under their respective belts. For Pittsburgh, it was their twenty-second game of the season, and for the Caps it was their twenty-first. Not surprisingly, both stars had played up to expectation, making this game the most anticipated of the young season.

Crosby recorded an assist in his first game, nothing special, but at least that first NHL point was over and done with. And it came on Mario Lemieux's fortieth birthday. Three nights later, in the team's third game, at home versus Boston, Crosby scored his first goal and jumped backwards into the end boards in celebration. He had five points in three games, but the Penguins were still winless to start 2005–06.

The early part of the season was a little overwhelming if not dreamlike for Crosby, but the bloom was off the NHL rose pretty quickly. The photos of first-goal pucks and scrums after those first games gave way to a numbing losing streak in October. The Pens lost their fourth game, and fifth, sixth, seventh, eighth, and then ninth, in a row. Four of those losses were in overtime, and a fifth in a shootout, and their tenth game, against a hapless Atlanta team, looked as if it would be the nadir.

The Thrashers scored four goals in the first half of the first period, but the Penguins finally showed some desperation and offensive magic, rallying for a 7–5 win on October 27. Two nights later, they lost again to close out the month in twenty-ninth place in the league (ahead of only those Thrashers). Crosby had two goals and 14 points in his first eleven games, an impressive start to say the least, but one buried in the mire of losing game after game.

November proved to be a brighter month. Crosby was now playing on a line with Lemieux and Mark Recchi, the kid dangling out of position, on left wing, alongside two veterans, and the team started to win some games. The first defining moment of the season came the night of November 10, a home game against Crosby's childhood team, the Montreal Canadiens. Crosby scored the first goal on a lucky bounce off a Montreal skate past goalie Jose Theodore, but after sixty-five minutes the game was tied, 2–2, forcing a shootout.

Each team got three shots, and the first five skaters had all failed to score. Crosby, the final shooter, stared at the puck at centre ice. A goal would win the game for the Penguins, a miss would force the continuation of the penalty shots. Crosby skated in with some speed, and between the circles he lifted his right leg as if to generate extra strength for a shot. Theodore went for the fake and froze, and Crosby moved in and roofed a backhand into the top of the goal.

He could hardly contain his joy after the game. "To do it in this type of game, with all the emotion, and against the Canadiens, it's awesome," he explained. "They were my favourite team growing up." The leg lift/fake came to be one of his signature moves, and a move many a player has since copied successfully, as it freezes the goalie more times than not.

Six nights later, Crosby elevated his play to another level, playing perhaps like an NHL superstar – and not as an eighteen-year-old hotshot prospect in the league – for the first time in his young career. The venue was the hated Wachovia Center in Philadelphia, home of the most uncouth and zealous fans in the game. The Flyers' hulking defenceman Derian Hatcher made a point of getting under Crosby's skin, and the strategy was abetted by some lax officiating. Hatcher cross-checked Crosby in the mouth, bloodying a lip, chipping his two front teeth, and forcing him to the stitch room for repairs. One shift later, Hatcher cross-checked him across the neck, but the only penalty went to Crosby for unsportsmanlike conduct, the result of his complaining to the referees.

Crosby made a nice play in the third period to set up the game's first goal, and he scored the second one to make it 2–0 for the visiting Penguins. The Flyers came back to tie the game and force overtime, but Crosby scored the winning goal on a breakaway thanks to a long and perfect stretch pass from Ryan Malone.

Vengeance was Crosby's, although he looked battered and bruised, not pretty-boy heroic, by game's end. But for all the vitriol a Crosby fan might have wanted to hurl at Hatcher, the Flyers defenceman also played the role of villain who forced the boy to become a man, who forced Mr. Wayne to become Batman before our very eyes. For that, the despised defenceman perhaps deserves some small credit.

Three nights later, still feeling beat up, Crosby was ineffective for the first time all season, as the Flyers reciprocated with a road win in Pittsburgh. And this is how the first twenty-one games went for number 87, as prelude to the first Washington-Pittsburgh meeting of the season.

Alexander Ovechkin had a much better time of things in Washington. He scored almost at will, and the team fared much better on the scoreboard as a result. To wit, the first game of the season, a 3–2 home win over Columbus. A scoreless first period gave way to five goals in the second. Columbus scored first, but Ovechkin tied the game on a one-timer half a minute later. The Blue Jackets went ahead 2–1, and a minute and a half later, Ovechkin scored again.

"I feel my dreams come true," he said in his broken English and with an enthusiastic smile afterwards. "I play in the NHL, first game. We win this game, and I scored the goals. And I'm very happy."

Ovechkin got points in each of his first eight NHL games, the Caps winning three and losing five. In the last of those, a 3–2 loss to Florida, he had his second multi-goal game and a total of ten shots on goal, exactly the kind of trademark game he came to produce with regularity. Just a few nights later, he had another two-goal game in another loss, 4–2, to Tampa Bay. On November 4, he was the only successful scorer in the shootout of a 3–2 win over Atlanta. Next game out, at home against Toronto, he had his fourth two-goal game of the young season in only his fourteenth NHL game.

"When I have a chance to shoot, I like to shoot," he said. "I love scoring goals, but I'm trying to help the team win games. If we win and I score, I'm really happy." Two days later, in the return visit of a home-and-home set with the Leafs, he did it again, scoring two more to bring his total to 12 goals in 15 games, registering seven shots on goal and being named the game's first star in his first game at the ACC.

Ovechkin continued his early-season heroics on November 15 against the Lightning. He scored a beautiful goal late in the game to force overtime by fighting off two defenders and getting a backhand past goalie Sean Burke, and then he scored the only goal of the shootout to win it for the Caps, making him three-for-three in the penalty shot contest to date.

The first Crosby-Ovechkin game, then, promised to be more than just another hockey game between two young and struggling teams. Both rookies had set the league on fire with their play, although neither team looked to be playoff bound. They showed poise and an ability to meet pressure head on and prevail, and now they were set to live through the media hype that preceded their first NHL clash.

In the craziness leading up to the game, Crosby was his usual diplomatic self. "Here you have two first overall picks," he began. "We've played each other before. He's had a great start to the season. I think there is competitiveness in both of us. It comes from wanting to be better, wanting to be the best. I'm sure he works hard. You don't get here by fluke."

The buildup was augmented by what is usually a most trivial league announcement – rookie of the month. That inaugural distinction for 2005–06 went to Crosby, but outraged fans in Washington groused about the pretty-boy saviour receiving preferential treatment over their own star, whose looks weren't so swell and whose English was a second language.

Still, when asked about this small honour, Ovechkin had a competitive response that signalled a long rivalry in the making: "It's a long season. We'll see who's better."

On game day, both players said all the right things about their adversary. Crosby said of Ovechkin: "He's a great player. Obviously, he has had a great start to the season so far. He's got good speed. He can do it all, I think. He's got a great shot, too. He's definitely dangerous when he's out there."

Ovechkin matched politically correct compliments with politically correct compliments. "He's a great passer, like

Gretzky, and he can see the ice. He makes a great pass; he's a really great player. I didn't see any of his physical game, but he scored ten goals."

Indeed, at this early stage of their careers, the two were "different players," as Ovechkin noted. Crosby had 10 goals and 15 assists to date, while Ovechkin had 15 goals and just 6 assists. Passer versus scorer.

Playing at home, and fired up by all the pre-game talk, Crosby came out and played a sensational game for the Penguins, making two all-world plays in the first two periods to lead his team to a narrow 5–4 win over the Capitals. Ovechkin had a lone assist but was a dangerous presence all night.

The Penguins stormed out to a 4–0 lead after twenty minutes, the period highlighted by the third goal, scored by Crosby. He knocked down a high pass at the Washington blue line and simply skated between two Caps defenders – Brendan Witt and Steve Eminger – and roofed a backhand over Olaf Kolzig. It was a confident, dramatic burst up the middle and a perfect finish.

In the second, the score now 4–2 for the Pens, Crosby showed the league another signature move. Coming down the left side in the Washington zone, he saw teammate Ziggy Palffy streak to the net. But rather than try to force a pass across, Crosby, a left-handed shot, turned towards the boards, as if to suggest he had run out of options and was looking to make a simple play. In one motion, though, he whipped a backhand pass across the slot to Palffy, who banged the puck home and diffused a Washington rally in the process. This spinning backhand pass has become a move he has used successfully with frequency, another great play in his repertoire.

Ovechkin nearly answered with a goal on a partial break-away, but he was stoned by goalie Sebastien Caron. "I thought I scored," the sniper admitted, "but it was a good save."

The Caps scored the only two goals of the third to make the game interesting, including a nice Ovechkin pass to spring Matt Pettinger for a breakaway on which he scored, but this was Crosby's night. He did all his damage in 19:16 of ice time, while Ovechkin was on for 25:17, the most of any player on either team, forwards and defence. More telling, Ovi played 1:38 while his team was short-handed, while Crosby was never utilized this way by his coach Ed Olczyk. Crosby was named the game's first star and Ovechkin the third, and each player complimented his opponent after the game through the media.

Said Ovechkin: "I think he scored a beautiful goal and did a great job, and he is good. He controlled the puck beautifully." Lost in the 87–8 hype was another personal aspect of the game for Ovechkin. It was the first time – and proved to be the only time ever – he played against his boyhood idol, Lemieux.

And poor Andrew Cassels. The Washington forward played in his 1,000th game on this night, but did anyone notice?

OLYMPIC DECISIONS

JANUARY 25, 2006: WASHINGTON 1 AT PITTSBURGH 8

As Crosby and Ovechkin were making their way through their rookie seasons, they did so in different worlds. From the second he was drafted by Pittsburgh, the eighteen-year-old Crosby was nurtured under the best conditions possible. The owner of the team was also its marquee player, one of the greatest players in the history of the game. And what started out as a jokey remark turned into a perfect domestic situation. When asked on draft day if Crosby would live with him, Lemieux answered playfully, "I've got plenty of room. He can stay on the third floor with the kids."

Crosby realized the value of such an arrangement, though. "I'd gladly take the offer," he said at the time, relishing the prospects of living with Mario in Sewickley, a tony neighbourhood just outside Pittsburgh. "To be around someone like that and learn, you know, that's a great opportunity." To another reporter, he said as much again. "That's the main thing, just being around him and seeing how he goes about things every day."

On road trips, Crosby roomed with another veteran, Mark Recchi, whose professional approach to the game couldn't help but rub off on the teenager. Even when he was rooming with Patrice Bergeron at the 2005 World U20 Championship,

Crosby was learning about the NHL. "He has played in the World Championship already and won a gold medal," Crosby explained. "He has played against great players and with great players, and I'm just trying to learn as much as I can."

Bergeron concurred. "We talk a lot about the NHL," he revealed. "I'm trying to tell him as much about it as I can."

And now, in the NHL, Crosby was living with the owner and playing on a line with that same Hall of Famer. He was learning every detail about the NHL on and off the ice from a man who had done so much in the game at the very highest level, from scoring the historic game-winning goal at the 1987 Canada Cup, to leading Canada to gold at the 2002 Olympics. A better situation did not exist anywhere in the world for Crosby.

Ovechkin, on the other hand, was coming to a new league and a new country completely unfamiliar to him. His English was as weak as his enthusiasm was over the top. What he did have going for him was that he was twenty years old, a veteran of four seasons in the Russian pro league. He also embraced Western life, celebrity status, fame, and late nights, so the cultural acclimatization was minimal. He lived across the Potomac River, in Arlington, Virginia, and had his family with him – mother, father, and brother Mikhail. But on ice he had no comparable mentor the way Crosby had with Lemieux. And a look at the lineup in D.C. indicated just how alone Ovechkin was in the task of providing the offence.

Numbers 87 and 8 were put in different situations in another way, too. Whereas Ovechkin was wiser but Crosby better guided, Crosby was also anointed the NHL's saviour. He was instantly promoted as the poster boy for the new NHL. Good-looking and polite, polished and almost incapable of controversy, he was the face of the league. In fact, if one stood on the Avenue of the Americas in midtown Manhattan and watched shoppers leave the NHL store, one would see large bags with Crosby's 87 sweater on them – not even the simplest promotional and commercial considerations were overlooked as the league marketed their Next One.

The pressure on Crosby to perform, to showcase the league and bring fans back after a miserable year, was colossal. Ovechkin, however, playing in a less hockey-crazy city for an owner without Lemieux's hockey pedigree, was allowed to skate under the radar. Time would quickly tell if he could handle pressure and expectations, but these weren't foisted upon him as they were with Crosby. Number 87 was expected to save a franchise, provide a new arena for the city, and bring the league back from the chaos of the lockout. Number 8 was expected merely to play like a first overall draft choice. Both players succeeded in spades.

Crosby's pressures were straightforward and always in the mirror, the newspaper, the microphone. Ovechkin, however, was quietly dealing with another matter that was never a serious threat to his dream but a significant distraction all the same. When he opted out of his KHL contract to sign with the Caps, his old team, Moscow Dynamo, was furious. It had provided him untold thousands of cumulative hours of ice time since he was eight years old, developed him into a world-class player in every way conceivable – and now was getting nothing for its efforts.

This was exactly the example the KHL and the Russian Ice Hockey Federation used when it refused to sign a new Player Transfer Agreement with the NHL, brokered by the IIHF. And so, on November 18, 2005, Dynamo filed a lawsuit against Ovechkin in U.S. District Court in Washington seeking not to bring its top player back to Russia but to receive compensation for their loss of the player – millions of dollars in compensation, in fact.

The next day, while practising in Montreal, Ovechkin was served his papers. This had to have been unsettling for him, even though his agent, Don Meehan, and the NHL supported him unequivocally.

Said Meehan: "I gather that the purpose of the lawsuit is to seek an injunction to prevent Alex from playing in Washington. It's their interpretation of 'their rules.' But we are very comfortable that the action will not be upheld."

Meehan's reference to "their interpretation . . . their rules" was to an arbitration board in Russia, made up solely of Russians, who decreed that Ovechkin's rights were owned by Dynamo and not by the Capitals. This decision came about because in the summer of 2005 Ovechkin signed with Dynamo's rivals, Avangard Omsk, which he had the right to do. But Dynamo also had the option to match the offer to retain his rights, which it did, thus making Ovechkin's KHL rights owned by Dynamo and not by Omsk, and making Ovechkin's "out" clause illegal since Dymano's contract did not include one. So surmised Dynamo, at any rate.

"That is the only thin, thin hook they have in this case," Ovechkin's attorney, Peter Sherwin, conceded.

Bill Daly, the NHL's deputy commissioner, agreed with Meehan. "Based on what I know, I am confident that the Caps will retain the rights to Alex's playing services."

On December 21, 2005, U.S. District Court Judge Emmet G. Sullivan heard arguments in the case and promised a swift decision. That came less than a month later, on January 18, 2006, when Sullivan ruled that the court "does not have . . . jurisdiction" to uphold the ruling of the Russian arbitration board. While mostly a legal technicality, its resolution gave

Ovechkin peace of mind, knowing that he could entirely, and without worry, focus on the NHL.

But by the time the two rookies played their second NHL game against each other an enormous amount had changed in their hockey worlds. In the intervening two months, their countries had announced rosters for the 2006 Olympics in Turin, Italy. Ovechkin was named to Team Russia, but Crosby was not on Team Canada.

The promising play of the Penguins in November led to a disastrous December in which the team lost eight of nine games. GM Craig Patrick, sensing the season was quickly slipping away, fired coach Ed Olczyk and installed a more system-oriented Michel Therrien in an attempt to salvage the year.

His second day on the job, Therrien raised eyebrows with a dramatic move – he named Crosby one of the team's assistant captains. "I don't think it's pressure," Therrien said of giving his eighteen-year-old even more responsibility. "He's a young kid, but sometimes a young kid has good, new ideas."

It still took the team nearly three weeks to win a game for their new coach, and then the Penguins closed out 2005 with three wins in four games. But if the Philadelphia game was the apotheosis of Crosby's young NHL career to date, the game against Atlanta on January 7, 2006, was surely the low point.

This was the second of back-to-back games against the Thrashers. The previous night, in Atlanta, Crosby took a retaliation penalty after being hammered into the boards from behind by Ilya Kovalchuk, and after scoring on the ensuing power play Kovalchuk gestured mockingly to Crosby. Then, in Pittsburgh, Crosby was high-sticked and hauled down on a breakaway – but it was he who got the only penalty, for unsportsmanlike conduct, after complaining to the referee. In all, Crosby incurred four minor penalties that game, and the Pens lost, 4–3.

Later that night, in the calm of Sewickley, Lemieux talked to his tenant and star charge. "You have to control your emotions," he intoned. "I know it's not easy. Every time you have the puck you're going to get hooked and grabbed. But it's always better to make [referees] your friends."

The next day, Crosby was a day older and a day wiser. "Sitting in the penalty box is tough," he admitted. "You're putting your team down . . . I want to lead by example, and sitting in the penalty box is in no way leading." Indeed, Crosby was leading his team in two disparate categories – scoring and penalty minutes. He knew this was part of the maturation process, but so did twenty-nine opposing teams who were more than happy to take advantage while he rode the steep learning curve that is the NHL.

But while the team's drama was playing out day by day, there was a parallel universe called the Olympics that was shifting into high gear. Teams named their rosters for Turin, and Canada had neither Lemieux nor Crosby. In the case of the former, the 2002 gold medal–winning captain had removed himself from candidacy for health reasons. He was suffering from an irregular heartbeat and didn't want to be named to the team if he might have to leave, a move that would have thrown a wrench into the team's preparation. He was also so frustrated by red tape in trying to get a new building for the Penguins that he formally announced the team was for sale.

Crosby's omission was another story, a huge one. Team Canada's executive director was Wayne Gretzky, who had held the same role in the 2002 Olympics and in the 2004 World Cup two and a half years later, both experiences leading to impressive victories for Canada. He was back for Turin, of course, but his selections were not as assiduous as fans had hoped. In particular, he showed a loyalty to Todd Bertuzzi that was mind-boggling for its bad timing. Bertuzzi's career had been turned upside down after he ended the career of Steve Moore two years earlier, having viciously attacked Moore from behind. It was one of the ugliest moments in NHL history, and when Moore refused to forgive Bertuzzi, even after Bertuzzi's tearful, televised apology, it was clear the league and its fans had a decision to make – side with Moore whose life had been irrevocably damaged, or side with Bertuzzi for sticking up for a teammate.

Gretzky, by naming Bertuzzi to the team, used the Olympics to make a point. But during the 2005–06 season, Bertuzzi was not having a good season and was nowhere near one of Canada's top NHLers. Crosby most certainly was. Gretzky was counting on his loyalty inspiring Bertuzzi to greater things, much as he had done when he named Theo Fleury to the 2002 Olympic team.

In some respects, the troubled Fleury had little business being on that team, but he promised to be only a positive force, and he was solid, if not spectacular, during that gold-medal run. Making matters worse, Moore filed his civil law suit against Bertuzzi just as the Olympics were beginning, shifting the team's focus from the collective challenge at hand to Bertuzzi's legal problems as fallout from his heinous act.

Of course, hindsight is wonderful, and given Canada's seventh-place showing in Turin, its worst in Olympics history, it's easy to say number 87 should have been on the team. What was symbolic about the horrible showing in Turin was how Canada lost to Russia in the quarter-finals, 2–0. Ovechkin scored the opening, and winning, goal, early in the third period – with Betuzzi in the penalty box.

For the first time in his hockey life, it might be said that Gretzky was caught with his head down. What every other top team in Turin had done was select a team of skilled players who could play the game at lightning speed. Bertuzzi was not such a beast. When Lemieux retired on January 24, 2006, because of the worries associated with that persistently irregular heartbeat, he said simply, "It's a young man's game." Gretzky failed to see this. He chose a team of veterans, and Canada and Crosby paid the price.

Crosby, though, ever the Gretzky-like diplomat, said all the right things after being excluded. He talked about not expecting to be on the team, the honour if he had been selected, the fact that he was eighteen with many more opportunities ahead of him. But his exceptional play in the NHL suggested he deserved a spot on the team.

Ovechkin had, of course, been named to Team Russia, and meanwhile, in the NHL, he just got better and better with every game. He used his size for big hits and his quick shot for scoring, becoming a seemingly nightly highlight reel of great plays. No night, however, could ever top that of January 16, 2006, in Phoenix.

The game had no particular meaning in the standings, but it was the first time Ovechkin played in front of Gretzky, coach of the Coyotes. The visiting Caps were chugging along to an easy victory, leading 5–1 midway through the third period, when Ovechkin scored "The Goal." Taking the puck into the Phoenix end down the right side, he tried to beat defenceman Denis Gauthier one-on-one.

Gauthier played the man perfectly, knocking Ovechkin to the ice as number 8 shifted to the left. Goalie Brian Boucher, however, moved across the crease sloppily, and as Ovechkin fell, his back on the ice, his head closest to the goal, he got the puck in the crook of his stick on the ice and whirled it into the gaping net. Even before he got to the bench Ovechkin was looking up to the scoreboard to watch the replay. So was Gretzky.

"That was pretty sweet," number 99 said after. "He's a phenomenal player, and he's been a tremendous influence in the game. It's great to see. He really is that good."

"The best goal I ever scored," Ovechkin said simply afterwards. A goal so good, in fact, it is still and likely always will be the best goal he ever scored. Many fans would argue it is, in fact, the best goal ever scored in recorded NHL history. It was his second goal of the game and 32nd of the season, and it came on the heels of his first career hat trick three days earlier, against Anaheim. That puck now resides in his house in a place of appropriate honour.

"As he fell, he had the presence of mind to change the angle of his hand and his stick so that he could kind of shoot with the stick behind his head," Caps goalie Olaf Kolzig explained. "Unless you've played hockey, you don't understand how difficult that is. Once we saw that on replay, we all lost our minds on the bench."

And so, game two of the Crosby-Ovechkin NHL rivalry was replete with side stories. One was named to his country's Olympic team; the other was not. One was given added leadership duties and was playing spectacular, consistent hockey; the other ran more hot and cold but was the most spectacular presence in the game. Ovechkin played in the shadows of Washington, while Crosby was in a *Truman Show*–like soap opera: the coach was replaced, Zigmund Palffy had retired; the owner had retired and was selling the team; Crosby was being accused of diving, while being molested every shift. There seemed to be no end. Ovechkin had only scoring to deal with; not so with Crosby.

But on January 25, 2006, there was one other intangible to consider. It was the first Penguins game of the post-Lemieux era. Only the previous day Mario had retired for good because of a heart ailment that wasn't going away and a decrease in general health and quality of play. "I feel the time has come," Lemieux said at a press conference announcing his final retirement. "If I could play this game at a decent level, I would come back and play. But I've not been able to do that this year. And I don't see it getting better as time goes on. I can no longer play at the level I was accustomed to in the past . . . The game is in great shape, and it's only going to improve from now on."

This last remark was, of course, a direct reference to his own team's Crosby and Washington's Ovechkin, both of whom could now cherish their memories of Mario. "I'm glad I saw his game, and I played against him in Pittsburgh. He was one of my favourite players. It's too bad," said Ovechkin.

For Crosby, the memories were far richer, not only because he and Lemieux had played and lived together but because Mario had taken on a father's role as teacher for the teenage Crosby. In Lemieux's final two NHL games, on December 3 and 16, 2005, Crosby was involved in the scoring with his landlord. On December 3, Crosby scored a goal, assisted by Lemieux, and thirteen days later the two had assists on a goal by Ziggy Palffy. These were Lemieux's last two NHL points.

The Washington-Pittsburgh game itself was anticlimactic, highlighted by numbers 87 and 66 while number 8 for the visitors played only the first two periods. During the first of the always-awkward television timeouts, fans were treated to a video tribute to their owner, Hall of Famer, and franchise saver. The result was a standing ovation from fans, from players from both teams, even from officials. Of course, sensing the magnitude of the night, it was also the occasion for Crosby to assert his presence.

The game was tied 1–1 early in the second period when Crosby set up two goals to make it 3–1 for the home side, both coming off one-timers from Mark Recchi on the power play after perfect set-ups from Crosby. Ovechkin scored the lone Caps goal on a shot from a bad angle, but he was laid low by a dirty play by defenceman Ryan Whitney just as the period ended. Whitney got his stick between Ovechkin's legs and lifted it into the player's groin, and as Ovechkin writhed in pain the Pens player was assessed a five-minute major penalty for spearing and a game misconduct.

After killing this off to start the third, the Penguins took over. In a five-goal third period, Crosby added another assist and a goal in an 8–1 rout of the Capitals. It was Crosby's first career four-point night and put an exclamation mark on Mario's final night of honour.

"He is gone, and he will be missed," Crosby said of his landlord. "You never can replace him or fill in his shoes. Now, there are a lot of us young guys who have to step up."

A FINAL GAME BEFORE TURIN

FEBRUARY 11, 2006: PITTSBURGH 6 AT WASHINGTON 3

It was only two and a half weeks between meetings, but this third Washington-Pittsburgh game of the season was perhaps the most psychologically difficult for Crosby. The Pens had defeated the Caps soundly last time but then had immediately gone on a seven-game losing streak, only ending the long slide with their win the night before against Carolina.

As well, this was the final weekend before the Olympics break. Crosby had three teammates going to Turin, including Russians Evgeni Malkin and Sergei Gonchar and Slovakian Tomas Surovy. And all Crosby saw on the horizon was a two-and-a-half-week break in the middle of winter without hockey until the next Pittsburgh game, March 1 against Ottawa.

The only thing Crosby could control was his own play, but as he had so often demonstrated, his play would only improve as the moment got bigger or the game grew in importance. Canada's Olympic team was announced on December 21, 2005. From that date to the Olympics break, Crosby had fourteen goals and thirty-two points in twenty-five games. If he were "in the mix" but not a selection originally, he was a no-brainer to be on the team by the time the Olympians actually packed their bags and headed for Italy.

Ovechkin cooled off noticeably between games against Pittsburgh, recording only one goal and four assists in seven matches, and the team posted a poor 2–5 record in that stretch. For different reasons, the Olympics played a role in the players' performances at this time, Crosby with something to prove, Ovechkin distracted by the prospect of the more important hockey just around the corner.

Both teams were at the same disadvantage, having played in a different city the previous night and flying to the American capital after the game. Washington lost in Philadelphia, 5–4, while the Pens beat the Hurricanes in Carolina, 4–3.

Crosby had the only goal of the first period in D.C., and he added an assist in the second. The goal came on a power play as he fought off a defender to the side of the net to bang home a loose rebound that goalie Olaf Kolzig couldn't control. It was one of four Pens goals with the extra man and came in a period in which the Caps dominated.

Meanwhile, Ovechkin answered with his 36th goal of the season in the third period while the Capitals were shorthanded. Dainius Zubrus did the work on the forecheck, making a quick pass to Ovechkin who had moved into the slot and who fired quickly for the goal to make it a 5–3 score. The game was never any closer.

Pittsburgh scored the only four goals of the second and coasted through the final twenty minutes once they had that 5–0 lead, but Crosby could take only so much satisfaction given the circumstances.

"It's always been like that," Crosby said of another game against Ovechkin. "You always try with that extra little bit of motivation when you're getting comparisons and things like that. You just try to use the energy from the game to utilize that in your play."

"If we wouldn't have lost the [last] game before the Olympics, I would have felt better," said Ovechkin, who could be forgiven for looking past this game to his first Olympics experience.

ONE GETS THE CALL,
THE OTHER A VACATION

2006 OLYMPIC WINTER GAMES

The 2002 and 2006 Olympic teams for Canada were like night and day. Recall in 2002 that after Canada tied the Czechs, 3–3, during the Preliminary Round, Gretzky stuck his neck out at a press conference in order to deflect the attention and colossal pressure from his players. In 2006, just the opposite happened. He wasn't even around when the players were named to the team because he had to return to Brampton to be with his dying mother. When the team was just about ready to fly to Turin, a gambling story broke that involved Janet, his wife – and, by extension, himself, to some unknown degree – and his assistant coach in Phoenix, Rick Tocchet.

Gretzky was questioned for including Bertuzzi and Bryan McCabe on his roster and for leaving off Crosby. And, once the team arrived in Italy, he had to field more questions about the gambling allegations, while Bertuzzi had to deal with Steve Moore's lawsuit. In all, these were not conditions remotely conducive to winning hockey. Gretzky even had to field questions about Dany Heatley (who some believed shouldn't have been allowed to represent Canada, after his reckless driving had caused the death of teammate Dan Snyder) or Shane Doan (who had been accused of hurling racist remarks to a French-Canadian linesman in a game in December 2005, charges that were never proved). Gretzky even brought along a "taxi squad" of three players to Turin in the event of injury, but, perhaps out of respect, Crosby wasn't even on this additional list (which included defence-man Dan Boyle and forwards Eric Staal and Jason Spezza, none of whom played).

What Gretzky knew as well as anyone was that selecting players for Team Canada was the most demanding part of the preparation. Whereas other nations had a clear knowledge of who were their top players and their second-tier players, Canada could easily field two Olympic-quality teams. It wasn't just picking twenty-three of the "best" players but picking twenty-three players who could work well together.

Most players on Canada's 2006 team deserved to be there. They had plenty of previous experience with Team Canada; they were having excellent seasons in the NHL in 2005–06. These choices were, more or less, beyond reproach. But two names stood out like scars on a smooth face – Bertuzzi and McCabe. McCabe was having an excellent year with the Leafs as a power-play point man, but his inclusion really seemed a media vote as much as anything, his name appearing in local and national papers on a daily basis as a maybe/maybe not selection. In the end, Canada's power play was dismal, and McCabe's play worse.

Bertuzzi's inclusion was out and out divisive, though, and was so patently political one wonders to this day why Gretzky put himself, and the player, in that position. Was there a tinge of jealousy? Did Gretzky believe Crosby should have to wait his turn? It couldn't be simply that he felt Crosby wasn't ready. After all, despite being the youngest player in the NHL, Crosby was leading the league in scoring and proving that he could play with the best players in the world – many of whom would be in Turin – night after night. In short, as per Gretzky's summertime dictum, Crosby had had a sensational start to the season and had played his way onto the team, really. He should have been there.

In fact, during the summer of 2005, when Gretzky was getting ready to announce the team's summer mini-training camp, Gretzky said Crosby wouldn't be invited but still could make the final team. "I hope we have to pick him," he said. "I hope he earns that right." Yet despite his stellar play in the first ten weeks of the season, Crosby's Olympics audition fell short in Gretzky's mind.

There were many reasons why Gretzky never had to answer directly for not taking Crosby. First, his mother passed away and he wasn't even in Vancouver on December 21, 2005, when the team selections were announced. Second, there was such an uproar over the selection of Bertuzzi that the exclusion of Crosby was a controversy that paled in comparison. Third, the rest of the executive group that did field questions spoke to the need for experience first and foremost, a logical strategy that could hardly be condemned, given that Gretzky had successfully selected the 2002 Olympic team and the 2004 World Cup of Hockey team.

Nonetheless, Crosby was disappointed at being left off. "There are so many good players in Canada," he said after the roster had been announced, "and being so young I don't think I expected to be picked. I prepared myself. I tried to have the best first half possible and give myself an opportunity, and I was right in the mix. I'm not there, but at least I can say I gave it a good shot."

Pat Brisson, Crosby's agent, politely disagreed with the decision. "I understand and recognize that it's not an easy decision for the Canadian selection committee . . . However . . . in my opinion, Sidney thrives under pressure and could play with anyone in the world and make a difference."

How right was Brisson. And how disastrous was Canada's performance. The country was shut out in eleven of its final twelve periods of hockey in Turin, an astounding degree of scoring ineptness given the skill and experience of the team on paper. It finished in seventh place, the worst showing in eighty-six years of participation in Olympic hockey.

Over on the other side of the pool, Russia started with a 5–3 loss to Slovakia and then won its next four games, the most impressive being a 5–0 shellacking of Sweden, the eventual gold medalists. Ovechkin scored in five of the first six games, and then like Canada's, the Russian offence dried up. The Russians were shut out in the semi-finals and bronze-medal game and went home empty-handed.

Crosby split most of the next three weeks between Cole Harbour and Rimouski, visiting family and friends before resuming workouts back on the ice in preparation for the second half of the season. He watched some of Canada's games but not all, surely believing at some points as he gripped the remote a little too tightly that he could have helped the team to a better result than seventh place. The big ice, no centre red line, huge passing lanes. He could have played on the fourth line, been used as a power-play specialist . . . anything.

OVI FINALLY WINS ONE

MARCH 8, 2006: PITTSBURGH 3 AT WASHINGTON 6

idney Crosby might have been the metaphoric Prime Minister of the NHL but he was losing the popular vote to Alex Ovechkin as the season went on. In pure statistical terms, they were of comparable value, but Ovechkin was off the charts on the entertainment meter. There was nothing Crosby could do about this, and he didn't want to do anything about it anyway.

To compare the two players using other metaphors, one might say Crosby was Zurich and Ovechkin was Las Vegas. Crosby was corporate and Ovechkin was the goofball in the mail room doing cartwheels. Crosby, Word Perfect; Ovechkin, Quark. Sid, Audi; Ovi, Ferrari. Sid, Matt Damon; Ovi, Jim Carrey. Sid, a deep Barolo; Ovi, a champagne.

When Ovechkin scored a goal, people in the next village heard about it. When Crosby scored, he went back to centre ice, put his stick down, and got ready for the ensuing faceoff. Where Crosby was responsible, Ovechkin was reckless. Crosby never stayed out on a shift too long, didn't get caught out of position trying to do too much, never gave the puck up in front of his own net. His first instinct was to pass, not shoot.

Ovechkin tried to beat an opponent one-on-one every shift. He shot from any angle, anywhere, so long as he could release the puck. He wanted only to score goals and jump backwards into the glass to celebrate. He literally ogled the giant scoreboard above centre ice with narcissistic delight to watch highlights of his shifts.

If one argued that Crosby was the new Gretzky, it wasn't so easy to find a player Ovechkin resembled. Think of previous great Russians like Pavel Bure, Alexander Mogilny, or Sergei Fedorov. They were shotgun-fast, sleek, skilled. But they weren't big. They didn't bulldoze their way through opposing players, and they didn't celebrate goals with the same 10,000 B.C. wildness.

Ovechkin resembled no Russian. And no Canadian was ever so cocksure. He shot the puck as often as Phil Esposito, but Espo went about his business without the same *joie de vivre*. And maybe therein lies the difference. Crosby, because of the league's expectations, couldn't afford to relax. Ovechkin, who could always go home to the KHL to play, could afford to play with a far less serious attitude.

But maybe, just maybe, this fourth and final meeting of the season between Washington and Pittsburgh put added pressure on Ovechkin's shoulders for a change. The Penguins had won the first three games of the season series, and Crosby was unquestionably the more dominant of the two so far. Ovechkin had just returned from Turin a week ago without an Olympic medal of any colour, and the Caps had lost their first two games after the break, before defeating the Islanders, 5–2, two nights earlier.

Ovechkin came out of Turin in good shape, though, scoring four goals and adding two assists in those three games. Crosby hadn't had such success. The Pens lost their first three after the Olympics, and their fourth this night against the Caps, and Crosby had been limited to just three points, to fall ten points behind his adversary in rookie scoring after this game.

In fact, the Penguins had won only fourteen games on the season to date, and three of those came against the Capitals. Adding to the drama of this game, the next day was the NHL's trade deadline, and several Washington players' names had surfaced in rumours, leaving an unsettling feeling in the dressing room.

Just as he had professed his desire to be drafted first over-all, Ovechkin was not shy about his ambitions on the race to the Calder Trophy. "I want to win rookie of the year," he stated. "I want to win all titles." Crosby answered the same question in a far more measured tone. "For me and him, it's a healthy competition," said Crosby, who, predictably, was taking a low-key approach to the rookie-of-the-year competition. "I think it's good we're both having healthy starts in our first year in the NHL, but our job is to play and it's for everyone else to talk about it."

On this night, Ovechkin went a long way to solidifying his place in the Calder voting. He helped rally the Caps from an early 1–0 deficit by scoring once and adding two assists in a 6–3 win, while his team limited Crosby to a single assist on that first goal two minutes into the game. It was Ovechkin's team-record seventh straight game with a goal, 18th on the power play, and 42nd overall on the season.

The Pens suffered from weak goaltending by Sebastien Caron, and coach Michel Therrien made no attempt to hid the fact after the game. "Sebastien gave up three bad goals," he offered. "It's tough to win when you give up one bad goal, and we gave up three bad goals."

The Caps made no bones about the fact this was a win for their young star against Crosby. Said coach Glen Hanlon: "We didn't want to see Ovi go out of here without winning this game. We tried to really take away the fact that it was Crosby-Oveckhin. We just wanted to make this a team game, and I think we played a strong game."

"We finally beat this team, and I'm happy," Ovechkin said. "He's a good player," he added, referring to his number 87 nemesis, "but we don't think about each other. We play for a team and try to help the team to win."

"The competition is always high when we play each other," Crosby added. "That's to be expected. It's just the way it goes. Someone has to come out on top."

CLOSE, BUT NO CIGAR

2006 WORLD CHAMPIONSHIP

t was a long season. The Penguins won just eight of twenty-three games after the Olympics, and Crosby was ever the consistent player on and off the ice, a professional and ambassador, as everyone had expected. He had points in seventeen of the final twenty-three games of the season, twice recording four points but only once getting two goals in a game. Clearly he was making his way through his first season as a passer first, someone who could draw the play to him before dishing the puck off to an open man.

Additionally, he was doing the little things right, keeping his shifts short, backchecking to his goal line, playing responsibly, as they say. And every day he worked on faceoffs. One of the worst on the draw at the beginning of the year, he improved by leaps and bounds over the course of the season, thanks to sheer industry and persistence. In spite of this, the Penguins finished with a miserable record of 22–46–14 and just 58 points, 29th overall and behind only St. Louis, which had 57 points.

The Capitals fared only a little better as a team. They finished in 27th position with a record of 29–41–12, good for 70 points. Neither team, of course, made the playoffs. Incredibly, Pittsburgh used 41 players over the course of the season and the Capitals 40, further proof these were teams just starting to build around their star players but a long way from settled.

Ovechkin was held pointless in only four of the team's final twenty-five post-Olympics games. He never recorded a hat trick during that stretch, and never had a four-point game as Crosby had, but he had eleven multi-point games as well. Coach Glen Hanlon was using him much more than Michel Therrien did Crosby in Pittsburgh, and like most stars Ovechkin thrived on the extra ice time.

Seven NHL players reached the 100-point mark in 2005–06. Crosby finished with 102 and Ovechkin with 107, while the Art Ross winner, Joe Thornton, had 125. Ovechkin got his 100th point on April 10 against Boston, a goal in overtime to give him 49 on the season. "I didn't score for four, five games and everybody is talking about it," Ovechkin said. "Coach [Glen Hanlon] came to me after the second period and said, 'Don't think about it; just go out and enjoy your time.'"

It was his first goal in six games, matching the longest drought of his rookie season. Three days later, in Atlanta, he scored his 50th of the season, midway through the first period, to ensure his place in rookie history as only the second player to reach 50 goals and 100 points in his first NHL season.

Crosby got his 100th point on a memorable night exactly one week after Ovechkin, April 17, the second-last day of the season. He recorded three assists in a 6–1 home win over the Islanders to become the youngest player to reach 100 points and only the second eighteen-year-old to reach the plateau (after Dale Hawerchuk with Winnipeg in 1981–82, who finished with 103). Perhaps more incredible was his consistency. He was held without a point for three games in a row only once, and two games twice, recording points in a total of 60 of 81 games.

"You're only a rookie once, and this is the only opportunity you have to achieve something like that," Crosby said. "It was nice to be able to do that here. I scored my first goal here, and this was a very similar feeling to that."

Still, when the regular season ended, both players felt they had still more in the tank, and both accepted invitations from their national federations to play at the World Championship in Riga, Latvia.

"It was tough a lot of times to go out there and get motivated when you know you're out of the playoffs with three months left in the season," Crosby said of the Penguins' dismal year. "We all tried to make good of the situation."

"There's healthy competition there – there's no hiding that," number 87 said of number 8. "I don't think there's hatred or anything like that. I respect him. I think he's a great player. I think it's great for everyone involved if we're playing good hockey and hopefully bringing excitement to the game. When we do play each other, I do think there's that level of competition where we want to show that we're good players and showcase our skill, and that goes for both of us. We both enjoy the challenge."

For Crosby, this was his first senior international event, his only other Team Canada appearances coming at the 2004 and '05 World U20 (Junior) Championships. Not so for Ovechkin, who was a Team Russia veteran at the ripe old age of twenty. He had played in two U18 tournaments, three U20s, two previous World Championships, a World Cup, and an Olympics, collecting five medals in those events along the way.

Indeed, an IIHF editorial during the Riga World Championship suggested Ovechkin shouldn't have qualified for Calder Trophy voting because he had already been a pro for three years in Russia, whereas players such as Crosby, Dion Phaneuf, and

Marek Svatos were playing in the pros for the first time in 2005–06, in the NHL. It's a point with merit, given that when Crosby was sixteen in Rimouski in 2004, Ovechkin was already playing pro with Dynamo, had played at the World Championship, and later had played at the World Cup among the top players in the game. Crosby wasn't even shaving then – yet somehow, two years later in their first NHL season together, they were equal?

The World Championship also gave both players another kind of motivation. For Ovechkin, a chance to wipe out the bitter memories of Turin; for Crosby, a chance to show what he could do at the highest level and maybe confirm or refute whether he had deserved a chance to be in Turin himself.

Russia had been in a terrible gold-medal drought in international hockey. It had not won Olympic gold since 1992 or World Championship gold since 1993. It had failed even to make the finals of the 1991 Canada Cup or the 1996 and 2004 World Cups, and only its two gold medals at the U20 in 2002 and '03 (with Ovechkin in the latter) could add a bit of shine to the country's once impeccable reputation.

Canada had disappointed at the Olympics, of course, but it had had gobs of success in other international events, including gold medals at the 2003 and '04 Worlds, not to mention gold at Salt Lake, victory at the '04 World Cup, and a plethora of titles at the U20.

Nonetheless, both players were going from one situation to something polar opposite. In the NHL, their teams lost more often than they won. Internationally, Canada and Russia fully expected to win every time they took to the ice.

"When you're losing it's an uphill battle and you're always fighting for wins which are so tough to get," Crosby explained. "When you're expected to win, there's not a lot of room for error. You always play to win, and as Canadians we always expect to win so I don't think things will change this year [in Riga]."

As well, there was the question of going from the smaller, NHL ice to the much wider European ice. Ovechkin, with his physical play and quick shot, preferred the NHL ice, as did Crosby.

"I think I'm more a small-ice player," number 87 suggested. "I wouldn't say I hate the big ice, but here [in the NHL] passes are shorter and you don't have to skate as much to get to the net, make plays out of the corner, stuff like that. Some guys like the bigger ice because they can slow the play down, but my preference is small ice. When you're on the big ice you try to control the play a little bit more instead of going all out all the time. There's more room to make plays so you want to take away their angles and not give them as much time to make decisions."

Crosby got two goals in his first game, a 5–3 win over Denmark. Both were assisted by Patrice Bergeron, the teammate he clicked so well with at the 2005 U20s. Crosby had a goal and three assists in the next game, an easy 7–1 win over Norway, two of those helpers coming on goals to Bergeron. The third member of the team's top line was Brad Boyes, no slouch around the net himself.

The Canadians then eked out a hard-fought 2–1 win over the Americans, a game defined by the goal of the tournament. Phil Kessel had scored in the opening period to give the U.S. a 1–0 lead, but midway through the game Bergeron gained quick control of the puck deep in his own end. Crosby immediately took off and Bergeron hit him with a long, perfect pass. Crosby blew between the two defencemen near centre ice, went in alone, and beat goalie Jason Bacashihua with a great deke to tie the game. The pro-Canadian crowd roared with approval. Crosby was now a World Championship star. Brendan Shanahan scored the only goal of the final period for the win.

Crosby had another goal and assist in an 11–0 rout of the home Latvian side, a bizarre game that featured nine power-play goals from Canada and seemingly countless Latvian penalties. Fans twice littered the ice with coins, forcing lengthy delays and even requiring Latvian forward Janis Sprukts to take the microphone to beg with the fans to stop.

Canada suffered its first loss of the Qualification Round, 6–4 to the Czechs, but Crosby had another goal thanks to a Bergeron pass and added an assist as well. He continued to lead the championship in scoring. A 4–2 win over Finland to close out the round-robin stage saw Crosby set up Bergeron and Boyes for goals, and now Canada faced Slovakia in the elimination quarter-finals.

Meanwhile, in another group of round-robin play, the Russians were dominating their competition. Ovechkin started with a hat trick over the weak Kazakhs in a 10–1 win, but he was held off the scoresheet in their next game, a close 3–2 win over Belarus. He was even less of a factor in a 4–3 win over Slovakia but came to life in a 6–0 win over Ukraine. Ovi had a goal and two assists and recorded eleven shots on goal. He had another quiet game against Switzerland, and scored once in an entertaining 3–3 tie with the Swedes, setting up a quarter-finals date with the Czech Republic.

Canada blew open a 1–1 game after two periods against the Slovaks, scoring the only three goals of the final twenty minutes to advance to the semi-finals and a date with Olympic champions, Sweden, for a chance to go to the gold-medal game. Crosby scored one of those three to extend his points streak to seven games.

Russia was not so fortunate. Ovechkin opened the scoring against the Czechs just 2:30 into the game off a pass from teammate Malkin, but it was the Russians who had to score with 65 seconds left in the third to force overtime. Zbynek Irgl counted at 7:58 to extend the Russians' goldless streak another year, ensuring there would be no final Crosby-Ovechkin showdown on the international stage to close out the 2005–06 hockey season.

Canada could get no further than the semis, but it wasn't for lack of effort from Crosby in a game that featured a scary moment for the NHL's marquee player. A wild opening period saw the Swedes take a 3–2 lead, and less than three minutes into the second they upped the lead to 5–2.

In the final minute of that middle period, however, all hell broke loose. Defenceman Dan Hamhuis kept the puck in at the Swedish blue line and fired a quick shot toward the goal. It went well wide, but the rebound came out the back side perfectly onto Crosby's stick. Goalie Johan Holmqvist stopped the initial shot, but Crosby went to the net and jammed home the rebound to make it 5–3. While Crosby was off balance and celebrating his goal, Mika Hannula viciously cross-checked Crosby to the jaw, and as Crosby fell to the ice in pain all remaining players became embroiled in pushing and shoving.

When the dust had settled, Hannula was assessed a five-minute major for checking to the head and an automatic game misconduct. A woozy Crosby went to the dressing room. He returned to start the third and declared his health by getting a breakaway just seconds after the faceoff. He was stoned this time by Holmqvist on this rush. Not the next time, though. Crosby made a sensational pass behind the Swedish goal back against the grain to linemate Patrice Bergeron, who drilled it high to the far side to make it 5–4.

Canada pressed relentlessly for the tying score but with goalie Alex Auld on the bench the last gasp came up just short. Hannula was given an additional one-game suspension for his hit on Crosby (missing the gold-medal game against the Czechs), and the IIHF's Disciplinary Committee later tacked on another four games to the 2007 World Championship and a fine of 5,000 Euros to make clear its distaste for hits to the head. Canada ended the tournament with a meek 5–0 loss to the Finns for the bronze medal and finished fourth.

This was not the only nasty incident in Riga. Other suspensions were doled out as a result of an altercation off ice toward the end of the Italy-Ukraine game. Tony Iob (Italy) was suspended for three games and Sergei Klymentiev (Ukraine) for two games after they engaged in a fight in the corridor leading to the dressing rooms, uncommon behaviour at an IIHF event, to be sure.

But now Crosby and Ovechkin were going home for the summer, to rest, to assess their rookie seasons, to get ready physically and mentally for their second seasons. They had proved they belonged in the league, and now they were destined to dominate it.

DIVVYING UP THE HARDWARE

JUNE 22, 2006: NHL AWARDS

t had been a long season. Crosby and Ovechkin had played exhibition games, the long regular season, and the World Championship, and had done an extraordinary amount to make fans forget the *annus horribilis* that was the lost season of 2004–05. Fans may have done without hockey for a year, but now there were two sensational players in the game *à la* Gretzky and Lemieux or Howe and Orr.

And a season that began with training camp in early September was now coming to a close with the NHL Awards show, on June 22, 2006, at the Centre in Vancouver for Performing Arts. Most of the talk focused, again, on Crosby and Ovechkin and their right to the Calder Trophy. Who was the more deserving recipient?

Ovechkin became only the second player ever to score 50 goals and 100 points in his rookie season (after Teemu Selanne, who had 76 goals and 132 points in 1992–93), but Crosby became the youngest player ever to reach the 100-point mark. Ovechkin was a pure scorer, while Crosby was also a sensational passer. Ovechkin loved to hit; Crosby was masterful at holding onto the puck while being clutched and grabbed. Ovechkin was Hollywood fun, but Crosby was the face of the league and excelled under far greater pressure.

In the end, it was no contest. The Calder was voted on by members of the Professional Hockey Writers' Association and they chose Ovechkin with almost unanimous support, giving him 124 of 129 first-place votes and 1,275 points in the voting system. Crosby got just five firsts and 831 points, and way behind, in third place, was Dion Phaneuf, with a bunch of third-place votes and a total of 580 points.

As usual, the two personalities remained consistent. Crosby downplayed the importance of winning beforehand when he said, "By no means am I going to measure my season based on this. It's a bonus if I get it, but if not, it's not something I'm going to be too disappointed about or put a lot of emphasis on. It'd be nice, but I'm not measuring my season on it."

After winning, Ovechkin did little to conceal his joy. "I'm very happy right now," he admitted. "I'm glad it's over. It means a lot. I think a lot about if I could win the Calder Trophy after the season."

His acceptance speech was short but genuine. "I want to say thanks to the whole Washington Capitals organization, the coaches and all my team guys. They are excellent boys," Ovechkin said as Crosby looked on. "I also want to thank my linemates, Dainius Zubrus and Chris Clark. They do a great job."

What's more significant was that the two shared the lime-light together this night and seemed to enjoy each other's company, the long grind of competing against each other all year giving way to a handshake that evening before parting ways for the summer.

"It's nice to get to hang out with him and talk a little bit," Crosby said. "Obviously, when we play each other, we don't get that chance. I think in the media it's always built up as such a rivalry, and we don't really know each other, so it was nice just to meet him. It's fun to see there's another guy going through a lot of similar things, and we can relate to a lot of the same things."

"We speak a little bit," Ovechkin concurred. "He's a great player, and he's a good person. I wish him good luck."

Perhaps Pittsburgh teammate and Russian friend Sergei Gonchar said it best in comparing the two stars. "It's a huge gap," he explained of the two-year age difference. "Alex isn't just older. He has played against men and practiced with men for the last three years," with Dynamo Moscow. Indeed, at this young age, that experience might have played a significant factor in Ovechkin's superior season.

Consider also the media coverage and the expectations the hockey world had foisted on Crosby. When Wayne Gretzky played his first year in the NHL, 1979–80 (the NHL refused to call him a rookie because of its lingering animosity with the WHA), there were twenty-one teams in the NHL, not thirty. There was no such thing as sports channels like TSN or ESPN, only *Hockey Night in Canada* and a game of the week in the U.S. There was no Internet, no team websites, no specialty channels, no Facebook or Twitter or blogs. And being Canadian playing in an American city meant a double whammy.

The media frenzy that Crosby endured on a daily basis far outstripped anything that Gretzky had to put up with, even when he was mobbed at the train station in Tokyo after arriving with Team Canada for the 1998 Olympics. Forget about the Calder Trophy. That Crosby stayed sane and wasn't committed to an institution is the greater miracle of his rookie season, age eighteen. Crosby, a native English speaker and a Canadian whose every move was followed by the entire nation, was far busier than Ovechkin, whose English was poor and who was followed by ardent fans but from a much greater distance and by far fewer media.

Having said that, Ovechkin's life was not simple, either. A proud Russian, he faced great expectations from fans back home. He alone represented Russia in the NHL, though he had compatriots in the league. As well, he arrived in Washington not knowing a word of English, having to adjust – albeit happily – to a truly foreign culture. He roomed with Brian Willsie on the road, to learn English and to fit in with the team, declining the easy option of rooming with Dainuis Zubrus, another Russian, which he was offered during training camp. In short, Ovechkin's problems may not have been as significant as Crosby's, but his life wasn't without complications.

Of course, the lingering image of the season remained Ovechkin's goal against Phoenix. But for Crosby, such a long and eventful season inside the Pittsburgh dressing room made it easy to choose a most memorable moment. "We played on Long Island and beat them 5–1," he recalled of the game on November 3, 2005. "I played on a line with Mario, and that's the first time we connected with a goal. He passed it to me, and I scored. I didn't think of it then, but now that he's not playing, it's something I will cherish for a long time."

2

CROSBY FRONT AND CENTRE

YEAR TWO BEGINS

DECEMBER 11, 2006: PITTSBURGH 5 AT WASHINGTON 4 (SO)

I t came to be the defining image of the 2006–07 season. On October 5, 2006, Jim Balsillie agreed to buy the Pittsburgh Penguins. The next day, every major sports page led with his smiling face and a hand holding a BlackBerry Smartphone with the Penguins logo as the background image. Balsillie, whose company, Research in Motion, produces the BlackBerry, is a billionaire and a hockey lover from Kitchener, Ontario. The sale, arranged by Mario Lemieux, was a clear sign that the owner had given up on the City of Pittsburgh in helping to build a new arena. He was ready to walk away and let someone else lose millions of dollars.

NHL Commissioner Gary Bettman, however, smelled a rat and made it clear the league would not tolerate any attempt to relocate the team. As a result, Bettman vowed to negotiate any arena deal moving forward, and if Balsillie couldn't – or didn't want to – keep the team in Pittsburgh, the league would take over its operation. On December 15, 2006, Balsillie withdrew his bid, sensing he would have far too difficult a time moving the Penguins to Southern Ontario, his real dream.

Apart from this off-ice drama, the Penguins were quickly building a playoff-quality team. It made two huge additions to its roster over the summer in the form of teenage draft choices Evgeni Malkin and Jordan Staal, younger brother of Eric, who had won the Stanley Cup with Carolina as a rookie the previous season.

As well, other parts of the team were coming together. Goalie Marc-Andre Fleury was a year older and wiser, as were other key elements to the team's offence, Ryan Whitney and Colby Armstrong. The team's GM, Ray Shero, also signed the aging wonder that was Gary Roberts, a player whose team-first dedication in the dressing room could have only a positive effect.

Ditto in Washington. The Caps brought in their top draft choice, Russian Alexander Semin, and its core of young players also carried another year's worth of experience to the rink, notably defenceman Mike Green and forwards Chris Clark and Brooks Laich.

Perhaps the most sensational news for the Caps over the summer was an event that did *not* take place. Captain and free agent Jeff Halpern signed a four-year contract with Dallas, leaving the leadership of the team open. Coach Glen Hanlon asked Ovechkin to be the captain, but Ovechkin wisely declined.

"This year, I'm not ready," he admitted. "My English isn't good enough. If I need to say something to the team . . . it's hard. The captain is very important. You must be a leader all the time."

One thing that did change was the curve in Ovechkin's stick. The NHL changed the limits of stick curvature from half an inch to three-quarters, and Ovechkin immediately went for the bigger bend. Crosby, on the other hand, played with an almost straight blade. Ovechkin's was a scorer's stick, which could get extra speed and more dipsy-doodle to the shots, while

Crosby's was a passer's blade, able to snap the puck equally successfully on the forehand or backhand side. The stick also accounted for Crosby's backhand shot, quite likely the best in the league alongside that of Toronto captain Mats Sundin.

It was a pity that because Pittsburgh was situated in the Atlantic Division of the Eastern Conference, and Washington was in the Southeast Division, the teams played but four times a year. As a result, the season was already a third over and Christmas just around the corner by the time the Pens and Caps played for the first time in 2006–07.

The teams were on opposite streaks heading into the game, the Penguins having won just two of their previous nine games but with a record just poking above .500, while the Caps had won five of six but were slightly below .500 on the season. Overall, both teams had improved significantly over the last year, and the Caps were now just three points ahead of the Pens in the overall standings.

What this meant was that the focus wasn't always just about Sid vs. Ovi so much as about the Pens vs. the Caps, a fact both stars noted with relief. Adding to the mix was the presence of two other Russians, Malkin in his rookie season with Pittsburgh and Semin back in the NHL, with the Caps, after playing three years in Russia. "This year, it's 'Capitals and Penguins meet' not 'Crosby and Ovechkin,'" number 8 said.

"These are meaningful games now," Crosby pointed out. "Last year, we were out of the playoff race pretty early. The first few times we played each other it was different because we had never played before. Now it's more regular."

Perhaps, but this was no Ex-Lax game by any standards. The 14,793 fans at the MCI Center in D.C. got their money's worth and more on this night, even though the home side came away with a disheartening loss. The Caps built an impressive 4–0 lead through the first twenty-six minutes of the game only to blow the lead and lose in a shootout.

"It was an unbelievable game to watch," Ovechkin said. "We dominated the first period and 10 minutes of the second period and then just stopped playing. Sometimes that happens. Nothing is a lock, you know? We're just disappointed right now."

Ovechkin did his part. He assisted on two of the four goals, and added a goal in the shootout. At the other end, Crosby was just as instrumental in the comeback, scoring late in the second period on a bullet shot in the slot to make it a 4–3 game and then making a great play to set up Malkin for the tying goal early in the third.

Crosby was checked hard near the crease, but as he fell onto his stomach he made a pass to Malkin cutting through the front of the goal. "Geno" snuck a quick shot as he also was falling past a stunned goalie, Olaf Kolzig, who was still watching Crosby.

"Anytime you play as bad as we did in the first period and you're able to bring it back up in the second and third, it's a good feeling," Crosby said. "I think it was fun to see the way we were chipping away."

A dejected Ovechkin held the opposite view. "It was our mistake," he said. "We scored goals, and then we stopped playing. We not concentrate in defensive zone, and they have shot and score more goals. It's our fault. We go up 4–0, and we stop playing."

In the shootout, Ovechkin scored as did Erik Christensen, and although Crosby was stopped by Kolzig, Malkin made a gorgeous deke on the goalie before sliding the puck in. Marc-Andre Fleury sealed the win by stopping Chris Clark on the final shot of the shootout, giving the Pens a stunning win after their slow start. The shootout loss drove down Washington's record to 0–5 in such games this season.

"There's no question there's more emotion, but it's natural for it to be like that," Crosby said of playing the Caps and Ovechkin. "I don't think guys are adding anything to it than what it is. Everyone knows when it's a bigger stage guys want to rise to the occasion. I don't feel I have to rescue a franchise or a league. I'm happy to be part of both, but I think there's a lot of young talent, a lot of guys who can bring excitement besides me and Alex."

One of those young talented players was Malkin. In fact, he began his career early in the season by scoring in his first six NHL games, a record matched only by three players from the NHL's inaugural season in 1917–18 – Joe Malone, Newsy Lalonde, and Cy Denneny. The difference was that all three had played previous seasons in the NHA, making Malkin's record all the more unique for a first-year player.

On this night, the Russian rookie who spoke little English stole the spotlight from 87 and 8 by speaking a language they all spoke fluently – hockey.

A RELAXING AFFAIR

JANUARY 24, 2007: THE 55TH NHL ALL-STAR GAME

Voting for the 2007 NHL All-Star Game came to a close on January 9, 2007, and Sidney Crosby was far and away the fans' choice to be in Dallas for the 55th edition of the mid-season exhibition. It was the first such game since 2004, the 2006 edition cancelled because of the Olympics and '05 wiped out by the lockout.

Crosby received 825,783 votes, the most of any player in either conference. The next closest player was Joe Thornton in the Western Conference, who received 663,931 votes. Ovechkin was third among Eastern Conference forwards with 475,297, meaning he and Crosby would be in the starting line-up as per fan ballots. Malkin was fifth in the voting at 399,081.

The voting produced another "youngest to" record for Crosby, who was now the youngest player to be voted to the All-Star Game starting roster. Among the many bits of business around the "glitter game" was Reebok's introduction of a new streamlined sweater and socks, designed to fit tighter to the body to reduce drag and therefore create extra speed for the players. Crosby was front and centre during the press conference, both as a key Reebok endorser and as a leading voice with the NHL. He was joined by Ovechkin, Nicklas Lidstrom, Marty Turco, and Jason Blake.

"We're in a new era in the NHL, why not do the same thing with the jersey?" Crosby answered rhetorically when asked what he thought of the new on-ice apparel.

At the Super Skills contest, both Crosby and Ovechkin took part in two events. Ovechkin, wearing a new, mirrored visor with a blue hue, competed in the fastest skater event but lost to Andy McDonald. Crosby scored in the team shootout for the Eastern Conference. Both participated in the In the Zone event, and Ovechkin also took part in the team shoot-out. The decisive contest was the one-on-one shootout, and Crosby scored the goal that gave the Eastern Conference the overall victory on the night. He beat Roberto Luongo, his future teammate at the 2010 Olympics.

The All-Star Game itself was the usual goalfest, this time won by the Western Conference by a 12–9 score. Despite playing together on a line most of the night, Crosby was held pointless and Ovechkin had but one goal. "It was an unbelievable time," Ovechkin enthused. "I waited for this time for so long. I will have great memories."

"There were 21 goals; you think I would have had one," Crosby joked after. "I guess it wasn't meant to be. I had a few chances; it just didn't work out."

Daniel Brière, with a goal and four assists, was the game's MVP after being named to the starting team with the two larger-than-life stars. "With Sid and Alex being the future face of the NHL, I was the other guy with those two," he said with due humility.

In the spirit of the occasion, Ovechkin sacrificed shots at several times to dish the puck to Crosby, trying to get a goal for his linemate.

"I tried to help him," he said with a smile. "Next All-Star Game, it will happen. There were a couple of times I normally would have shot, but I wanted to play for the fans. I tried to help him, but it didn't work."

Indeed, Crosby's lack of production this night recalled Wayne Gretzky's first All-Star Game in 1980. The Wales Conference beat the Campbell Conference, 6–3, and Gretzky was held without a point. After the game, Walter Gretzky gave Wayne a puck. "What's that?" Wayne asked innocently. "It's the game puck," his dad responded wryly. "I thought you'd like to touch it since you didn't all game."

SID GETS INTO A RHYTHM

FEBRUARY 3, 2007: WASHINGTON 0 AT PITTSBURGH 2

Sidney Crosby's ascendancy was as clear as a blue sky on a cloudless day. By the time this February game rolled around, the Penguins had won five games in a row, including a 5–4 shootout win at home to Montreal two nights earlier when he had three assists. They were in the hunt for a playoff spot with a 26–17–8 record, the most improved team in the league and some twenty-six points better in the standings to this point from a year ago.

Crosby himself was at the top of the scoring leaders with 25 goals and 82 points. He had his first career hat trick against Philadelphia on October 28, and had a six-point night against the Flyers on December 13 (1 goal, 5 assists). That came during a ten-game point streak during which time he had 23 points and took the lead among individual scorers. He had cut down on his penalty minutes, the result of being a year older and learning how to argue his case more effectively with referees, and wearing the A on a young team he was becoming more of a leader in the dressing room.

Not so the Capitals. They had a 21–24–7 record coming into this game and had won just two of their last nine games. Ovechkin was doing his part, though, having scored 33 goals, including six game-winners, but the supporting cast wasn't yet pulling its weight. A playoff berth was looking less certain with every mounting loss.

To make matters worse, the team had run into injury trouble on the blue line and had acquired Milan Jurcina the previous day from Boston for a conditional draft choice.

The Penguins had now won five of six games in the year-and-a-half-old Sid-Ovi rivalry, but this 2–0 win marked the first time one team had been shut out in Washington-Pittsburgh games. It was also the first time – and remains to date one of only two occassions – neither player recorded a point. More specifically, it was the only NHL regular-season game Crosby had ever played against Ovechkin without recording a point, until 2011 (to go along with one in the playoffs). Ovechkin, on the other hand, has had four pointless games against Crosby during the NHL's regular season.

Goalie Marc-Andre Fleury stopped thirty shots to earn the shutout and was the star attraction on this night. Crosby's pointless game also ended a most incredible streak. In his year and a half in the NHL to this point, the Penguins were 0–30–1 in games he was held off the scoresheet. Not tonight. Ronald Petrovicky scored in the second period, and Jordan Staal added an empty-netter to seal the win for the home side. The win was a season-high sixth in a row for Pittsburgh.

Other statistical facts worth recounting include that this marked the ending of their respective point streaks, Ovechkin having had a point in his previous thirteen games and Crosby in his last eight. Crosby still led all players with 82 points, but Ovi still was the goalscoring leader with 33. Coming off the ice after the game, Ovechkin snapped his stick in half in frustration, a rare outburst of anger for the Russian. "I'm just very, very mad," he later explained. "We have to score. We have many chances."

Despite playing twenty-four minutes Ovechkin was limited to three shots, all in the final period, and he was on for both Pittsburgh goals. Crosby had two shots in 18:46 of ice time.

"Sometimes I think about Crosby, and sometimes I don't think about Crosby," Ovechkin once said philosophically. "Right now I don't think about him because he is he and I am I."

And frequently the twain shall meet.

SID AND OVI MAKE HAPPY

"ROAD TRIP" COMMERCIAL

On February 16, 2007, the NHL launched a successful TV spot called "Road Trip" to help advertise the NHL game of the week. Shot a few weeks earlier in Dallas during the all-star break, it featured several NHL stars, notably Crosby and Ovechkin.

It begins with Ovi ordering room service, but we quickly realize something pranky is going on because of the size of the order:

Ovechkin: "Hi, I'd like to order some food. How many people in the room? Just me. Three pizzas, four chicken fingers, two meatloaf dinners, six large French fries, some sausage, five lobsters – lots of ketchup – chicken corn dogs, Canadian bacon, six Pepsi . . ."

As he places the order, the scene is intercut with other all-stars who are wreaking havoc in other rooms and hallways of the hotel. Eric and Jordan Staal are engaged in a knock-down-drag-out pillow fight; Joe Thornton is stuffing his face with fancy food from an unattended room-service tray in the hall; Roberto Luongo and Ryan Miller are pulling the shaving cream prank on a sleeping Marty Turco; Brendan Shanahan and Sheldon Souray are tossing water balloons out the window; Dion Phaneuf, Martin Havlat, Phil Kessel, and Patrick Eaves are racing luggage trolleys down the hallway; Dany Heatley, Justin Williams, Martin St. Louis, and Brian Rolston are playing mini-hockey with reckless abandon, knocking furnishings over with guilty – and mischievous – pleasure.

And then comes the punchline from Ovechkin, who has finally finished ordering. "That's it . . . My name? Sidney Crosby."

After which a promo appears:

> NHL players are just like you & me
> Plus they're really good at hockey.

And then the final joke. Room service arrives at the door of the unsuspecting Crosby in the form of several valets, each with many dishes on their trays. Crosby opens the door to a chorus of "Room service!" He looks away knowingly and scowls into the camera: "Ovechkin."

Of course, the ad played up the rivalry between the game's two young stars. The "Road Trip" spot was great for the league, because of its popularity, and also for increasing the profiles of the two players, who clearly enjoyed the ad even as it poked fun at them.

"It took a lot [of takes], just because of the lighting or I didn't say it the right way," Crosby said. "They have to be so precise for a two-second clip."

Game on, indeed.

SID WINS AGAIN

FEBRUARY 18, 2007: WASHINGTON 2 AT PITTSBURGH 3

Personality, reputation, performance. These make a player.

Ovechkin? He has a great shot. He loves scoring. He connects with the fans through crazy celebrations. He's a wild guy with hair poking out from his helmet to frame an unshaven face. He's fun-loving and incredibly talented. He scores more highlight-reel goals than anyone. He's a big hitter.

Crosby? He works harder in practice than anyone else on the team. The pressure he is under is immense. He can do it all: pass, shoot, make great plays. He's incredibly strong on his skates. He knows how to lead his team to victory. The smartest player in the game. The bigger the game, the bigger he plays.

Perhaps the finest compliment paid to Crosby was that even when he wasn't playing his best, he had a way of making those around him play better. With Ovechkin, when he was "on" he could win the game on his own, but if he was "off" he couldn't motivate those around him either. These different styles reflected a definite Canada-Russia dichotomy, where Canadians learned the team game from an early age and Russians focused on individual skills. The former style might not be as highlight-reel glamorous, but it usually trumped the latter where it mattered most – on the scoreboard.

The last time these teams played, just two weeks earlier, the Penguins had won the game, 2–0, their sixth straight victory of the season. After that game, they lost to Montreal, 4–3, in overtime, but this win against the Caps tonight was again their sixth in a row since that lone loss squeezed between twelve victories. In all, though, the team had earned points in the last sixteen successive games and was well on its way to the playoffs for the first time since 2001, even though Crosby had just one goal in the last ten games. Malkin, however, had 10 goals and 26 points in that time to pick up the slack.

The Caps could not boast equal success, going 2–3 in their games between meetings, and after the loss tonight they had won only two of the last eight games. The chances of making the playoffs were not good. "When Ovechkin gets only one goal in seven games, it's tough to win," Capitals coach Glen Hanlon said of his star's scoring slump. "Don't mistake that. It's not his fault we're not winning. But if you're asking where the offense has gone, he's a big part of that."

"My luck go away," Ovechkin admitted. "I just hope my luck come back soon."

And therein lies the rub. As Ovechkin goes, so go the Caps, but every now and then Crosby can run dry and still be supported by his teammates. More problematic for Ovechkin was that he had to deal not just with the Crosby matchup but also with going against his friend and compatriot Malkin, who scored the go-ahead goal in the second period.

"Yeah, of course, I enjoy playing against him especially when we win the games – and he's getting pretty mad," Malkin said good-naturedly.

Indeed, it was a quiet night for both top stars, Crosby limited to a single assist and Ovechkin held without a point for the fifth time in his last seven games. Crosby was still tops in the league's scoring, though, with ninety points. In their seven head-to-head meetings, Pittsburgh had won six times, and Crosby had four goals and twelve points. Ovi had three goals and eight points in those games. The rivalry would always be there, but for now it was pretty one-sided.

Mark Recchi got the opening goal, for Pittsburgh, on the power play, but just 65 seconds later, Richard Zednik made a nice deflection past Jocelyn Thibault to tie the score, 1–1. Malkin got the only goal of the second period with only 1:16 remaining, catching goalie Brent Johnson off guard. Malkin was standing near the end red line when he ripped a shot on goal, beating the goalie over the glove despite the bad angle.

Maxime Talbot made it 3–1 early in the final period, and Alexander Semin got a lucky one in the final minute, his 31st of the season but only his second in the last nine games. The Caps, last in the Southeast Division, had a long way up to get to the playoffs.

A CLEAN SWEEP FOR CROSBY

MARCH 27, 2007: PITTSBURGH 4 AT WASHINGTON 3

There were now many great days ahead for hockey in the Steel City, thanks to the historic events of two weeks earlier, when Penguins owner Mario Lemieux reached an agreement with the City of Pittsburgh to build a new arena. The cost was pegged at $290 million and the opening scheduled for October 2009 (it was eventually delayed a year).

Later in the year, the team signed an agreement with the new arena to remain in Pittsburgh until at least 2040. Pittsburgh's rich hockey heritage included three principal arenas in its history. At first there was The Casino, which hosted the city's first hockey game on December 30, 1895, between a team from Queen's University in Kingston, Ontario, and a local team made up of players from Western University and Holy Ghoset. The arena was destroyed by fire just a year later. It was replaced three years after that by the Duquesne Garden just down the street, which hosted its first hockey game the day after opening, on January 23, 1899.

The Pittsburgh Yellow Jackets of the United States Amateur Hockey Association used this rink, and when the team was sold and joined the NHL as the Pirates, it played out of this arena for its four years in the NHL. The Yellow Jackets later returned, and in 1936 the Hornets of the IAHL (International-American Hockey League, precursor to the AHL) were formed. The team played out of Duquesne for the next twenty years until the building was razed for an apartment complex development. The Igloo opened in 1961, and it remained the city's main arena until the fall of 2010, when the Consol Energy Center hosted its first Penguins game.

Hockey in Washington, D.C., did not have as rich a history prior to the Capitals joining the NHL in 1975, but it is there all the same if one looks hard enough. Everything really revolved around one man, Miguel Uline. He built the eponymous Uline Arena in 1941 so that his Washington Lions team could play in the Eastern Amateur Hockey League. The Lions played on and off in various minor leagues for the better part of two decades, but the arena was renamed the Washington Coliseum in 1959.

The Lions, too, were later known by other names, variously as the Eagles and the Presidents. After 1960 the Coliseum wasn't used much for hockey, and the team didn't have another pro team until the Capitals came along in 1975. Incredibly, the building survives to this day, though it is currently used as a transfer station for the city's garbage. It has been put on a preservation list in the hopes it can be renovated and another, more civic purpose found for the barn.

Sidney Crosby became part of Pittsburgh's arena history pretty much the day he was drafted by the team. It's unlikely Mario Lemieux could have kept the Penguins solvent without number 87, and no doubt the team would have failed to finance a new arena without such a franchise-defining player. When the building was near completion, the Pens announced capacity would be set at 18,087, the last two digits, of course, tribute to Crosby himself.

Ovechkin's role in the hockey history of D.C. is also

impressive, though. Prior to his arrival, the Verizon Center was struggling financially. Opened in 1997 as the MCI Center, it was a state-of-the-art building with a mediocre-to-poor hockey team. Its only Ovechkin-like star previously was Jaromir Jagr, and his two-and-a-half-year stay with the Caps could at best be described as uninspired, at worst, disaster.

The Caps had signed Jagr to a seven-year, $77 million contract in 2001, the richest in league history to date, and he failed to deliver top individual results, team results, attendance results, or off-ice results. The Caps had gone to the Stanley Cup finals in their first season at the new arena (1997–98) but were swept in four games by Detroit and hadn't been near the Cup since.

Ovechkin's career did not immediately signal a change for the fortunes of the team at the box office and bank, but within a couple of years a team that was losing many millions of dollars had moved into the black. Today, it is one of the most financially successful American teams in the NHL, and sellouts at Verizon are the norm, not the rare exception.

To understand the importance of Ovechkin, consider Atlanta, which drafted Ilya Kovalchuk first overall at the 2001 draft. Arguably an equal talent, Kovalchuk has none of the singular personality of Ovechkin and failed to capture the hearts, minds, TV sets, or wallets of sports fans in Atlanta. By the time he was signed by New Jersey in the summer of 2010, Atlanta was in financial turmoil equal to the more public problems of the Phoenix Coyotes and moved to Winnipeg a year later.

If one were to go around the NHL and look at franchises whose operations have been on the border of make or break, it'd be clear that none has been as heavily influenced one way or the other as Pittsburgh and Washington have been by, respectively, Crosby and Ovechkin.

The Penguins' victory on this particular February evening was significant for many reasons. First, it guaranteed the Penguins a spot in the playoffs for the first time since 2001. Second, it gave the Pens 98 points in the standings, an incredible improvement over the meagre 58 they'd accrued the previous season. Third, the team prevented Ovechkin from scoring, leaving him without a goal against them all season. Not surprisingly, this success translated into four straight wins for Pittsburgh over their rivals. Washington, meanwhile, lost for the fourth time in a row, and had now lost 13 of 15 to fall well out of playoff contention.

The Caps jumped out into a 2–0 lead before a packed house of 18,277 at the Verizon Center, much to the dismay of the thousands of Pittsburgh fans who had made the four-hour drive to D.C. for the game. But Pens coach Michel Therrien called a timeout to calm his troops down, and soon enough the visiting fans had something to cheer about.

The Penguins got one goal back later in the opening period with Bryan Muir in the penalty box, and then Crosby cued a rally in the second, assisting on the tying goal and scoring the go-ahead goal in a five-minute span near the start of the period, both scores coming with the extra man. The Penguins made it 4–2 later in the period.

Pittsburgh's three goals with the extra skater were not lost on Ovechkin. "They do great job on the power play, but five on five, I think we beat them," he opined. Maybe, but the chants of "MVP! MVP!" directed at Crosby were certainly unsettling to the home Caps and their star, Ovechkin.

Crosby had six shots to lead all players while Ovechkin had four for the Caps, tops on his team. Ovi's 23:31 of ice time also led all skaters in the game, but he couldn't muster a goal.

He did set up his team's first goal, though, making a nice pass to Alexander Semin early in the opening period.

Washington coach Glen Hanlon pulled goalie Olaf Kolzig with fully two minutes left in the game, and although the Caps made it closer with a late goal from Milan Jurcina, they couldn't get the tying goal.

CROSBY CONTROLS THE HARDWARE

JUNE 14, 2007: 2007 NHL AWARDS

n their first season in the NHL when Crosby was eighteen years old and Ovechkin twenty, the consensus, in the form of Calder Trophy voting, was overwhelmingly in favour of the Russian as the best young player in the game. But 365 days later, Crosby now nineteen and Ovi twenty-one, Ovechkin had been pulled off the throne so that the hockey world could anoint Sidney as the world's greatest player. The only question was his title – King Crosby? King Sid? King Kid? They all worked.

Said Martin Brodeur at the 2007 NHL Awards ceremony at the Elgin Theatre in Toronto: "I think he is the new player in the NHL. Two years in the NHL, and he has been dominating. His leadership, whatever he does out there, is tremendous. The fans love him . . . Like Wayne Gretzky, he is going to make the NHL a better sport."

The Awards were significant for two reasons – the domination by Crosby, and the absence, in physical presence and word, of Ovechkin. Crosby led the league with 84 assists and 120 points, becoming the youngest player ever to win the Art Ross Trophy and the only teenager in any team sport in North America to lead his league in scoring. He was also the youngest to win the Lester B. Pearson Award, and after his name was called for the Hart Trophy, to finish his silverware hat trick, he became the youngest winner of that trophy since Wayne Gretzky in 1980.

Interestingly, the young Russian who was decorated at the Awards was Ovechkin's friend – and Crosby's teammate – Evgeni Malkin, who won the Calder Trophy by beating out their Penguins teammate Jordan Staal and Colorado's Paul Stastny.

Ovechkin finished the season with 46 goals and as many assists, his 92 points placing him 13th in the overall scoring race, a distant 28 points behind Crosby. But perhaps more than any other stat on the season, one stands out like a sore thumb. Among the top 20 scoring leaders for 2006–07, only two players were in the minus of the plus-minus stat – Boston's Marc Savard and Ovechkin, both of whom were a disastrous –19. Crosby, on the other hand, was a +10, by no means the best in the league but a very respectable figure all the same for an offensive-minded player. Ovechkin's number was worrisome because despite scoring 46 goals, he was still on the ice for 19 more goals against than goals for, a clear indicator of poor defensive play.

After the NHL season, Ovechkin returned to Moscow, his home, to play once again in the World Championship, desperate to win gold for his country on home soil. He managed only one goal in eight games, however, and the Russians were stunned by a Mikko Koivu goal at 5:40 of overtime in the semi-finals to lose to Finland, 2–1. They rallied to beat Sweden, 3–1, for the bronze medal, but this wasn't the way Ovechkin wanted either to end his season or to begin his summer.

Crosby was not invited to play for Canada this year, but that was because after the team lost to Ottawa in five games in the opening round of the playoffs, he let slip that he had played the end of the regular season and the playoffs with a broken bone in his left foot. Rehab was his only activity after the final game.

Well, that's not entirely true. At the team's send-off luncheon on May 31, Crosby was named captain for the upcoming season, making him the youngest wearer of the C in the NHL's ninety-year history. Vincent Lecavalier was captain in Tampa Bay at age nineteen years and eleven months, but Crosby was two months younger. He continued Pittsburgh's captain's lineage, which had ended a year and a half earlier when Mario Lemieux retired.

"Sidney has done so much for this franchise in his first two seasons, made so much history, that you have to keep reminding yourself that he is only nineteen years old," Penguins general manager Ray Shero said in a statement. "It is obvious to all of us – coaches, players, management, staff – that he has grown into the acknowledged leader of the Pittsburgh Penguins. It is only appropriate that he wears the C as team captain."

"I was always told that age is just a number," Crosby said. "I try not to let it get in the way of anything."

On the subject of numbers, another, much bigger number played a role in the summer of 2007. On July 11, Crosby signed a five-year contract extension worth $43.5 million, including a $5 million signing bonus. His entry level, three-year deal had one more year left on it, but the new deal would average out to, appropriately, $8.7 million a season. Although a large deal, this was a team-oriented one as well. The CBA permitted a top salary of 20 per cent of the salary cap, which for this season was $50.3 million.

Crosby could have reasonably asked for $10.06 million a season, but doing so would have jeopardized the team's chances to sign the many other young superstars on the team, notably Evgeni Malkin, Jordan Staal, and Marc-Andre Fleury. Indeed, when it was time for Malkin to sign, he agreed to a similar deal, knowing there was no way he could ask for more than what Crosby was making.

"Individual honours and scoring championships are great," Crosby said after signing on the proverbial dotted line, "but my number-one goal is to win the Stanley Cup. I'd love to be part of bringing the Cup back here to Pittsburgh."

"Any projections I'd done had Sidney at the max, because you never knew what was going to happen," general manager Ray Shero admitted. "Sidney is interested in winning the Stanley Cup. He's interested in winning in Pittsburgh. This is a great first step, obviously."

Crosby said that, "it was important to do what was right, for everyone," but was happy the number turned out to be his lucky one.

"I was right around that ballpark, so I said I might as well go 8.7," Crosby said. "That's my number, and it's always been that way. It's always been good to me, so, hopefully, maybe it will bring a little luck."

The stage was set for 2007–08. Crosby was now the undisputed, unifying NHL champion of the world. The league was his to control and to guide. And Ovechkin had plenty of catching up to do.

3

OVECHKIN TAKES CONTROL

MISSING TEETH TELL A STORY

OCTOBER 20, 2007: PITTSBURGH 2 AT WASHINGTON 1

True story. At the 2006 Olympics, Finland's Teemu Selanne lost most of his front teeth during a game. He came in to the House of Hockey, where players and family could relax, smiling proudly, the lost "Chiclets" a clear indicator of the sacrifices needed to win hockey games. He looked ten years older, but he said if it would help his team win a medal, it was worth it. The Finns won silver, so it was a fair trade for the "Finnish Flash."

Such is the nature of hockey players that dental appearances have a full range of importance. Some players get fitted with dentures so that off ice they look, well, more socially acceptable. Others won't get their teeth fixed until after their career, and others want to get the damage fixed immediately and permanently.

When Sidney Crosby suffered cracked teeth against the Flyers during his rookie season, he got the damage repaired right away. He had to. Or, at least, it was in his best interest to. As the face of the NHL, he had to have the pretty-boy look for the cameras, a job requirement, so to speak.

But just a couple of weeks before this first meeting between Pittsburgh and Washington early in the 2007–08 season, Ovechkin lost his front tooth, which created the gap for which he has been famous ever since. The event occurred in a game in Atlanta, October 5, 2007, when he was high-sticked. He stayed in the game and assisted on the game-winning goal in the third period of a 4–3 road win over the Thrashers.

After the game he spoke of wanting to get the tooth replaced, but then he thought otherwise. "It makes me look hot. Girls like it," he said. "Like a warrior."

And so the gap has stayed, and his smile, with the black hole in the middle of his mouth, has become part of his persona. On this night, though, "Handsome Sid" edged "Gapboy Alex" by a 2–1 score thanks in large measure to the play of these two. Crosby made a great play to set up the winning goal, a power-play score from Ryan Whitney late in the second period. Ovechkin, on the other hand, was held without a point for the first time of this young season, and for the third time in the last four Pittsburgh-Washington matchups.

And the crowd was into it. The capacity 18,277 fans at the Verizon Center booed Crosby whenever he touched the puck, but they were stunned to hear a large Pittsburgh contingent counter by booing every time Ovechkin had the disc. It all made for a lively atmosphere that got both players' attention.

"Maybe from each guy's side, there's a little more motivation," Crosby conceded, "because there's more attention, more eyes on the game."

Ovechkin dismissed the ongoing media interest in a personal rivalry he suggested had passed its due date. "We can't think about matchups, Crosby and Ovechkin," he explained. "It's over, I think. It was over after the first year."

Not true. In fact, the rivalry was only getting started. After all, Ovechkin played with as much pride as any great star, yet to date he had taken a whuppin' almost every time his team had faced Crosby's. And with playoff battles and Olympics showdowns in their near future, fans were just warming up to an 87–8 battle every time they met.

Ovechkin suffered no Samson-like loss of strength from losing his tooth; in fact, he played twenty-two minutes and fired eight shots on goal. He also nailed Crosby with a hard check early in the third period that got everyone on ice involved in a little group discussion. Crosby was unfazed. "That was a good hit," he admitted. "He's a strong guy. He plays a complete game. I don't expect him to take it easy against anybody, especially me."

Of course, the victor has an easier time making such diplomatic remarks, and for Crosby the satisfaction was substantial, knowing he had beaten Ovechkin in eight of the nine NHL games they had played against each other.

BOUDREAU ERA
BEGINS IN D.C.

DECEMBER 27, 2007: WASHINGTON 3 AT PITTSBURGH 4 (OT)

The Edmonton Oilers didn't know how lucky they were to have Glen Sather as their coach. Sather came by the job honestly and moved into it seamlessly, back when the team was still playing in the WHA. He had been a player with the Alberta Oilers, then a playing coach, and finally just a coach. He knew how to nurture the incredible talent the team was acquiring, from Wayne Gretzky and Mark Messier to Glenn Anderson, Jari Kurri, Paul Coffey, Grant Fuhr, and Kevin Lowe. Sather played a parental role for these players, being protective when need be and a disciplinarian on other occasions. Sather was the driving force behind the Oilers' dynasty of the mid-1980s, during which the team scored more goals than any other in NHL history.

The same can't be said for many other teams and coaches. It took years of experimentation in Detroit before Scotty Bowman came on board and made a difference to their Stanley Cup fortunes in the 1990s. New Jersey became a force only when Lou Lamoriello established a style of play for the team and then brought in first Jacques Lemaire, and later Larry Robinson and Pat Burns, Montreal men who knew how to win the big prize.

The Pittsburgh Penguins had to make adjustments over-night when they acquired Sidney Crosby in the 2005 Entry Draft. One minute they were a dying team far away from the playoffs in need of a new owner and new arena; the next minute they were one of the league's marquee teams. But they needed a general manager who could acquire players to go with Crosby, and they needed a Sather-like coach as well. Ed Olczyk wasn't that coach, and Michel Therrien definitely wasn't, as time would tell.

So, too, in Washington. The Capitals not only had Alex Ovechkin, they had a core of young star players around him who needed to be coached in a particular way, on ice and off, during games and during practices, at home and on the road. Stars didn't necessarily deserve star treatment, as it were, but a player like Ovechkin needed more ice time, extra time on the power play, and greater confidence from the coach in criti-cal situations. After another mediocre start to this season, Ovechkin's fourth, GM George McPhee fired coach Glen Hanlon on November 22, 2007, and brought up Bruce Boudreau from the farm team.

The Caps were 6–14–1 at the time, dead last in the league despite the optimism of their new team motto of "New Look. New Season. New Attitude." Their dismal ranking, combined with the training-camp dictum of owner Ted Leonsis that "the rebuild is over" and the raining of boos by the home fans during the team's recent losing streak, made it clear some-thing had to be done.

Not only did the Caps bring in a new coach with a new attitude, they brought in someone who was one of the best feel-good stories in coaching history. As a player, Boudreau was one of the highest scoring juniors in Canadian history, but his small stature meant he was never going to become a regular in the NHL. He was called up many times for short stints with the Maple Leafs (seven in all) but always sent back to the minors, where he played for some seventeen seasons (1975–92).

After retiring, Boudreau became a coach and the pattern repeated. He coached in the minors for an incredible eighteen years, having success virtually wherever he went. He won the Calder Cup with the Hershey Bears of the AHL in 2005–06, and prior to that he had won the Kelly Cup in the ECHL with the Mississippi Sea Wolves in 1998–99. The Bears were Washington's AHL affiliate, and it was that connection that got him to the NHL in November 2007, albeit at first on a temporary basis. In short, no one deserved a chance to coach in the NHL more than Boudreau. "I've sort of waited thirty-two years for the opportunity, so I'm looking forward to the challenge," he said the day the Caps hired him and made him a full-time NHL employee for the first time in his life, at age fifty-two.

Boudreau was immediately classified as a temporary coach for the rest of the season. That gave McPhee time to assess Boudreau, and it gave the coach time to prove his worth without the pressure of knowing the franchise depended on him. Boudreau was, as they say, a players' coach, and had spent his life in hockey. If anyone were qualified for the job, it was him. If anyone would be determined to make a success of this ridiculously fortuitous chance to coach Ovechkin et al., it would be him.

Front and centre, Boudreau's job was to manage Ovechkin, not just watch in awe: to coach and guide and develop the young star. But an enormous part of that task involved making the most of the other players, trying to make Ovechkin feel like the most important player but not the one who had to single-handedly win every game.

The transformation was immediate. The Caps had started the year 6–14–1 under Hanlon, their worst start in twenty-six years, and looked sure to miss the playoffs. But in his first five weeks with the team, Boudreau produced a record of 7–5–3, not great, but a vast improvement. The power play was better; the penalty killing, better; and, most telling, the atmosphere in the dressing room radically improved. As a result, McPhee soon named Boudreau the full-time coach for the rest of the season.

It was a sage confirmation of Boudreau's abilities. By the end of the year, the Caps produced a record of 37–17–0–7 under their new coach and finished first in the Southeast Division. Boudreau was named Jack Adams Award winner for his transformative effect on the team. He had Ovechkin firing on all cylinders, playing on one of the top lines in the league with Nicklas Backstrom, a passer by nature, and Alexander Semin, who could shoot or pass, depending on the situation.

But in this game, Boudreau's first against Crosby and Pittsburgh, he returned to the dressing room after 61 minutes and 33 seconds of play, more than a little disappointed. The Caps allowed a power-play goal late in the third period to give Pittsburgh a 3–3 tie, and in overtime Crosby made a great pass to Sergei Gonchar who scored the game winner. What looked like a win turned into a loss, and no one knew better than Boudreau that those were the kinds of games that could become habit-forming.

"I thought we had total control over the last half of that game, until we took a penalty," Boudreau said in measured tones. "It is a game we have to win."

Crosby had a hand in the go-ahead goal late in the first period, but Ovechkin capitalized on a defensive miscue in the slot and ripped a quick shot past Ty Conklin to give the Caps that 3–2 lead late in the second period. He suffered a cut to his leg early in the third period and didn't return after requiring twenty-five delicate stitches, leaving Boudreau without his top scorer for the final period and overtime.

The Penguins got their chance late in that final period when Shaone Morrisonn took a roughing penalty at 15:48. Darryl Sydor scored the tying goal off a faceoff, ripping a hard slapper past Olaf Kolzig to send the game to overtime. Kolzig had replaced starter Brent Johnson, who was injured on Pittsburgh's second goal scored late in the first period by Colby Armstrong.

On the winning goal, Crosby took the puck from behind the Washington net in front, and while the two defencemen both focused on him he dropped the puck back to Gonchar, who had moved in from the point. Gonchar could see plenty of net and made no mistake with his hard shot at the 1:33 mark.

"Sid made a great pass," Gonchar noted. "When he started skating toward the net, both defencemen are paying attention to him and not even looking at me. I had a wide-open net."

It was the ninth win in ten regular-season meetings between Crosby and Ovechkin, but this one had an asterisk beside it because of number 8's third-period absence. The Caps had played at home the previous night, beating Tampa Bay, 3–2, while the Pens had the night off, waiting comfortably at home for the visitors to arrive.

Boudreau was not impressed. "We have chances to put the game away, and we have to have the killer instinct. I don't know how you get it. I don't know if you're born with it. But somehow we have to find it."

CAPS PUT ACCENT ON VICTORY

JANUARY 21, 2008: WASHINGTON 6 AT PITTSBURGH 5 (SO)

O f course, it's naive not to be aware of the business side of the game, and both Crosby and Ovechkin will leave hockey with colossal amounts of money in the bank, invested, available to care for them and their families for the rest of their days, till they shuffle off their mortal coil. But the ways in which they have gone about acquiring their millions to date have been radically different.

Agent Pat Brisson of CAA Sports has been with Crosby since the start of Crosby's career. He has advised the Crosby family and helped develop the teen into a man, and brought carefully chosen endorsements to the table in the form of huge contracts with, particularly, Reebok and Gatorade.

Ovechkin played things differently. First, when he was still in Russia, a long way from the NHL, his agent was Don Meehan, perhaps the most respected agent ever to represent players. Meehan was by Ovechkin's side in January 2003 at the World U20 (Junior) Championship in Halifax when Ovechkin first held a press conference, and he got Ovechkin his first contract at a time when it looked like he'd have to play another year in Russia. Meehan hired a good Russian friend, Anna Goruven, the only woman certified by the NHLPA to be an agent, to help, and she in turn had her daughter, Susanna, move to Washington to act as Alex's translator. By the time Ovechkin was twenty-one, pretty much everything he and his family had was through the efforts of Meehan.

But on November 15, 2006, Ovechkin fired Meehan and decided to go it alone with the help only of his mother, Tatiana. He knew he'd be signing a big contract in the next year or so and decided that (a) he could negotiate directly with owner Ted Leonsis and GM George McPhee and (b) it was like throwing money out the window to pay an agent 3 to 5 per cent of a huge contract to do what he believed he could do equally well.

The classy Meehan said only that he "wished him well," and the financial umbilical cord was cut. On January 13, 2008, Ovechkin signed the largest contract in NHL history, a thirteen-year deal worth $124 million – and no agent's fees. The signing came during a period when several mega-length deals had been arranged, many of which turned out to be unwise signings by the team.

Rick DiPietro, for instance, signed a fifteen-year deal worth $67.5 million with the New York Islanders, a sum that so far has been close to a total waste for the team. Scott Gomez signed a seven-year $51.5 million deal with the New York Rangers, one that was such a failure he was traded two years later to the Canadiens.

But Ovechkin's signing doesn't have the smell of failure to it so much as an element of selfishness not present in the Crosby deal. By earning nearly $10 million per season, he will cut into the potential of the team to surround him with quality players, meaning Ovechkin will be well paid for a long time – and will no doubt deliver with hundreds of goals – but the team will have a tremendous challenge building itself into a Cup contender.

"I signed a long-team deal. I want to be here," said Ovechkin. "I like Washington. Right now, I can't believe it. I'm happy to stay here. It's my second home. I like the fans. I like the team. I like everything here."

Ever the puck philosopher, whittling the game down to the bare bones because of his minimal English, Ovechkin concluded, "Hockey is my life, and money is money. If you think about money, you stop playing hockey."

And the pressure to bring a Cup to D.C. with that kind of income? "I know it's extra pressure, but I have to play the same," he said. "If you think of pressure, it's hard for you. I have to play the same way – play more, play better."

So Crosby and Ovechkin, who made a total of about $5 million together in their rookie season, were now making nearly $20 million a season together. They entered the league star prospects; they met and exceeded all expectations to date; they were now being very handsomely rewarded for their efforts.

Unfortunately, the first meeting between Crosby and Ovechkin in 2008 had to be delayed because of injury. Three days earlier, Crosby had fallen hard into the end boards and suffered a high-ankle sprain, which would keep him off ice for several weeks. More serious than a standard issue ankle sprain, the high version involves the ligament that connects the tibia and the fibula.

This was the first time a Crosby-Ovechkin matchup failed to materialize because of injury, and it came at a time when the Penguins were putting together a good streak of play. They had won nine of their last ten games prior to the 3–0 loss to Tampa Bay when Crosby was injured, and the other game was a shoot-out loss. They were leading the Atlantic Division but now had to rely on Evgeni Malkin for most of their offence.

"It's a huge loss," said coach Michel Therrien with plati-
tudinous predictability. "He is the heart of the team, and he
is our leader. We are going to face adversity, and we are going
to have to battle through it."

"The big thing with this is time," Crosby said, evaluating
the injury. "You really can't do very much . . . We'll see how
fast I heal."

Indeed, it was Malkin and Ovechkin who shone brightest
with Crosby out, both Russians scoring twice and adding an
assist. The Capitals, however, prevailed in the shootout,
thanks to goals from Ovi and linemate Alexander Semin.
Ovechkin led all skaters with eleven shots, but Malkin was
sensational playing in place of Crosby as the marquee Penguin.
Crosby, in a boot cast, watched the game with owner and
landlord Mario Lemieux from a private box.

"We lost our best player and you can't really replace him,"
Malkin said. "It's not only me; everybody has to keep up with
every game."

Both teams had leads and scored two goals in the opening
period, and the same thing happened in the second in reverse.
In the opening twenty minutes, Pittsburgh scored first and last,
with two Caps' goals in between, and in the second it was
Washington that had the early and late goals and two Pens
scores in the middle. The teams traded goals in the third, setting the stage for overtime in a 5–5 game after sixty minutes.

The Penguins had a huge opportunity to win, getting a
rare five-on-three power play in the extra period but muster-
ing only one shot. In the shootout, the Caps prevailed, 2–1, to
earn a 6–5 win, their first in Pittsburgh since 2002. Ovechkin's
two goals launched him to the top of the leaderboard for the
Rocket Richard Trophy with 38, one more than countryman
Ilya Kovalchuk of Atlanta.

OVI SHINES AS
CROSBY SITS OUT

JANUARY 27, 2008: THE 56TH NHL ALL-STAR GAME

Crosby and Ovechkin were wildly different – even in the expression of their similarities. They both, for instance, were very media friendly, accommodating any and all requests to the best of their ability. But where Crosby was the politically correct spokesman for the league, Ovechkin was the less responsible one who spoke without thinking of the repercussions. Crosby was the sheriff; Ovechkin the outlaw. Sid was serious – Ovi, fun-lovin.'

Still, Ovechkin rarely got in trouble for what he said. He wasn't an idiot like Sean Avery; he was just the kid who said what was on his mind, and often that was self-promoting and self-centred, whereas Crosby never talked about himself unless asked.

They also played the way they spoke. Crosby worked tirelessly in practice and demanded his teammates do the same. One never got the sense that Ovechkin was a first on the ice/ last off kind of guy. Crosby practised many details of the game – from faceoffs, to tip-ins, to passing to teammates for one-timers. One always got the sense, rightly or wrongly, that Ovechkin worked on his shot and little else.

To this point in their careers, Crosby was the more

popular player, if All-Star Game voting was any reference point. For the second straight year he led all vote-getters, this year with 507,274, well ahead of the player with the second-most votes, Nicklas Lidstrom, captain of Detroit, with 477,787. Crosby, however, couldn't make it to the All-Star Game because of his ankle injury. Ovechkin, nowhere near the top in votes, was, of course, named to the roster in due course.

Ovechkin took advantage of Crosby's absence by wowing the crowd during the Skills competition the day before the game. On the shootout drill, he came in on goal, flipped the puck to his stick and bounced it in the air several times, and then fired a shot. It wasn't the craziest play ever executed, but it showed that when Ovechkin had a chance to be the hot-dog performer, he'd happily steal the spotlight and get the fans going.

Crosby may have been voted to the starting lineup of this All-Star Game, but Alex Ovechkin scored two first-period goals. "I'm good," Ovi said after, with a big smile appropriate to the casual occasion. He played on a line with Martin St. Louis and Jason Spezza and propelled the East to a 5–1 lead after the first period.

Number 87 was joined in the press box (metaphorically speaking) by a veritable all-star team in itself: goalies Martin Brodeur and Roberto Luongo, both of whom pulled out because of personal reasons, and skaters Dany Heatley, Sergei Zubov, Paul Stastny, and Henrik Zetterberg, all of whom withdrew for one reason or another.

As a result, Ovechkin not only attracted the spotlight, he revelled in it and shone brightest under it. He accommodated the incredible media demands, signed hundreds of pucks, pennants, and cards, and whatever other memorabilia fans thrust in front of him.

In the third period, coach John Paddock briefly put together a modern "Russian five" comprised of Ovechkin, his good friends Ilya Kovalchuk and Evgeni Malkin, and defence-men Sergei Gonchar and Andrei Markov. "It was pretty cool," the Great 8 said of the opportunity.

More than being cool, it gave Ovechkin the opportunity to be the star of the show – and he was.

SID BACK WITH A VENGEANCE

MARCH 9, 2008: PITTSBURGH 4 AT WASHINGTON 2

Sidney Crosby had returned to game action only a few days before the next Pens-Caps meeting and pronounced himself fit before taking the ice against Ovechkin and the Capitals on this night. For fans who had tickets to the game at the Verizon Center, they could not have been disappointed by what they saw, even though the home side lost. The top guns played up to expectations, and although the game ended on a bizarre note, it was a highly entertaining evening all the same.

Crosby had returned to action March 4 against Tampa Bay – ironically the team he played against when he injured his ankle some forty-five days earlier – and was the star of the game, creating many scoring chances before setting up the 1–0 goal late in the third period for Maxime Talbot. "I had some great chances that I would have loved to put in," he admitted after game one of his return. "It didn't happen. Sometimes that's the way it goes. I'm a little rusty."

He was anything but rusty this night of March 9 against the Caps in a critical game for the home side. While Pittsburgh was chugging along at or near the top of the Atlantic Division, life wasn't so comfortable for the Capitals, who were fighting for their playoff lives.

Indeed, Malkin had stepped up to fill the void when Crosby was injured, and with both playing so well, Ovechkin was up against more than he alone could handle. The teams exchanged goals early in the second period after a scoreless first, but Crosby put the Pens ahead at 18:08 when he banged in a rebound from the side of the goal. It came at the end of a penalty to Sergei Fedorov, but he had just returned to the ice so it didn't count as being a power-play goal.

Despite the score, Fedorov was having a positive impact on the team. Acquired just a dozen days ago from Columbus, his was a symbolic uniting with Ovechkin. Fedorov defected from the old Soviet Union in 1989, sending shockwaves throughout the hockey world. He formed one of the greatest lines in his country's history, teaming with Pavel Bure and Alexander Mogilny, and was the first great superstar from the Soviet Union to establish himself in North America. And now, at age thirty-nine and nearing the end of his career, he was playing alongside a player who owed him a debt of gratitude for paving the way – Ovechkin.

Even before the period ended, though, the Caps tied the game with a man advantage, Ovechkin getting the assist on a goal by Alexander Semin. The Pens were badly outplayed through two periods and were lucky to be tied after being outshot, 33–13, but the final twenty minutes were the polar opposite. The third period was dominated by Pittsburgh, and they deserved to win, though the go-ahead goal was hardly one to brag about.

In the final minute of regulation, with the Penguins pressuring the Caps, Crosby took a shot that goalie Cristobal Huet saved. The puck came to Caps forward Nicklas Backstrom, who tried to push it back to the goalie, but Huet wasn't expecting the play and Backstrom made the pass with speed and force, resulting in the puck going directly into the net. Crosby got credit for the score but realized the luck involved.

"We've been on the other side of that before," he said. "Obviously, it's not fun. It's a big break for us."

Indeed it was, and it was a tough loss for the Caps to take. "That was officially heart-breaking," coach Bruce Boudreau conceded. "I feel bad for Nik. He was doing everything that he could, and he ends up shooting it in his own net."

Upon seeing his linemate and good friend score this miserable own goal, Ovechkin dropped to the ice and covered his head in disbelief. It was the tenth Crosby win over Ovechkin in twelve NHL meetings to date, none more fluky than this. After this game, Crosby's ankle flared up and he was off skates for another eighteen days.

The playoffs were another story altogether and pointed to the differences between the two teams. Think of Crosby as the hub of a wheel: everything revolves around it, but all the spokes are vital to the hub. Think of Ovechkin as the hood ornament on a BMW: it's the very symbol of success – but all on its own.

In the opening round of the playoffs, Ovechkin scored the winning goal in a game-one, 5–4 win over the Flyers. He then went goalless for four games, and the Flyers took a 3–2 series lead. Ovechkin scored twice in game six on the road to force a deciding game, but even a goal and an assist in the last game weren't enough and the Caps were out of the playoffs in the opening round. In three years, Ovechkin had just these seven playoff games as post-season experience.

Said an exhausted Ovechkin: "It's hard, but it's good experience for us."

Crosby, meanwhile, recovered from the injury and, fresh from the long rest, captained his team to game six of the Stanley Cup finals against Detroit, before losing. He had 27 points in 20 games and was a leader throughout, but afterwards he revealed two injuries that didn't help the cause. "It wasn't so much my ankle as it was my ribs," he said, deflecting attention from the one injury that was well known and shedding light on another that had been well guarded.

But his final thoughts on the season were perhaps most emblematic of his personality. "We just came up short. It's pretty tough. It's not a fun time. We have to remember this feeling for sure."

Remembering the bad experiences is vintage Crosby. It's what motivates him, whether it's the memory of losing the World Junior gold before winning it, or of losing a playoff series or a vote for a top individual trophy. Crosby remembers these bad moments as motivation for making sure they never happen again.

Next year, he would back up these words in spades.

YEAR OF THE OVI

JUNE 12, 2008: 2008 NHL AWARDS

Early in life Sidney Crosby was praised by Wayne Gretzky as a star who might one day break some of 99's records. Late in this 2007–08 season, Gretzky chimed in on Ovechkin, with similar praise. "He's just a bull," Gretzky began. "He's got a little bit of everything. He's got the release and the hands that Bossy had, the quickness that Kurri had, and the toughness that Messier had. He's the whole package, and he loves to score goals . . . I think he can get 90 [in a season] one day," he predicted. "The thing about scoring goals is that it's one thing to score, but there are some guys who really enjoy scoring goals more than other guys. He's one of those guys who likes to score. If he could, he would keep the puck for every one. But it's great for the game. He brings excitement to the game. He's fun to watch. He's a good player."

The gods of cyberland agreed wholeheartedly with Gretzky, for even when the NHL Awards ceremony was still a week away, NHL.com was already selling T-shirts emblazoned with Ovechkin's name on them announcing "2007–08 Hart Trophy winner"!

Of course, once the gaffe was detected, the sale was stopped, but it was clear neither of the two other finalists – Jarome Iginla and Evgeni Malkin – stood much of a chance

The 17-year-old Crosby settles into a chair in his family's basement to watch the draft lottery and discover which team will have the right to claim him.

Crosby is selected by the Penguins at the 2005 Entry Draft after Pittsburgh won first overall choice via a lottery to determine the order of drafting after the lockout.

A pre-NHL Ovechkin undergoes the rigours of testing during the league's annual combine to determine physical (and psychological) strength and performance.

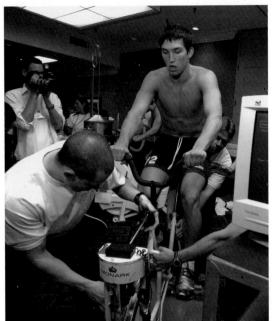

Getty Images

Reuters

Ovechin is front and centre at the 2004 Entry Draft when the Caps select him first overall.

An injured Ovechkin congratulates Crosby after Canada defeated
Russia 6–1 to win gold at the 2005 World Junior Championship.

Ovechkin and Crosby
share a friendly moment at
the NHL Awards ceremony
in Vancouver in June 2006.

The golden goal! Crosby beats Ryan Miller with a quick shot at 7:40 of overtime to give Canada Olympic gold in 2010.

Crosby and Ovechkin match each other stride for stride during the quarter-finals at the Vancouver Olympics, a game in which Canada overwhelmed the Russians by a 7–3 score.

The most memorable on-ice contretemps between the two great rivals occurred on February 22, 2009, when Sid and Ovi pushed and shoved, and yapped a little more, during a line change.

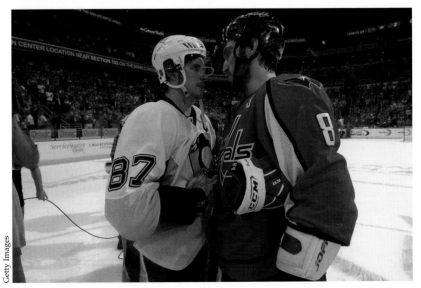

Crosby and Ovechkin shake hands after one of the most memorable playoff series of the modern era, a seven-game showdown won by the Penguins in 2009.

Ovechkin celebrates a goal in trademark style, jumping off the glass with typical excess.

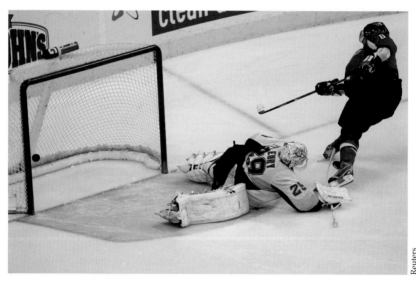

Ovechkin beats Pittsburgh goalie Marc-Andre Fleury with a deke and easy finish into the open net.

Although the respect on ice is mutual, there is no love lost when Crosby and Ovechkin meet, as this mid-ice collision indicates.

Reuters

Reuters

Crosby bats the puck out of mid-air into the net during the 2009 playoffs.

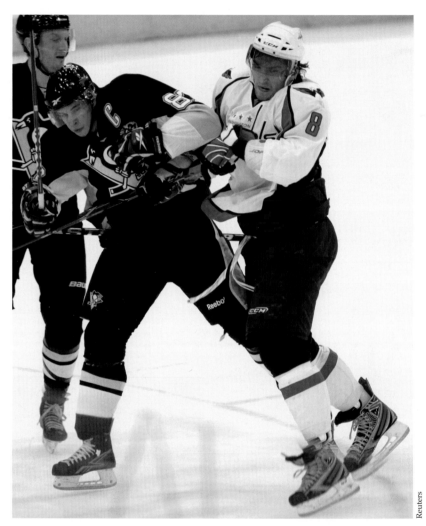

Crosby and Ovechkin eliminate each other from play as they check each other hard.

against Ovechkin after the season he had had and Crosby's extended absence that had eliminated him from contention.

"If I win it," Ovi said the day of the awards show, in Toronto, referring to the Hart Trophy, "it will be a dream come true. It's MVP. It's for the best player in the league. It means you're the best. It will mean so much to me and my family."

This was unquestionably Ovechkin's year, and he knew it. Not only did he play his usual great game consistently, but it's entirely possible he drew extra motivation from Crosby's lengthy injury, realizing he didn't have to share the spotlight with anyone and that the league was, in a manner of speaking, his for the taking.

In the first 46 games of the season, playing when Crosby was healthy, Ovechkin had 57 points, but in the final 36 games of the season, mostly played without number 87, Ovi had 55 points. And, during the days of Crosby's absence, Ovechkin's point production increased from 1.24 per game to 1.61. As important, his defensive play also improved by leaps and bounds, and his weak plus-minus of −19 from the previous season turned into a +28 this season.

Regardless, Ovechkin was the dominant player this season and was feted on Awards Night with an impressive collection of silverware, notably the Art Ross, Hart, and Rocket Richard Trophies and the Lester B. Pearson Award. Crosby was, understandably, shut out from the gifts because he had played too few games to make a season-long impression.

"I want to win everything," Ovechkin said after the ceremony. "Next time, the Stanley Cup. These awards and all awards are all about my teammates, coaches, training staff and everything, all Capitals organization. They gave me a great chance. They gave me trust to prove what I can do on the ice. And the fans are unbelievable. They support us and love us; it doesn't matter what happens, we still have our fans. I think we have a great future. We have great young guys who play well. We had a great experience this year, and I hope next year we improve more and more."

"I think I'm the happiest 22-year-old guy on the planet right now," continued Ovechkin. "I have a great family. Everything I have I made myself from working hard. And I know it's improving. I'm happy right now with what I'm doing and how everything is going. One more day here and my summer will start right away," Ovechkin declared. "I'll go to Turkey for vacation, relax and forget about everything, and I'll be ready for next year."

Asked if he could ever win the Selke Trophy for defensive play, Ovechkin joked, "If I play more defensively, Bruce [will] kill me because my goal is to score goals. I play defensively how I can. It was good for me when I worked with Glen Hanlon. He taught me a lot. He said, 'You're good, but sometimes you have to work for the team; block shots and do some hard work.'"

Joining Ovechkin on the winner's podium was his coach, Bruce Boudreau, who was named Jack Adams Award winner as coach of the year in honour of the incredible turnaround he helped orchestrate, taking the dormant Caps to an unexpected playoff berth.

One added bonus for Ovechkin in winning the Hart Trophy came from D.C. mayor Adrian M. Fenty, who had promised to give the hockey star a key to the city if he won. Ovi did, and the next day Fenty kept his word, making the ceremonial gift on the steps of the Wilson Building in downtown D.C. The city belonged to Ovechkin, but the playoffs were still Crosby's bailiwick.

YEAR FOUR
BEGINS WITH A BANG

OCTOBER 16, 2008: WASHINGTON 4 AT PITTSBURGH 3

For the first meeting of the 2008–09 season, Crosby earned two assists, but the Caps got the two points in the standings. In fact, it was a meaningful and memorable game for several reasons. First, the Penguins blew a 3–0 lead that they had built twenty-two minutes into the game. Second, to go with his two points, Crosby also made two mistakes, leading to the tying and winning goals. And third, the game made clear the new hostility Ovechkin felt towards countryman and former friend Evgeni Malkin, as Ovi hunted him down at every opportunity.

The Penguins got the only two goals of the opening period, both on the power play. Crosby played a bit part on the first one from Alex Gologoski, and made a nice pass to Malkin for the second one. Miroslav Satan, also with the extra man, made it 3–0 at 1:51 of the second period, and with the Penguins seemingly in control the fans sat back and enjoyed the proceedings.

Tomas Fleischmann got one back for the Caps to make it a 3–1 game after forty minutes, and then it was all Washington in the third. Alexander Semin scored at 3:38 to make it a one-goal game, and then midway through Crosby gave the puck up inside the Caps' blue line on a blind pass and Michael Nylander wound up tying the score.

Then, late in the period, Crosby lost a key faceoff in his own end to Boyd Gordon, who let go a quick shot that went in and out so quickly play continued. It wasn't until the first whistle, two minutes later, that video review confirmed the shot beat goalie Marc-Andre Fleury – and that the Caps had rallied to win on the road, 4–3.

"We tried to sit back," Crosby said. "Sometimes when you get a lead like that you think it's going to be easy. We didn't play the right way."

Ovechkin felt the same about his team's first forty minutes. "We didn't shoot the first two periods. Maybe we were afraid. Maybe we were sleeping, but we don't play our hockey. We just change our minds [in the third period]."

For Washington coach Bruce Boudreau, the game had some symbolic importance. "I don't know if it's a 'statement game' per se," he noted, "but I think it [the comeback] is the identity of our team. No matter what happens, we don't quit."

Malkin had a goal and two assists but was genuinely perplexed by Ovechkin's physical play towards him. "Ovechkin is a great player, but every time he hits me – I don't know why," Malkin said.

"It's just a hockey game," Ovechkin said when pressed for a comment. "I hit hard with everybody."

Just a few days after this game Ovechkin returned to Russia for a few days to be with his ailing grandfather, Nikolai Kabayev, who died soon after Ovi's visit. Ovi had had just two goals in his first eight games and was likely preoccupied by his grandfather's illness such that the start of his season was adversely affected. Taking his emotions out on Malkin probably both helped his psyche and harmed it at the same time. When he returned to the NHL, Ovechkin was more relaxed and reverted to his old scoring ways pretty quickly.

RIVALRY HEATS UP

JANUARY 14, 2009: WASHINGTON 6 AT PITTSBURGH 3

A rivalry that began as media interest in 2005 promoting the game's two bright stars turned to something greater and, not coincidentally, more appealing over time. This 2008–09 season took the rivalry from the close quarters of Crosby and Ovechkin to the larger context of Pittsburgh versus Washington, and, in a very real and curious way, to that of Canada versus Russia. And, with the Olympics only a year away, all of these permutations had greater meaning on a global stage.

To start, it seemed Ovechkin was taking over from Crosby as the league's marquee player, the one for whom the epithet "most exciting" might most easily apply. But Evgeni Malkin and Ovechkin, long-time friends and countrymen, playing on opposite NHL teams, had been feuding off ice, putting Malkin more in Crosby's camp and creating an offshoot rivalry between the two Russians. In their first game of the season they exchanged several hits, Ovechkin in particular going out of his way to try to nail Malkin.

Adding fuel to the fire, Washington-Russian Alexander Semin made denigrating remarks about Crosby in an interview published by Yahoo.com soon after the teams' first meeting of the year. Semin pointedly attacked Crosby's skill and character, perhaps feeling entitled to vocalize because at the time, October 31, 2008, he was actually leading the NHL in scoring, with 16 points at that early stage of the season.

Said Semin: "What's so special about [Crosby]? I don't see anything special there. Yes, he does skate well, has a good head, good pass. But there's nothing else. Even if you compare him to Patrick Kane from Chicago . . . [Kane] is a much more interesting player. The way he moves, his deking abilities, his thinking on the ice and his anticipation of the play is so superb. I think that if you take any player, even if he is dead wood, and start promoting him, you'll get a star, especially if he scores 100 points. No one is going to care about anyone else. No one is going to care whether he possesses great skill.

"Let's say you put someone in front of the net and let him deflect pucks in, and he scored 50 goals. Everyone will say, 'Wow!' and then hand him a $10 million-per-year contract. That's what they like here."

Crosby responded in typical understated fashion: "It's not like I need a reason to be motivated," Crosby said. "I feel like I'm a pretty motivated person anyways. I don't feel like that kind of stuff changes the way I play. I've been criticized before. It's one of those things I have to deal with. I don't read into it a whole lot."

And so the rivalry spread its wings. There was Crosby the Canadian and Ovechkin the Russian, doubly competitive because they played for different NHL teams. Then Russian teammates and NHL adversaries – Malkin and Ovechkin – added to the intrigue, and Semin, another Russian, weighed in on Crosby as well.

Pittsburgh drew first blood tonight on the power play, not surprisingly a passing play from Crosby to Malkin for the only goal of the first period. Washington outscored the Pens

2–1 in the second period, but in the third it was all Caps as they pulled away midway through the final period.

Ovechkin scored an early power-play goal to make it 3–2 for the Caps, but Crosby set up Ryan Whitney at 3:12 to tie the game again. Then Ovechkin took control, setting up one goal and scoring another, to put the game away and end a four-game goalless streak and a three-game losing streak for the Caps in one fell swoop.

Incredibly, Ovechkin had 10 of Washington's 42 shots, and he was clearly the best player on the ice. "When he gets in a slump and then breaks the slump, he doesn't break it just to break it," coach Bruce Boudreau noted. "He gets two or three . . . That's what Alex does. He's a really emotional guy and he plays on that passion. And when he gets going, he's pretty hard to stop."

More than other games in Pittsburgh, on this occasion Ovechkin was booed every time he touched the puck, giving him added motivation. "I love it!" he enthused. "They push me hard all the time."

Crosby stumbled over David Steckel in the third period and left the game with an injured knee. He missed the team's next game, against Anaheim, but played some twenty-six minutes against Carolina a few nights later. However, because of tenderness in his left knee, team doctors suggested he take a few days' rest. Crosby relented and missed the All-Star Game, though this decision was not without controversy. And, prophetically, this was not the only time Steckel took Crosby out of a game.

The win was Ovechkin's fourth against Crosby in fourteen career NHL games to date.

A HINT OF CONTROVERSY

JANUARY 25, 2009: THE 57TH NHL ALL-STAR GAME

I f there was a hint of controversy about the Sidney Crosby persona – and hint is an apt grade – then it was about his participation in special events such as the NHL All-Star Game.

His first misdemeanour occurred in 2005 while he was still in junior with Rimouski. That winter, the CHL's Top Prospects game was played in Vancouver, and local organizers advertised the game as a showdown between Crosby and another sensational junior, Gilbert Brule. Crosby pulled out of the game, though, leaving promoters red-faced about his last-minute decision.

"Sidney missed the Prospects Game because he was really banged up," his agent, Pat Brisson, tried to explain. Rimouski's coach and GM, Doris Labonte, also came to his player's defence: "Since he won the gold medal with Team Canada at the world juniors, he hasn't been in top shape. Emotionally, he is drained . . . the time has come for him to rehabilitate physically and mentally."

The promoter of the Top Prospects Game, Ron Toigo, had an opposing view. "For the guy who wants to be the next Wayne Gretzky . . . the history of Wayne Gretzky is that he would be here with one leg if that's what it took because it's good for the game."

Then, in 2008, Crosby withdrew from the All-Star Game with a very legitimate injury, a high-ankle sprain that had kept him out of the lineup for some six weeks (January 18–March 4). But this year, in 2009, things were a little different.

Crosby led all players with a whopping 1,713,021 All-Star votes in 2009, the most ever garnered by one player, and teammate Evgeni Malkin was close behind with 1,585,936 votes, for a game to be held in Montreal as part of the Canadiens' 100th anniversary celebrations. Both Penguins stars were named to the starting lineup, while Ovechkin was well behind in the calculations and hearts of ballot-stuffing fans and had to settle for being added to the roster at a later date.

Because of his junior career in Rimouski, and his connection to the Habs through his father's being drafted by the team, Crosby was as popular a player in Montreal as any in the league who didn't play for the Canadiens. But three days before the game, he withdrew. "It's an unfortunate situation," he posted on the team's website. "It's going to be a really special event. I would have loved to be part of it, but the injury is something I have to deal with, and I believe I made the right decision."

General manager Ray Shero backed him up. "Their [The doctors'] recommendation was to take four or five days off and let the injury heal, and go from there," he wrote.

The withdrawal grew into part of a larger and more symbolic controversy, though. Just a day earlier, two members of the Stanley Cup champion Detroit Red Wings also withdrew. Pavel Datsyuk and Nicklas Lidstrom begged off from the game because of "nagging injuries." As well, the Young Stars game suffered four player pullouts – goalies Steve Mason and Erik Ersberg, and forwards Milan Lucic and Nicklas Backstrom.

The problem in every case was that these withdrawals were announced as the players were still competing with their club teams and showed no signs of serious injury that truly required medical supervision or time off ice. In the case of Crosby, he injured his knee towards the end of the game against the Caps on January 14, but after missing the game against Anaheim on the 16th, he played in the team's last two games leading up to the All-Star break. In fact, his ice time wasn't affected at all. He played 20:23 against the Rangers on the 18th and 25:55 against Carolina on the 20th.

To his credit, commissioner Gary Bettman called the players' bluff, being at once sympathetic for genuine injuries that were a consequence of bad timing vis-à-vis the All-Star Game while issuing a none-too-veiled threat for those that weren't.

"For any player who is selected to be on the team and can't be here," he began, "it's disappointing for everybody, particularly for the fans who want to see the player here. But again, it's not unusual for players to sustain injuries and be unavailable to play. What we don't expect," he added, dagger in tongue, "is injuries that last just for the weekend. And we rarely get those."

The message was simple. If you're injured, you'd better not be playing in league games. And if you're playing and aren't really injured, I'll suspend you, because All-Star participation is obligatory, not voluntary.

And that's just what Bettman did. Datsyuk and Lidström maintained their "nagging injuries" status and were suspended for the Red Wings' first game after the All-Star break. To avoid suffering a similar fate, Crosby flew to Montreal and made some appearances in street clothes during the All-Star showcase.

At the end of the day, who could argue with all three? The NHL season was long and gruelling at the best of times, and guess what? Detroit and Pittsburgh made it to the Stanley

Cup finals this year. Maybe that bit of extra rest was a contributing factor to the teams' success. Maybe one or all three players might have suffered a big or little injury during the All-Star game in Montreal that could have hampered that run to the Cup finals. The withdrawals, then, really spoke to a greater issue – the complete and total meaninglessness of the All-Star festivities.

Withdrawal, however, was not in Alexander Ovechkin's vocabulary. He was in Montreal, in full equipment – and he stole the show. While the Crosby drama of "rest for the Cup race vs. play in the All-Star Game" played out, there was another drama on stage. Ovechkin and Evgeni Malkin had had a falling out some two years ago, to the extent that they were no longer friends or even on speaking terms. Such personal animosity is rare in the hockey world, but this season it had gotten so bad it was impossible even for the casual fan not to notice.

It was an extraordinary change in their relationship. The countrymen had been roommates at the 2006 Olympics in Turin and spent much of their free time together as well. It was only recently that Malkin had finally spoken of the problem. Triggered by Ovechkin's attempt to hit Malkin's agent, Gennadi Ushakov, at a Moscow nightclub, Malkin admitted in a Q&A on a Malkin fan's website on January 16, 2009, just days before the 57th NHL All-Star Game in Montreal, that he "hadn't talked to him in two years." Why the nightclub confrontation? The reason for that remains a mystery, but the fallout was that the two top Russians, friends, had turned on each other.

In a long NHL season, such a rivalry was probably good for business, as they say, but for fans of Team Russia looking ahead one year to the Vancouver Olympics, such animosity could be absolutely detrimental to success on the world's biggest stage.

"Maybe we'll be friends again by that time," Malkin ended on his own fan's site, not sounding particularly optimistic.

Cue to the Skills Contest during the All-Star festivities. Ovechkin was one of the skaters involved in the trick shot contest of the shootout, the NHL's attempt to replicate the NBA's slam dunk contest. For his final shot, Ovechkin skated over to Malkin at the blue line, and Malkin was ready to help him out.

He fitted Super 8 with a fisherman's hat, a small Canadian flag poking out of it, then with sunglasses, which he cleaned with a towel, and finally with a squirt of Gatorade into Ovechkin's waiting mouth. Malkin gave him a second stick, and then Ovechkin went in on goal, stickhandling with two sticks before tossing one aside and taking a shot. The crowd ate it up, and when he was done, Ovechkin threw the accoutrements into the stands. The schtick was endorsed by 45 per cent of players and fans as the winning shot in the entertainment event.

More important, the partnership in preparation for the event signalled the end of the Ovechkin-Malkin feud. Team Russia would be ready for Vancouver after all.

"We've talked before. Now we talk too much," Malkin confirmed. "Yeah, now we are good friends."

"It's fun for the fans to see who we are and how we are," Ovechkin said.

The truce was brokered by Ilya Kovalchuk, who arranged a dinner for the three to hash out differences and clear the air.

At the game itself, Ovechkin had a goal and two assists and scored the clinching goal in a shootout against Roberto Luongo to give the Eastern Conference a 12–11 win. He played on a line with Marc Savard and Dany Heatley. He and Savard combined on a quick give-and-go early in the game for the first goal, Ovechkin finishing off the final Savard pass with a great shot past J-S Giguere.

Ovechkin also had a chance to rub elbows with the great Gordie Howe and later chatted with Guy Lafleur and Jean Béliveau. "I ask [Howe] everything what I can ask him. Lots of legends were here and I shake hands with them. It's history. They play before us in the NHL."

But the game itself was secondary to the symbolic importance of the festivities. Crosby may have been more popular before the game, but Ovechkin had taken over in Montreal.

Still, for Crosby, who played for his team, he couldn't have cared less about Ovechkin's popular success. Sure, he was shown up and a no-show in Montreal, but by the summer he was the one who had a day with the Stanley Cup.

OVECHKIN TOO HOT

FEBRUARY 22, 2009: PITTSBURGH 2 AT WASHINGTON 5

General manager Ray Shero had had enough of coach Michel Therrien. Although the Penguins were an excellent team, something just didn't feel right to Shero, and on February 15, 2009, he pulled the trigger, firing Therrien and replacing him with Dan Bylsma.

Dan Who-sma?

Bylsma was lucky enough to be in the right place at the right time, but his future in coaching might well have been predetermined years before he joined the Penguins. The Michigander had been an outstanding student and fine athlete in several sports (notably golf and baseball) during his four years at Bowling Green University. In a lengthy, mostly minor-league hockey career, he played 429 games at the NHL level with Los Angeles and Anaheim, and immediately after retiring in 2004 he turned to coaching, first as an assistant with Cincinnati in the AHL.

He and his father, Jay, meanwhile, wrote two books on hockey that offered advice to young players about becoming professional players. Bylsma later started a website devoted to helping kids prepare for and understand the pro game.

Bylsma had a mere 54 games' experience as a head coach with the Penguins' farm team, Wilkes-Barre/Scranton Penguins, before getting the call from Shero to take over the big club. Young, and with an academic bent and a knowledge of the game as a checker and plumber, Bylsma was the mirror opposite to Therrien. He stepped into the dressing room with a fresh approach, identified Crosby and Malkin as the players who drove the offence, and took charge of the bench with a command the players admired and respected – and responded to.

The Pittsburgh-Washington game on February 22 was only Bylsma's fourth game with the Penguins (two wins and a loss coming into the game), but it was a combination of events on both sides that led to the lopsided score on this night. Pittsburgh had earned a hard-fought, 5–4, win over state rivals Philadelphia the previous night, while the Colorado Avalanche had manhandled the Caps with a 4–1 score two nights earlier. The loss led coach Bruce Boudreau to put the team through a gruelling practice the next day, leaving them huffing and puffing from the bucket skate. "When you don't play well," he exhorted, "you have to make them understand that it's unacceptable."

Both teams, then, came into this Monday night game with tempers short and nerves frayed, in no mood for anything out of the ordinary. But, no, extraordinary is exactly what they got.

Emotions flared, emotions erupted – the warriors whose rivalry had been documented umpteen times by the media in words, on paper and onscreen, met centre stage, live, on ice, before dozens of cameras, the encounter relayed to millions of rock 'em-sock 'em diehards. Yes, Sid and Ovi had a bit of a set-to during the game!

Perhaps unsurprisingly, the war broke out during one of the most one-sided Sid-Alex games. The Penguins had not been having a great season and were now 29–26–6 for the year, while the Caps were 38–17–5 and in first place in their division. The win was also the third in a row by the Caps over Pittsburgh this season, and they were 4–1–1 going back to the start of the Bruce Boudreau era after being 1–7–1 previously against their rivals.

Regardless, simmering emotions finally boiled over late in the second period as Crosby and Ovechkin skated to their respective benches on line changes at the same time. The two pushed. Crosby said something. Ovechkin, happy with the team's 5–2 lead at the time, dismissed his opponent with a condescending wave of the glove, a gesture he knew would be picked up by cameras.

Post-game, both players were provocative and passionate. "Like it or lump it, that's what he does," Crosby said with uncharacteristic heat in the moments just after the game. "Some people like it, some people don't. Personally, I don't like it."

Ovechkin was not silent on the contretemps, by any means. "What I can say about him?" he said. "He is a good player, but he talks too much. I play hard. If he wants to do something like hit me again, try to hit me again, and I'll talk to you guys [about] who plays dirty. That's my game."

Each player had a version of how things started. Said Sid: "I was skating to the bench, and he pushed me from behind, so I gave him a shot back. That's hockey, and he likes to run around these days. That was it."

Ovechkin's view was different. "It was not a cheap shot; it was a game moment. If he don't like it, it's his problem."

Boudreau thought he understood what happened. "Sidney was jawing at everybody. Every time he would come off, you see him talking to our bench and our bench talking to him. I think he got frustrated because he wasn't getting the freedom he's had in this building before."

And with that observation, the Caps coach laid out his strategy to limit Crosby's effectiveness – take away his space. This night, and all season, it had worked. Sid was held to a single power-play assist and had just three shots on goal despite playing 27:08, the most ice time by any player in the game. Ovechkin, meanwhile, had nine shots. He scored the game's first goal to set the tone, added an assist later in the game, and was a force to be reckoned with all night.

Perhaps this was a night Crosby let other emotions get to him. Since the teams had last played, Ovechkin had had two sensational games against Montreal, a team of special importance to Crosby because, of course, his father had been drafted by the Canadiens, and Crosby always played well against the team he had adored as a young boy.

On January 31, Ovechkin scored four goals against the Habs, including the overtime winner. And, just four nights previous, Ovi had scored one of his greatest goals.

Here's what happened. A long pass from deep in the Montreal end out to centre ice failed. Canadiens defenceman Roman Hamrlik and Ovechkin raced to the left-wing boards right at the red line, but Ovechkin got there first. He had a choice to make – either go in straight and collide with Hamrlik, or do what he did. Ovechkin slid towards the puck, stopped, and spun around. As he did so, he backhanded the puck off the boards behind Hamrlik, and then chased after it, avoiding contact in the process so he could claim the puck cleanly and with speed.

He then roared down the left wing, chased only by Kyle Chipchura, who cut Ovi's legs out from under him at the face-off circle. Ovechkin, sliding on his back, managed to raise himself enough to get off a quick shot that beat a stunned Carey Price just before he collided with the goalie and knocked the net off. It was a goal for the ages, not to mention YouTube, and one Crosby no doubt saw many times over the next four days on any sports news show leading up to his next meeting with Super 8.

Against Pittsburgh on this afternoon game, the result was never in doubt. Washington led 3–1 early in the second period and scored two more goals later in the middle period. Ovechkin got the first goal, on the power play, finishing a nice series of passes with a bullet shot in the slot. It was his league-best 43rd goal of the season and was followed by a tying goal by Maxime Talbot to make it 1–1. After that, the game was dominated by the Caps.

Bylsma made a goalie change when the score was 5–1, but Washington played with a confidence that now had it 3–0–0 against the Pens this season. "We are growing up as a team," Ovechkin explained. "We played well on the power play, penalty kill. We just didn't give them any chance."

For three years he couldn't have spoken with such bravura, given the Penguins' domination over the Caps, but Washington, thanks to coach Bruce Boudreau, had learned how to play against Pittsburgh. And, while it lasted, Ovechkin was enjoying every minute of it.

SID SHOOTS OUT THE LIGHTS

MARCH 8, 2009: PITTSBURGH 4 AT WASHINGTON 3 (SO)

As far as Sid vs. Ovi matchups go, this was a pretty good one that extended two streaks. The Penguins won their sixth game in a row and ended their road trip a perfect 5–0–0 under new coach Dan Bylsma, giving him a record of 8–1–1 since taking over. The Caps, meanwhile, lost their fourth in a row, their longest slump under coach Bruce Boudreau. The game also marked the return of Ovechkin, who had missed the previous game with a bruised heel.

This was the first game since the two players got involved in a well-documented pushing and shoving match between the players' benches, and this game was equally intense without the marquee set-to. There were big hits, broken glass, pushing and shoving matches, great scoring chances, and big saves. It had the feeling of a playoff game. Of the sixteen minor penalties called, ten were for roughing.

Both players were asked to comment on their last meeting when emotions had spilled over, and both were diplomatic but testy. "We're emotional guys, and we play hard," Ovechkin explained, "and when we have something on our mind, and we want to say something, we say it."

Offered Crosby: "A lot of things happen on the ice, and that's where they need to stay. But there's a certain point, too, a certain respect level. It comes down to respect. There are just little things you don't do. That was more frustrating than anything. The pointing."

On the rivalry side of things, Crosby had a goal and an assist and scored the only goal of the shootout, while Ovechkin had an assist and was stopped in the shootout. But this win was Crosby's first of the season after three losses to Ovechkin and the Caps.

"Great ones seem to have the game on the line when it's their turn," Boudreau said. "Tonight it was Sidney's time to have the game on the line, and he's a great one. And he made no mistake when it was his turn."

Crosby opened the scoring at 4:29. The goal came on a quick transition in which Bill Guerin took the puck down the left side and waited for Crosby to charge up the middle. He fed number 87 a perfect pass in the slot on the two-on-one and Crosby fired it into the half-empty net for the early Pittsburgh lead.

Alexander Semin tied the game for Washington in the first period but the Penguins scored the only two goals of the second. Sergei Gonchar got an early power-play goal and then Crosby set up Guerin for a goal, returning the favour from the first-period combination. It was a typically quick, beautiful play by Crosby, all hand-eye coordination and little razzle dazzle, that led to the goal.

Kris Letang merely poked the puck along the right-wing boards to keep the puck outside his blue line. The puck went to Crosby, his back to the Washington goal, at the Caps' blue line. He simply redirected the puck to Guerin, skating hard over the line unguarded. How he saw Guerin is anyone's guess, and how he made the pass while keeping the play onside is also for the Fates to discuss. Guerin moved into the slot and ripped a shot past goalie Jose Theodore for a 3–1 lead.

Not to be outdone, Ovechkin keyed a third-period rally, scoring on a power play in the first minute. He ripped a hard screen shot in the slot past Marc-Andre Fleury to make it a one-goal game at 0:29, his league-leading 47th goal of the season. Less than a minute later Brooks Laich tied it, 3–3.

The rest of the period and overtime settled nothing, so they went to a shootout. Alexander Semin and Slava Kozlov missed for Washington, as did Kris Letang for Pittsburgh, leaving the next Penguins shot to Crosby. He moved in on goal and resurrected his right-leg-lift move, freezing Theodore before beating him with a quick shot over the right-hand glove.

Washington had one last chance to score, and that was left to Ovechkin, but his shot was kicked out calmly by Fleury. The two best players in the league were the two best players in the game, and the two points in the standings came down to one penalty shot each. It couldn't get better than that, and on this night, as Boudreau noted, the scale tipped in Crosby's favour.

The game, marked as it was by a playoff atmosphere, was an appropriate end to the regular season series between the teams. One fan handed out hundreds of pacifiers in mocking reference to Crosby as a cry-baby, and number 87 was booed much of the night. "I don't love it," he said of the jeering, "but it doesn't change the way I do anything out there. I've played in some tough rinks before. Philly comes to mind as a tough building. But this one is gradually making its way up there."

The next time Crosby and Ovechkin would face off was seven weeks later, with the Stanley Cup in both players' sights.

4

CROSBY GETS TO THE CUP FIRST

CHASING THE CUP DREAM

MAY 2, 2009: PITTSBURGH 2 AT WASHINGTON 3

Two major events had occurred in the life of Alex Ovechkin since he last faced Crosby and the Penguins, now nearly two months ago. First, on March 11, 2009, he had signed with IMG to represent him. Now that he had his career-defining contract – without agents' fees – he wanted to focus on endorsements and on promoting the AO brand and image, as it were, and who better than IMG to help?

Ovi was coming off a season of 65 goals and three individual awards from the previous June, and had another 50-goal season already under his belt. He had continued scoring YouTube-popular, spectacular goals, and he was charismatic and personable off ice. And, his English was improving every day.

But for every positive to Ovechkin's personality, there was a negative. He loved doing crazy things, which kept his antics public. Perhaps the most famous incident was his ride with Mike Green on a golf cart underneath the seating at the Verizon Center. Driving at a pretty good clip, Ovi approached a big industrial door that was sliding down to close. Ovechkin accelerated, and both players had to duck to avoid being decapitated as they sped under it. The clip went viral, of course, but owner Ted Leonsis and general manager George

McPhee were none too thrilled to see their $124 million man taking such risks.

It also couldn't help but make one wonder what Ovechkin might do in one of his high-powered sports cars away from the camera's watchful eye.

"We're a little worried about his driving habits," McPhee acknowledged in sublime understatement.

Ovechkin loved America like a kid discovering a new game. He was like a young David Letterman, willing to try anything and everything once, be it bungee jumping, roller coasters, or Segways. He loved fast cars, so much so that he souped up even the fastest. Indeed, his automobile collection was fast becoming the stuff of legend in D.C. Ovechkin owned three AMGs, a Porsche Cayenne GTS, a BMW M6, and a Mercedes SL 65 AMG Black Series, one of only 350 in the world and capable of speeds in excess of 320 km/h.

Asked how quickly he drives, Ovi said, "Here [in the U.S.] I drive 160 miles [per hour]. In Russia, I put max like 220, 240, probably." He explained: "My dad say, 'Don't think about tomorrow; think about right now. If you want to do something, do it.'" Perhaps, but chances are pretty good his dad wasn't talking about driving a car 240 miles per hour on a Moscow highway. And with a licence plate that read AOGR8 he would hardly go unnoticed on the roads.

In a profile of Ovechkin for the *New York Times*, Charles McGrath wrote: "Off ice, he enjoys full rock-star privileges. He lives in an immense pad and markets his own line of Ovi-wear. He enjoys techno-pop, fast cars, beautiful women, torn Dolce & Gabbana jeans and loud parties."

Does any of this sound remotely like Sidney Crosby?

By the time Crosby was fifteen he already had endorsements with Sherwood and Frameworth. Soon after, the big boys followed and deals totalling millions of dollars with Gatorade, Reebok, and Pepsi were established. Reebok was the first, a $500,000 deal in March 2005 while Crosby was still playing in Rimouski and only seventeen years old. The deal was worth more than most future Hall of Famers currently in the NHL had; Reebok knew Crosby was the face of the future, the face of the next generation, the face of young, great hockey. Ever the gentleman, Crosby made sure every member of the Oceanic roster and staff was given a full line of Reebok attire.

Early in 2008, Crosby came out with his own line of clothing, SC87, featuring T-shirts, pants, and shoes, casual, sporty clothing that reflected Crosby's persona as a sports-loving innocent far happier playing tiddlywinks for competition than having orgies with women pouring vodka on his chest.

What Crosby had, Ovechkin wanted, but number 8 wasn't willing to play the marketing game. Ovechkin was paid good money to go to card shows and do signings, but he eventually got bored of these, treated fans badly, and probably did his image more harm than good. Crosby never did trade shows because he knew the trouble wasn't worth the time.

Crosby relied on his "team" to develop his business strategy, while Ovechkin relied on his own instincts as well as on his mother's opinions. Crosby was a sponsor's dream because those large companies that invested millions in him didn't have to worry about a middle-of-the-night phone call from a jail, or, worse, from a tabloid asking to confirm some salacious rumour.

But one thing above all other considerations made Crosby more marketable. One word that defined any athlete in any country, in any language and from any sport. Winning. Crosby was a winner wherever he went. No, not every game, or every prize, or in every situation. But he chose his spots well and won when it mattered the most.

Even small things counted, like the outdoor game in Buffalo on New Year's Day, midway through the 2008–09 season. The game went to a shootout, and after a pretty quiet sixty-five minutes of play, guess who scored the winning goal? Crosby. The spotlight ended on him.

Head-to-head battles between Crosby and Ovechkin? Crosby won the majority. Later in their careers, who won the playoff series between the two? Who won the Stanley Cup? Olympic gold? Crosby. Ovechkin got on YouTube, but Crosby's basement had the more important trophies.

It's easy to say Ovechkin was the more spectacular player, that he was the guy with the missing tooth, the wild hair, the unkempt appearance who transformed North America's feelings about the once-stuffy, Communist-era hockey country. It's a lot easier to market Crosby neat and in a suit, wearing Olympic gold around his neck.

The second important event occurred the night the Capitals went to Tampa Bay to play a game, Friday, March 20. Ovechkin started the game with 49 goals, and he talked with teammates Mike Green and Jose Theodore about doing something special when he got number 50, hopefully on this night. The teammates raised their eyebrows and laughed, and nothing more was said.

Sure enough, Ovechkin got number 50 that night, less than eight minutes into the game, but his teammates would have nothing to do with the NFL-style celebration that followed. Ovechkin dropped his stick off to the side of the Lightning goal and then bounced his hands up and down over it, suggesting the stick was too hot to handle. Green laughed briefly from a distance, but few others were impressed. "He wanted me to join in, but there was no way I'd join in on that. I just kind of stood back and let him do what he does," Green said afterwards.

"I grew up in the old days in the Spectrum where the first period after that happened might have been a three-hour period," Tampa Bay coach Rick Tocchet offered by way of suggesting a brawl would follow any breach of hockey's code of conduct. "It's not something I like, and it's hard for me to see that in our building."

The scorer made clear his intentions afterwards. "I don't want to show them [the Lightning] any disrespect. It's all about my team, and it's all about me."

Ovechkin's coach didn't exactly endorse the unique move, but he did offer a pithy parallel: "As Canadians, we tend to be conservative. Twenty-five years ago, we got mad at the Russians for showing no emotion. Now they're showing emotion, and we're mad at them again."

Over the years, Crosby has celebrated goals with exuberance, but only the big ones. His first goal at the World Junior Championship was likely overdoing it, but he was sixteen years old playing on a world stage, so an extra jump or two late in a blowout hardly was unconscionable. His first NHL goal, age eighteen, was also memorable, as was his shootout winner outdoors in Buffalo. But most of the time Crosby lifts his arms, grabs his mouthguard, and hugs his teammates. End of story. Ovechkin was as famous for his wild celebrations, his jumping backwards into the glass as he waited to be mobbed by teammates, as he was for the actual putting of the puck into the net.

As Ovechkin once said, "He has his style and I have mine. Everyone is different. My style is me. Sid is Sid."

That being said, there was no greater moment of truth arriving for these two star players than game one of the Conference semi-finals of the 2009 Stanley Cup playoffs. The winners would get to play for the Stanley Cup; the losers would go home and have nightmares about the chance that had been lost.

The teams got to this series under different circumstances. Washington needed seven games to squeak by the Rangers, 2–1, in the final game, a game and series in which Ovechkin wasn't much of a factor. The Penguins needed six games to beat cross-state rivals, the Flyers, and Crosby was the dominant player in that series.

The Capitals trailed the Rangers three games to one and rallied to win game seven, but Ovechkin was a factor only in the first game of the series when he had two assists in a 4–3 loss. The Caps were shut out in game two, and although Ovi had two more assists in game three, the story was Semyon Varlamov, an unknown goalie inserted into the lineup during the previous game when Boudreau had been unimpressed with starter Jose Theodore. Varlamov played incredibly well and took the Caps the rest of the way during their playoff run that year.

Ovechkin got his first goal in game four, but in another losing cause, and he scored the final goal in the final minute of a 4–0 win in the next game. In game six, he scored again, but it was a goal to make it 5–1, not what one might call a big or pressure goal. In the deciding game, he was all but invisible.

Crosby, on the other hand, rose to the occasion of playing the hated Flyers. He opened the scoring early in game one to get the series started on the right note and later added an assist in a 4–1 win. He was limited to one assist in game two, an overtime win, and he had two more assists the next game in a 6–3 loss.

Crosby scored the first goal in game four of a crucial 3–1 road win but was held off the scoresheet along with everyone else in a 3–0 loss in game five. Game six, in Philadelphia, produced an incredible comeback. The Penguins trailed 3–0 early in the second period only to score three times before heading to the dressing room tied, 3–3, the final goal thanks to Crosby. He added a second goal into the empty net to seal the 5–3 victory in the game and the series, sending the Pens on to a best-of-seven-game set against the Capitals.

Pittsburgh joined the NHL in 1967 and Washington joined eight years later, and in the thirty-four years they shared membership in the league the teams had met in the playoffs seven times. Pittsburgh had won six of those series, twice trailing 3–1 in games before winning game seven. They last played in 2001, a Pittsburgh win. The only time the Caps won was in 1994.

The most famous game between the two franchises was undoubtedly the night of April 24, 1996, the fifth-longest game in league history. The Caps had won the first two games of the series, in Pittsburgh, and headed home with a chance to sweep the best-of-seven if they won both games at home. But Pittsburgh won game three, and game four went to the last minute of the fourth overtime period. Pittsburgh's Petr Nedved scored the winner sometime in the wee hours, and the Pens rallied to win the next two games and eliminate the Caps after falling behind in the series, 2–0.

Although the game-one summary of 2009 showed both Crosby and Ovechkin with goals, the deciding factor in the Saturday afternoon matchup was another Russian, goalie Varlamov. Crosby got the opening goal of the series on a beautiful play. He skated hard in over the Washington blue line, cut to the middle, and, as the two defencemen backed in a bit, let go a quick shot from the slot that beat Varlamov cleanly.

The Pens had the start they wanted, but the Caps responded with two goals late in the period. David Steckel tied the game at 13:50 and then, with just 2:57 left in the period, Ovechkin put his team ahead when he one-timed a pass on a five-on-three situation.

Mark Eaton tied the game at 12:54 of the second when his point shot fooled Varlamov, but the goalie atoned a short time later with a game-saving play off Crosby. Crosby and Chris Kunitz came in over the blue line and criss-crossed. Crosby went to the net and Varlamov came well out to challenge Kunitz, who fed a pass to Crosby. Sid had beaten defenceman Tom Poti to the net and took the pass, in one motion shooting the puck at the wide-open net. Varlamov dove back, however, and got the paddle of his stick on the puck just as it reached the goal line.

"That's got to be the highlight of the year. It's got to be," enthused Caps defenceman Mike Green.

Varlamov was demure in describing what happened. "There was no other option left to me. I had to play it with my stick. If he put the puck anywhere else, it would have been in the net, so I guess it was lucky."

Crosby had his own version of events. "I didn't get a lot on it," he suggested, not wanting to give the goalie a psychological advantage. "I just tried to direct it into the net. He kind of made a desperate save. You end up losing the game, 3–2, and you don't want to say, 'what if?'"

Tomas Fleischmann then scored the only goal of the third for the win, but the talk afterwards was all about Varlamov's save off Crosby. Numbers 87 and 8 played as everyone expected, but Washington's masked number 40 was already the X factor after only one game.

As a result, the series stood at Washington 1, Pittsburgh 0.

ONE FOR THE AGES

MAY 4, 2009: PITTSBURGH 3 AT WASHINGTON 4

There have been great quotes in the world of sports, words that are inaptly expressed but still capture a moment with a memorable turn of phrase. Yogi Berra was a walking *Bartlett's* of *bons mots* and *non sequiturs* phrasing. And then there was an ancient boxing promoter, Joe Jacobs, who made famous the complaint, "We wuz robbed." One time, he went to a World Series game in Detroit when it was bitterly cold, and Jacobs remarked, "I shoulda stood in bed."

And then came Bruce Boudreau, who offered his own linguistic gem on the heels of one of the most memorable playoff games ever contested. The score line showed nothing particularly special, the Caps winning by one goal in a home game to take a 2–0 series lead. What was extraordinary was that Crosby for Pittsburgh and Ovechkin for Washington each recorded a hat trick. The best players were at their absolute best. And this prompted Boudreau to remark afterwards, "That's why they are they."

The red-clad thousands who made up the majority of the crowd on this night had plenty to cheer about, and only a fantastic left-pad save by Pittsburgh goalie Marc-Andre Fleury early on kept the score 0–0. Ovechkin skated through the crease and redirected a Sergei Fedorov shot beautifully, but Fleury bested number 8 with a great play of his own.

Crosby got the only goal of the opening period, on a power play at 6:38. Stationed off to the side of the goal, he swiped home a rebound after goalie Semyon Varlamov couldn't control Sergei Gonchar's point shot. Later in the period both star players had incredible scoring chances but were denied by goaltending just a hair better. That was the only scoring of the opening period, but the two stars of the night were only just getting warmed up.

Ovechkin tied the score at 2:18 of the second period on a patented one-timer from his off wing. Slava Kozlov teed up a pass for him perfectly, and Ovechkin rifled a shot past Fleury, who couldn't get across the crease quickly enough to make the save.

Crosby then got his second of the night, again by being in the right place at the right time. Bill Guerin took a quick shot from a bad angle that Varlamov failed to handle cleanly, and Crosby, to the back side of the play, scooped the puck into the open side at 10:57, to make it 2–1 for the visitors.

David Steckel scored the only non-Crosby-Ovechkin goal of the night five minutes later, finding a loose puck to the side of the goal and whipping it high over a sprawling Fleury to tie the game, 2–2.

The third period was tense with the drama such a game would naturally produce, but Ovechkin broke the game open to give the Caps their first lead of the night, scoring a goal almost identical to his first. This time, though, it was Mike Green who fed him the puck on the off wing, but the rest was the same. Ovechkin one-timed the puck and ripped a slapshot past Fleury at 12:53 to make it 3–2 for the Capitals.

Ovechkin then gave the Caps a two-goal lead just two and

a half minutes later. His hat trick goal was another classic from his repertoire of great plays. He came in over the blue line alone, going one-on-one against countryman and NHL opponent Sergei Gonchar. Instead of trying to beat his man, though, Ovechkin skated right at him, and just a flash before the two would collide he fired a wrist shot, using the defenceman as his screen. The puck rocketed over Fleury's glove – an Ovechkin wrister was easily as speedy as most NHLers' slapshots – and it was now a 4–2 game with just four minutes left.

The crowd tossed every conceivable kind of hat to the ice, prompting Crosby to request the public address announcer to ask fans to stop littering the ice.

The game was far from over, though. In the final minute, with Fleury on the bench, the Penguins pressed for a miracle comeback. A mad scramble in front saw Crosby take five whacks at the puck, the last one successful as he batted the puck out of mid-air past a stunned Varlamov. The goal, Sid's third of the night, came with 30.4 seconds remaining, but in the ensuing half minute, the Pens couldn't find that tying goal. Washington had won both games at home to start the best-of-seven and was going to Pittsburgh with a legitimate chance of taking a stranglehold on the series.

The stats of Sid and Alex in game two were amazing. Crosby had five shots and played 22:26, while Ovechkin had an incredible 12 shots on goal and played 23:32. The Caps had only 33 shots, and Ovechkin accounted for more than a third of those.

The praise afterwards was as expected. "It's everything the media has made it out to be, a battle of the two best players in hockey, and tonight they both carried their teams," said Washington defenceman Mike Green. "We were fortunate that Alex was at the top of his game."

"It's good for the fans to see great players play against each other and two great teams play against each other," Ovechkin said. "It's an interesting time and an interesting game. It's unbelievable when you play against great players and you win a game like this.

"I just try to do my best," he continued. "And you can see how I score goals. My partners do their job. They give me puck in empty space. That's what I need to score goals. Without them, probably I didn't score three goals right now."

Crosby registered his frustration at his team's solid play, which nonetheless had his team needing to win the next game to stay in the series. "I'm sure it's entertaining for people to watch. If I were to look at it from a fan's point of view, obviously that would be the case. As a player, seeing a guy like him get a hat trick is not a good sign. But at the same time, I realize people are entertained by that."

"Sick game," Ovechkin added. "Three goals by me and him." He didn't care about Crosby's output – his team won.

Crosby agreed with that. "It's nice to score," he said, "but it's better to win."

"When you build that hype of superstars playing against each other and then the superstars play like superstars, it's a neat thing, fun to talk about," Capitals coach Bruce Boudreau said. "Not too many people can do what they did tonight."

That is, indeed, why they are they.

CROSBY RALLIES THE TROOPS

MAY 6, 2009: WASHINGTON 2 AT PITTSBURGH 3 (OT)

Players can talk all they want about a playoff series being seven games, but when you're trailing 2–0 the next game *is* the series. For a team to go down 3–0 is virtual suicide, with the number of teams coming from 3–0 down to win a series countable on one hand (with digits to spare), and the task is all the more difficult because the team leading 2–0 is relaxed and playing well.

But this was a night starring not only Crosby and Ovechkin but two other Russians, Malkin and Varlamov. Malkin, who had been invisible the last several games, played his best game of the playoffs, and Varlamov, despite seeing twice as many shots as his opponent, Marc-Andre Fleury, kept the Caps in the game all night long.

The Mellon Arena fans had barely sat down when Ovechkin silenced them. Mike Green rifled a routine shoot-in from centre ice, but when Fleury went behind the net to play the puck, it hit a stanchion and came out in front of the open net. Ovechkin was skating in on the forecheck and drilled the puck in for an easy goal and a shocking 1–0 Washington lead.

The Penguins settled down, but the visiting Caps played a good road game as well, keeping the scoring chances to a minimum. Finally, midway through the second period, Ruslan

Fedotenko tied the game, and the score remained 1–1 until late in the third, overtime looming.

With just 4:59 remaining, though, Malkin scored his first goal of the series on a power play, with Alexander Semin in the penalty box for hooking. It was one of seven Washington penalties all night (to only two for the Penguins), and a costly one at that.

"They have only two penalties. It's kind of a joke, I think," opined Ovechkin later.

The go-ahead goal was one of many great passes Crosby made over the course of the game. He came in over the blue line, and dropped the puck to "Geno" who moved into the slot and fired a high shot through a maze of players that beat a screened Varlamov. The home side had a late 2–1 lead, but the game was not over just yet.

With two and a half minutes left in the third period, Penguins defencemen Chris Kunitz got the puck inside his faceoff circle and made a pass up ice. In the process, Ovechkin was hunting him down. The two collided – exploded into each other, really – and went flying. It was the kind of play that would have resulted in a riot during the regular season, but at this stage of the game, in the playoffs, both players dusted themselves off and got back in the play.

Moments later, Pascal Dupuis took an interference penalty, at 17:32, and on the ensuing power play the Caps tied the game. Nicklas Backstrom banged in a loose puck to the side of the goal, forcing overtime and crystallizing a season into one goal for Pittsburgh. If the Pens didn't score in overtime, the season was pretty much over.

Fortunately for the Penguins, they scored. They had an early power play when Brian Pothier cleared the puck over the glass, but couldn't capitalize, even though Varlamov lost his stick at one point, leaving him vulnerable. At the other end, the Pens avoided disaster when Ovechkin had a great chance to score but missed. Moments later, midway through the fourth period, Kris Letang beat Varlamov with a slapshot. It was the result of a unique Crosby play.

When Crosby came into the NHL as an eighteen-year-old, the weakest part of his game was faceoffs. He wasn't as quick as his opponents, and he didn't know the little tricks of the trade about stick position, timing, and preparation. After four years and countless hours working on this part of his game in practice, however, he was a master of the draw. And he employed a similar strategy for all four possible important faceoff scenarios – defensive zone forehand and backhand, offensive zone forehand and backhand.

Rather than try to scoop the puck back to a defenceman, Crosby liked to slap the puck to the boards where his winger, expecting the slap-pass, could quickly gain control of the puck. It was an unorthodox method, to say the least, but sheer genius, as this goal proved.

In the Washington zone on his forehand for the faceoff (that is, to Varlamov's left), Crosby snapped the puck to Mark Eaton on the boards. In one motion, Eaton swept the puck back to the point to Letang, and his quick shot beat Varlamov. The time it took for Crosby to win the draw, snap it to Eaton back to the point and in? Three seconds.

Malkin led all skaters with 29:38 of ice time and an Ovechkin-like nine shots, but it was Crosby's faceoff win that kept the Penguins alive in the series. And Ovechkin now had a hand in six of his team's nine goals. He was doing it all. The stars were playing like stars, and the fans were getting their money's worth.

A SERIES NOW ON RESTART

MAY 8, 2009: WASHINGTON 3 AT PITTSBURGH 5

Psychologically, Washington still had the advantage before the start of game four. After all, the Caps had won their two games at home and needed only one road win to go home with a chance to close out the series. And being down 3–1 wasn't much better than 3–0 for the Pens in terms of odds-on chances to rally and eliminate their opponents.

And, as in game three, the Caps struck for an early goal, possibly to Pittsburgh's advantage. If the Pens weren't awake before the game, they certainly were when trailing 1–0 and with the series on the line. This time it was Nicklas Backstrom who scored on the first shift, just thirty-six seconds after the opening faceoff. He got the puck at centre, skated down the left wing, and blasted a long shot that fooled Marc-Andre Fleury over the glove side.

Three minutes later, Sergei Gonchar tied the game for Pittsburgh on a long shot from just inside the blue line, and at 10:47 the Penguins went ahead to stay. Chris Kunitz kept the puck in at the Washington blue line and spotted Crosby in behind everyone. Crosby made a couple of fakes and had a couple of whacks at the puck, but Varlamov made the saves. He couldn't corral the disc, though, and Bill Guerin knocked it in for a 2–1 lead.

Ruslan Fedotenko made it 3–1 by the end of the period, one of the rare occasions that either team had a two-goal lead in the series. In between, Sergei Fedorov had two incredible chances to score, but he hit the post on the first try and was stopped by the glove of Fleury on the second.

The turning point of the game, however, occurred at 14:55 of the period. Washington was on the power play, and Gonchar had the puck in the corner of his own end when Ovechkin came at him hard, clipping his countryman with a vicious knee-on-knee hit.

Penguins teammate Brooks Orpik was none too pleased with the play. "That's three games in a row where he's out there trying to hurt guys," he said. "You just watch the way he hits. He likes to target the Russian guys for some reason."

Ovechkin got a two-minute penalty for the hit, nullifying a crucial power play, but Gonchar, the key to the Pittsburgh defence, went to the dressing room and was finished for the night. It was the kind of hit Ovechkin was periodically guilty of committing, one that crossed over from aggressive to dirty, power-forward to vicious.

"It was an extremely negligent hit," Gonchar's agent, J. P. Barry offered, "and if anyone else in this league does the same we all know they will face serious discipline."

Ovechkin maintained his innocence after. "I tell a couple guys – Guerin, Eaton – it was accidental. I didn't try to hurt him."

Regardless, the incident got the Pens fired up, no doubt about that, as they scored just thirty seconds later during the ensuing four-on-four situation.

Washington's Chris Clark brought the Caps within one, scoring the only goal of the second period, but Crosby made it a two-goal game early in the third on a beautiful play. Miroslav

Satan came in on a two-on-one and slid the puck perfectly between the legs of defenceman John Erskine. Crosby merely had to redirect the puck into the open side.

Milan Jurcina for Washington and Maxime Talbot closed out the scoring, but for the first time in the series Varlamov looked weak and Ovechkin was not a factor. Number 8 recorded the second assist on Clark's goal and had only three shots on Fleury, none particularly dangerous. And, his hit on Gonchar may have inspired the Pens in one of those playoff moments that great teams use as a rallying point at a time when focus is paramount.

No matter what the spin, both teams had won their games at home and were heading back to Washington for game five. Said Penguins' coach Dan Bylsma with mathematical succinctness: "It's a best-of-three now."

ROAD WIN SHOCKER

MAY 9, 2009: PITTSBURGH 4 AT WASHINGTON 3 (OT)

To squeeze the pressures and expectations of an entire season into seven games is thrilling for the fans and demanding for the players, but to squeeze all of those juices into three games was even more intense. The teams had two wins each and the Caps still had home-ice advantage, but the Pens had momentum, and they'd proved Varlamov was human and beatable and was not going to play like Ken Dryden in 1971.

"You have to work hard to get the bounces. We've created a lot of good opportunities and sometimes they haven't gone in, but they've found a way to even out. You work hard for those breaks. That's just the way hockey goes."

So said Crosby after a game that was decided by a lucky goal in overtime. He was skating hard to the net on a two-on-two play with Malkin, the puck carrier streaking down the right wing. Malkin made a hard pass across for Crosby, but Washington defenceman Tom Poti put his stick on the ice to intercept the pass. He succeeded, but the puck slid between the pads of goalie Semyon Varlamov at 3:28 of the first extra period to give Pittsburgh a 3–2 road win and a chance to close out the series two nights later at home.

Playing without a day off, both teams were strong from the opening faceoff, knowing the pivotal importance of game five in a 2–2 series. This game it was Crosby who was pretty quiet and Ovechkin who did everything possible to give his team a victory, but it wasn't enough.

Jordan Staal gave Pittsburgh a 1–0 lead early in the second period, but just fifty-nine seconds later Ovechkin tied the game on a long wrist shot that should have been stopped by Marc-Andre Fleury. Ovechkin later drew the second assist on a Nicklas Backstrom power-play goal, but Pittsburgh struck for two early goals in the third period to re-take the lead, 3–2.

Again, though, Ovi responded. As the clock ticked down and a goal became critical, Washington had a three-on-two in the Pittsburgh end. Backstrom, with the puck in the slot, dished it off to Ovechkin to his right, and number 8 wasted no time in drilling a shot past the sprawling Fleury. With just 4:08 left in the third period, overtime loomed large. Teams knew the next mistake would end the game, and as a result a cautious ending to regulation set up the need for a fourth period.

Just 1:29 into the overtime, however, Milan Jurcina took a tripping penalty, and that's when Malkin and Crosby broke out to create the winning goal, scored with just one second left in the man advantage. Ovechkin was excellent in this game, but it wasn't enough to beat a team full of determined Penguins.

That, and a little bit of luck, gave Pittsburgh a massive advantage heading to game six.

ROAD SHOCKER II

MAY 11, 2009: WASHINGTON 5 AT PITTSBURGH 4 (OT)

O n the day of game three of this playoff series, May 6, Russia had defeated Belarus 4–3 in Bern, Switzerland, to advance to the semi-finals of the World Championship. That night, the Caps lost. On the day of game four, May 8, Russia beat the United States, 3–2, to advance to the gold-medal game in Switzerland, and the Caps lost again.

Two nights later, May 10, between games five and six of this Caps-Pens series, Russia edged Canada, 2–1, to win gold for the second straight year over its great rivals. Ovechkin was not there to celebrate with friend Ilya Kovalchuk, the tournament MVP, as he had been the previous year, but he drew inspiration from that win and made sure he played with a commensurate pride in a game that the Pens expected to win, ahead 3–2 in the series, playing on home ice in an elimination game.

Game two was the one that had given this series meaning, that had allowed people to use words like epic and classic, because of the play of Crosby and Ovechkin. Game six confirmed the reports.

Although the deciding goal in game six was scored by the then little-known David Steckel in overtime, the sixty minutes of regulation featured classic play from numbers 87 and 8, in the form of great passing, dramatic goals, and an intensity that belied the more languid training camp in September when the season had begun.

"I was telling a couple of people after the game, 'This is so good for our game when the best players can shine on a bright stage like this,'" a jubilant Caps coach Bruce Boudreau said after. "I just wish it was for the Cup."

Offered Crosby: "There was a lot of talk before the series started, and it's everything it was made out to be. We would have loved to finish it off here and it could have worked out that way, but let's just say we're all not surprised that it's going seven."

"I think the league wants us to play seven games," Ovechkin said with a smile, "Pittsburgh-Washington, so they got it. Fans probably happy, too."

Think of how this pivotal game went from the perspectives of players and fans of both teams.

The Pittsburgh perspective: You score an early goal in the first period to send your team on its way to winning the series. The Caps surge ahead, but you wind up tying the game late in the second and going ahead early in the third. Again, the Caps surge ahead, but you score late in the game to force overtime. The Caps win in the fourth period, and now you have to go to Washington for game seven. Shocking. Missed opportunity.

The Washington perspective: You give up the critical first goal but then rally to go ahead late in the second period. You give up a late goal in that period and an early one in the third again to be in the precarious situation of trailing in an elimination game. You rally to go ahead, only to give up the tying goal late in the third period. You win in overtime, to force game seven, at home. What a relief. Do unto others. . . .

And that's how game six played out. The Penguins scored the only goal of the first period when Crosby and Bill Guerin came in on a two-on-one and converted the play to perfection. Crosby made the exact pass necessary, and Guerin took aim and drilled a high hard shot over the outstretched arm of Varlamov for the 1–0 lead. Just forty minutes to go and a one-goal lead. But the Penguins started the middle period disastrously as they couldn't cope with the more desperate Capitals.

Viktor Kozlov tied the game for Washington early in the second period on a play in which everyone in the Mellon Arena was watching Crosby. He blocked a Mike Green shot and went down in pain, and as he struggled to the bench Kozlov ripped a wrist shot past Fleury. Crosby recovered, but his team's lead was gone.

Tomas Fleischmann put the Caps up, 2–1, but Mark Eaton tied the game at 19:26 of the period. Now, just twenty minutes to go in game six with the game tied, 2–2, with no margin for error either way.

Kris Letang put the Pens up with an early goal on the power play in the third, with Steckel in the penalty box, but then a minute later the Caps scored twice in twenty-nine seconds to stun the Mellon Arena crowd and take a 4–3 lead. The early goal spelled victory; the immediate collapse spelled defeat.

Brooks Laich scored on a power play off a bad-angle shot, and then Kozlov caught Fleury slow to react to a puck that went around behind the net and snapped it in the open side before the goalie knew what had happened. Ovechkin was involved in both those goals, but Crosby was on the bench, none too pleased with what had transpired after the team took another lead.

The tying goal came off a harmless-looking play that quickly turned in Pittsburgh's favour. A ring around the boards in the Washington end was missed by Matt Bradley along the right side, and Brooks Orpik fired a quick shot on goal to keep the puck in. Varlamov failed to control the simple shot, and Crosby was right there to flick the puck in with just 4:18 left in regulation. Another rally, another blown lead, another overtime.

That set the stage for Steckel's OT winner to force game seven two nights later at the Verizon Center. It came on a play similar to the decisive moment of the gold-medal game of the 2006 Olympics. To start the third period of that game between Sweden and Finland in Turin the score was tied, 1–1. But on the opening faceoff between Mats Sundin and Saku Koivu, Koivu's stick broke, and he went to the bench to get a new one. As he did, Sundin got the puck, skated in over the Finland blue line, and dropped the puck to his defenceman, Nicklas Lidstrom. Lidstrom ripped a shot past goalie Antero Niittymaki, and that turned out to be the only goal of the period. Sweden won gold, thanks to a broken stick off a centre-ice faceoff.

On this night, Steckel was involved in a faceoff in the Pittsburgh end with Maxime Talbot. Talbot broke his stick on the play, and Steckel went to the net after getting the puck back to the point. Brooks Laich fired a shot towards the goal, and Steckel redirected the puck past goalie Marc-Andre Fleury to give the Caps an overtime win. Their record was now 6–1 in elimination games with Boudreau behind the bench.

"They're incredible, both of them," Boudreau said of Crosby and Ovechkin. "They play on a level that, boy, other people can't attain because they're that much more superior. If I wasn't behind the bench, I'd sure enjoy watching them. I think a lot of people will want to see game seven."

"It's time for everybody to play their hardest," Ovechkin said after. "This is the best group of guys. They never give up. It doesn't matter who scores . . . what matters is we win the game, and we go back to our building and our fans."

CROSBY EARNS THE LAURELS

MAY 13, 2009: PITTSBURGH 6 AT WASHINGTON 2

The NHL's worst nightmare was coming true. A playoff series between the two best players in the game, going to a decisive game seven, and no national broadcast in the United States because of a poor rights deal between the league and the Versus channel. Be that as it may, this was the most important game Crosby and Ovechkin had ever played against each other to date, notwithstanding their gold-medal showdown at the World U20 Championship in 2005.

Ovechkin was his usual effusive self in the day off between games, feeling perhaps a little too good after the Caps' huge road win in game six to avoid elimination. He had six goals and six assists in the series, and was thriving on the added media attention. "All the time, I love it," he admitted of the spotlight. "I say, 'Wow! It's me! It's good!' Why not? I am who I am, and if I'm in this position, why can't I read the news about me, what you guys are writing about me, and what you have to say about me? I love this kind of stuff. When I came here, it was my dream, and my dream was to be the best. I work hard, and right now I am who I am, and I don't want to stop."

Crosby was more succinct in his philosophy: "It's a game seven, and somebody is going home. There's nothing to think about except leaving it all out there."

In retrospect, the game wasn't close. This in itself was stunning given its importance and the fact that five of the six previous games were decided by one goal, three in overtime. But in examining the details, one realizes this game could have been radically different. Think first of all about how the previous games had gone. Neither team held a two-goal lead for more than a few minutes. Crosby and Ovechkin were the two best players, playing their best against each other as everyone had expected.

And so, in game seven, two events in the first period pretty much decided the game. First up, Ovechkin. He had a breakaway just three minutes into the game, but goalie Marc-Andre Fleury snapped out his glove and robbed Super 8 of a sure goal. "I didn't score on the breakaway. If I score the first goal, maybe it's a different game," Ovechkin acknowledged afterwards.

A little later in the period, Crosby did score on his chance. Parked to the side of the net on a power play, he stopped a long Sergei Gonchar shot from going into the corner by controlling the puck with his skate, moving it in one motion to his stick, and snapping it into the open side to give the Pens a 1–0 lead. It happened so quickly, you needed the slow-motion replay to realize just what superb hand-eye coordination Crosby possessed to make that play a reality. Gonchar's presence was inspiring for the Penguins. He was playing in his first game since being sidelined by a questionable Ovechkin hit in game three, and although his knee wasn't fully recovered, he was in the lineup to do his bit.

Just eight seconds later, Craig Adams scored to make it 2–0 off a bad giveaway after the faceoff at centre ice. The early 1–0 Capitals lead that might have been, if not for a great Fleury save, was instead a 2–0 Pittsburgh lead, and the advantage shifted irrevocably from home to visitor.

In the second period, the Penguins turned on the after-burners. On the first shift, Crosby skated down the right side, waiting for the trailer, Bill Guerin, and pushed a perfect pass to him. Guerin got his full body behind a great shot, beating Varlamov cleanly just twenty-eight seconds into the period to make it 3–0.

Less than two minutes later, Kris Letang ripped another long shot past Varlamov, making it 4–0. As soon as the goal was scored, TV cameras panned to Ovechkin at the bench, head hung low, knowing the game – and series – was pretty much over. Jordan Staal made it 5–0 on a lucky bounce in front soon after, leaving no doubt which team would win this game.

"After the third goal, I was thinking of pulling him because he looked really dejected, and maybe I should have called a timeout at that point," Boudreau admitted of the struggling Varlamov in goal. "And then, after the fourth goal, I think the wind completely came out of his sails emotionally."

By the midway point in the game, Ovechkin's breakaway miss seemed light years ago. He scored late in the second to make it 5–1, but if the Caps were hoping for a dramatic and historic comeback in the final twenty minutes, Crosby laid that hope to rest at 2:02 of the third when he scored on a breakaway of his own. Ovechkin got too fancy inside the Pittsburgh blue line while killing a penalty. He was checked off the puck, and Crosby got the loose disc with only the goal in sight. He had a 140-foot breakaway, slowed down when he got to the crease, and snapped a quick shot between the goalie's pads to make it 6–1.

Brooks Laich scored several minutes later to make it 6–2, but that was the final goal of the night. "I don't know what happened. It's very disappointing," Ovechkin said later. "They played better."

And they played with more discipline. The Penguins did not incur a single penalty all game while Washington had four minors.

"This was Magic and Bird from back in the day," Guerin said. "It was just a great series for the league and a great series for the game of hockey. I don't know if I've been involved in a series with as many ups and downs as this one. I'll never forget this one."

"It feels good just because of the way the series went, not particularly because of me and him," Crosby explained.

Ovechkin tried to remain upbeat at a time when he couldn't help but be down. "No answers. They played better. It's good steps for us, for sure. We can take good experience from this, but bad experience, too. We had 2–0 lead [in the series], then twice lost in overtime. A little bit more push. We were so close, but close is not good enough. It will feel terrible."

Boudreau himself found praising the opposition captain easy on a night like this. "I always thought he was a great player," he said of Crosby, "but I didn't know how great a player. He's always on. He doesn't take time off."

Perhaps the greatest difference in the series came out of the fundamental difference between Crosby and Ovechkin. Ovechkin was always about doing it himself, figuring if he scored enough goals his team would win, carrying the team on his stick and relying on that alone for victory.

Crosby realized this was a Herculean, impossible task. But, if you could get all the players around you to play better, to be at their best, the team was going to have a much greater chance of winning. Crosby not only played well; he inspired great play in others.

Sidney Crosby shares the same initials as Stanley Cup, and in 2009 the two SCs were, indeed, fast becoming friends.

OVI GETS THE HARDWARE, BUT CROSBY GETS THE CUP

JUNE 18, 2009: 2009 NHL AWARDS

Team player versus individual was never so in focus as this spring when Alex Ovechkin swooped down to nab three of the NHL's top individual awards – Hart Trophy, Lester B. Pearson Award, and Rocket Richard Trophy. Sidney Crosby didn't win a single award. Well, check that. He didn't win an individual award that night in Las Vegas when the hardware was being doled out, but he did captain the Penguins to the Stanley Cup, a trophy he'd take any year over ones named Hart, Ross, Richard, or whatever else was on offer at the June awards show.

"It's pretty important when people and players give you this," Ovechkin said, holding the Hart Trophy. "I don't want to stop. I want to be the best again next year." He then put it down on the dais and reached for it several times, making fun of his controversial 50th goal celebration when his stick was "too hot" to handle. "Just having fun," he said.

To quote Ovechkin from several months later, "It [was] another good day to be Alex Ovechkin."

After eliminating Washington in seven gruelling games in the Conference semi-finals, the Pens still had two more play-off series to win if they hoped to capture the Cup. And this was where teamwork came into play. Crosby had been a key player in the first-round victory over Philadelphia, and then he was brilliant in eliminating the Caps. These efforts seemed to take the starch out of him and he was never as good the rest of the way, but Evgeni Malkin came in to fill the breach. Malkin had been nearly invisible the first two rounds, but he came to the fore in the Conference finals against the Carolina Hurricanes, spear-heading the Pens to a four-game sweep and a much-needed four-day break before the start of the Cup finals against Detroit.

Only the first two games were close, and even then they weren't exactly spine-tingling. The Penguins had a 2–0 lead after twenty minutes of game one, but Carolina halved the lead on a goal midway through the second. The Penguins made it 3–1, and the 'Canes scored late to make it a 3–2 final. Malkin had a goal and assist for the winners.

In game two, Crosby opened the scoring and added an assist later, but Malkin stole the show with three goals and an assist. Carolina led 3–2 after the first period, and even after the Pens rallied it was still a 4–4 game early in the third. Malkin scored twice, though, and Tyler Kennedy added an empty-netter to make it an impressive 7–4 victory and a 2–0 lead in the series.

The teams headed to Raleigh, North Carolina, for the next two games, but the 'Canes simply couldn't handle the powerful Penguins. The 'Canes got the early goal before a sellout crowd, but Malkin scored twice and Crosby added another to make it 3–1 for Pittsburgh. The closest the home side came was 3–2 early in the third, but Pittsburgh pulled away with three unanswered goals later to produce a 6–2 win and a 3–0 series lead. They shook hands two nights later. After getting another early goal, Carolina didn't score again and the Pens eliminated them with a 4–1 win.

Malkin was also key in the seven-game series against Detroit for the Cup, and Crosby came back to be effective as well, notably in a crucial moment of game four. The home team had won the first three games, meaning Detroit had a 2–1 series lead, and the fourth game was tied 2–2 in the second period. Malkin blocked a pass at his blue line and tore down the right wing as Crosby bolted through the middle towards the goal on a two-on-one. Malkin made the pass over, and Crosby made no mistake snapping the puck in midway through the period to give the Pens a 3–2 lead.

Three and a half minutes later, Crosby played a starring role in the prettiest goal of the playoffs. Chris Kunitz got the puck along the left-wing boards just inside the Detroit blue line. He whipped a pass across the full width of the ice to Crosby who knew what he was going to do well before the puck got to him. Near the front of the goal, ahead of Kunitz, was Tyler Kennedy. Crosby had the puck on his stick only long enough to zip another cross-ice pass back to Kennedy, and poor Chris Osgood was still getting ready to position himself for a Crosby shot when Kennedy had already put the puck in the back of the net.

It was a sensational goal. Kennedy had made the initial play by chasing Henrik Zetterberg down. Zetterberg thought he was doing the smart thing by just backhanding the puck along the boards and out, but it was a blind shot and he didn't see Kunitz trailing the play. Kunitz saw Crosby even before he fired the puck cross-ice, and Crosby saw Kennedy go to the net immediately after checking Zetterberg. Three players thinking together, two passes of lightning speed, and one shot into the empty side of the net. That made the score 4–2, and the Red Wings never recovered.

Both teams won their next home games, Detroit by a comfortable 5–0 score and the Pens by the narrowest of margins, 2–1, setting up a game-seven showdown in Motown for the Stanley Cup on June 12. This was what Crosby had been waiting 365 days for, the chance to atone for losing the Cup the previous year, to Detroit, on home ice. The Red Wings, more experienced, playing at home, would surely have the advantage, but the Pens had been here now and knew what to expect and how to prepare.

A scoreless first period gave way to important developments in the second. For starters, Maxime Talbot, hero in no one's eyes except his wife's and kids', scored the only two goals to give the Pens a stunning 2–0 lead. But sandwiched between those goals was an innocent-looking play at centre ice along the boards. Crosby collided with Johan Franzen at 5:33 and injured his knee. The captain hobbled to the bench and played only one more shift, a token and symbolic appearance for half a minute in the third, staying on the end of the bench the rest of the game, encouraging his teammates as they went for the Cup.

Jonathan Ericsson scored for Detroit at 13:53 to make it a 2–1 game for Pittsburgh, but the outcome wasn't decided until the very second before time expired, when goalie Marc-Andre Fleury flung himself across the crease to stop a sure goal from Nicklas Lidstrom to preserve the 2–1 win. The Penguins had done what Crosby vowed to do – not to experience the disappointment of 2008 again. In so doing, he became the youngest captain to win the Cup, and after lifting it high above his head he turned to thirty-eight-year-old Bill Guerin and handed it off to his linemate who was hoisting the Cup for the first time since 1995, when he had won as a young unknown with the New Jersey Devils.

"Everything it took to win, we did it, you know," Crosby enthused after. "Blocking shots. Great goaltending. Different guys stepping up. I mean, we did exactly everything it takes to win. We're really happy with the result. We've been through a lot."

Alexander Ovechkin was rested and fresh-looking when he carried off his three trophies on Awards night in Las Vegas, but Sidney Crosby was sleeping with the most desired prize of them all that night, the Stanley Cup.

Said Ovechkin, surrounded by his trophies: "Personal stats is good. Personal awards is good. I just want to win one award, and that's the Stanley Cup."

He knew what Crosby didn't have to say.

5

FULL-ON RIVALRY

CAPTAIN OVI
A LOOSE CANNON

JANUARY 21, 2010: WASHINGTON 6 AT PITTSBURGH 3

Recall that the newly retired Wayne Gretzky said that Crosby could one day break some of his records. It was a stunning compliment, and it turned out to be a prescient one, too, regarding Crosby's skill, but it was completely inaccurate in the literal sense.

Which records could Crosby break? Fifty goals in thirty-nine games to start a season? Ninety-two goals or 215 points in a season? No. Neither Crosby nor Ovechkin were going to touch these records, and as both players entered their sixth NHL season it was patently obvious that all of number 99's scoring records would be safe for many, many years to come.

The truth is that today's hockey doesn't allow such ridiculous offence, not even for a single game. Perhaps there'll be a few lax moments in the occasional game but that's not the 1,500 career games that Gretzky played. The term "coaching system" did not exist until the mid-1990s, but when it arrived, with Roger Neilson and the Florida Panthers, it was here to stay.

The under-talented, expansion Panthers (who joined the NHL in 1993) stressed defence first, last, and in between. Incredibly, they made it to the Cup finals in 1996, their third year in the league, before being swept aside by the more talented Colorado Avalanche, but the style of hockey proved so successful that every coach at every pro level and down started to use some sort of "system."

A system was a way of negating the Gretzkys of the game, a way of saying, "We don't have a 99 on our team, so we'll just suffocate him rather than watch him beat us." Thus was born an unprecedented era of hooking, holding, slashing, clutching, grabbing, and interfering. Coupled with the ever-increasing size, speed, and strength of the players, which has, in effect, reduced the size of the ice, offensive players simply don't have the room and are not allowed the freedom to work their magic as Gretzky did in his prime.

To wit, when Gretzky was leading the high-flying, record-setting offence in Edmonton in the 1980s, his coach, Glen Sather, stressed offence because, well, he could. Thus, Gretzky became one of the team's most oft-used penalty killers. Sather's philosophy was simple. If there were nine players on the ice instead of ten, a player like Gretzky would have an additional 11 per cent of room out there. No matter that his team had one fewer skater.

In the twenty-first century, top players like Crosby and Ovechkin rarely kill penalties. Through their first five years in the league, Crosby had a grand total of *two* short-handed goals and Ovechkin four. Gretzky, after his first five years, had twenty-nine "shorties"! Twenty-nine! And, the Oilers were always near the top of the ratings for killing penalties. Imagine your team has a power play, and all you can think of is, "Don't let Gretzky steal the puck or we're done." Sather brilliantly countered the defensive situation with offence.

Today, Dan Bylsma and Bruce Boudreau would say that that philosophy is not responsible. In 2006–07, Crosby averaged

14 seconds – yes, *seconds* – of short-handed ice time a game and has never played more than, on average, a minute a game. Ovechkin's numbers are even more staggering. In 2005–06, he averaged 44 seconds a game, then in the next four years averaged 9 seconds, 7 seconds, 74 seconds, and 3 seconds.

In his rookie season, Crosby scored his 100th point in the team's 81st game of the year. Here's what then coach Michel Therrien had to say of his teen star reaching the century mark. "When he started to get around 80 points, you really started to believe he could do it," Therrien said. "But I didn't want to take away from the team concept. He did it within a team concept." Such words would never have occurred to Sather.

No, Wayne, 87 and 8 are amazing players, but your records are safe.

For Alexander Ovechkin, the 2009–10 season went from sensational to just excellent pretty quickly. He started the year scoring 14 goals in his first 14 games, generating obvious talk of "50 in 50" as he was reaching the prime of his career. But on November 1, 2009, in a home game against Columbus, he suffered an "upper-body injury" and missed the next two and a half weeks, shelving any talk of breaking records.

Then, on November 25, he scored early in the first period but in the third ran Patrick Kaleta into the boards from behind, taking a five-minute major penalty and game misconduct for his efforts. Just five nights later, in a 3–2 win over Carolina, Ovechkin crashed into Tim Gleason with a knee-on-knee hit that left both players limping off the ice. Even earlier, in a game on October 22, Ovechkin was fined $2,500 for slew-footing Rick Peverley of Atlanta, one of the dirtiest and most danger-ous kinds of plays in the game. Ovechkin again received a five-minute major and game misconduct for the Gleason play, but he also drew criticism from two sources.

First, coach Bruce Boudreau called Ovechkin's play "reckless," and then NHL disciplinarian Colin Campbell suspended him for two games. What's more, Ovechkin's incredible start had now been clouded over by an injury, two game misconducts, and play detrimental to the success of the team, as it had to try to kill off two five-minute major penalties in close games.

One thing was certain. Ovechkin seemed to learn from this brief outburst. In the next thirteen games he incurred just two minor penalties, and then his season got better again on January 5, 2010, when he was named the team's captain, replacing Chris Clark who had been traded on December 28. The announcement came inside the team dressing room prior to a game against Montreal, and the Ovechkin Era began with a 4–2 home win (although number 8 was held without a point).

"If I need to say something, I will say something," Ovechkin said of his expanded team duties. "But I will show what I can do on the ice. It's a big honour for me. I'm going to do my best, but I don't want to concentrate on having a C on my heart. I'm just going to play the same."

"It will be totally different," Boudreau said of the outgoing and incoming captains' styles. "Clark was an organizer. His wife took care of the [players'] wives. If there was a problem, Clark took care of the room and everything else. Ovi is taking care of the ice. That's what Ovi is going to do."

Coming into this game, the first since they faced each other in game seven of last year's playoffs, both Washington and Pittsburgh were feeling good. The Caps had won four in a row and seven of their last eight games, during which time they had averaged five goals a game. The Penguins were coming off a 6–4 win over the New York Islanders in which

Crosby matched his career best with a six-point night (two goals, four assists), but the memories of game seven were still fresh for everyone.

"It's pretty hard for us to see what happened last year in the seventh game," Ovechkin admitted, "but we can't do nothing about it." He was happier talking about the one-on-one rivalry with Crosby. "It's the same with the Lakers and the Cavaliers," he enthused. "Two players play against each other, and the media say who is better and who deserves to win. It's the same in soccer, like when Real Madrid and Barcelona play. The top players play against each other, and everybody says, 'Wow, this is going to be a sick game,' and they can't wait for it. It's the same. They can't wait for it."

On this night, captain Ovechkin played a significant role in the win even though it started off as Crosby's night. Crosby took advantage of a puck-handling miscue from Jose Theodore to push the puck over the line at 4:22 for the early Penguins lead. Later in the period Ovechkin drove down the left wing, cut nicely to the middle, and got a shot off. Goalie Brent Johnson made the save, but the rebound came right to Mike Knuble, and he smacked it in to tie the game, 1–1.

The teams exchanged goals early in the second, and then the Pens took the lead on a Kris Letang shot at 10:46. Five and a half minutes later, Ovechkin tied the game. He took a pass in the high slot and ripped a snap shot past Johnson on a power play, the team's first man-advantage opportunity of the game. The third period was all Capitals on the scoreboard, though Pittsburgh had the better of the play. The Pens simply couldn't score. Washington scored two early goals to take control, and then Ovi added an empty-netter to complete the scoring. He now had thirty-two goals for the season, just one behind Crosby.

"I don't think we played a bad third; they just played a little bit better," Crosby said.

"We have won five in a row, and we just want to continue it," Ovechkin said. "Today we started great and we finished great. It's a big sign for us. All this group was very concentrated, and I think we deserve this win. It was a pretty big game for everybody, and mentally we were ready."

OLYMPIC FEVER RUNS HIGH

FEBRUARY 7, 2010: PITTSBURGH 4 AT WASHINGTON 5 (OT)

This was perhaps the most dramatic and exciting regular season game between Crosby and Ovechkin, ranking second all-time only to game two of the 2009 playoffs when each recorded a hat trick. On this night, the Caps extended their team-record winning streak to an incredible fourteen games. And they did it in impressive fashion, rallying from a 4–1 deficit to win, 5–4, on the strength of Mike Knuble's power-play goal in overtime.

"This is what people pay to see," a jubilant Washington coach Bruce Boudreau said after. "The superstars [shone], and there is tension and excitement and physical play. You could see the passion on both sides. This is what hockey is all about."

Ovechkin had three goals and an assist (his ninth career hat trick but first in fifty-one weeks) and Crosby two goals. "It is always intense and people expect an emotional and intense game when these two teams play each other," Crosby said. "I think that is just the result."

What wasn't said but was patently obvious was that this game marked the final buildup to the Olympics. Just one week later the NHL-Olympics break would start, and with this matchup fans could start thinking – dreaming – of a Crosby-Ovechkin meeting with a gold medal on the line. In fact, the teams played in total six more games before the break, losing five. Only a Penguins win, 3–1 over the lowly Islanders, prevented a complete shutout. Olympics on the brain? You better believe it.

Crosby got this game underway with two goals in the first period to give the Pens a 2–0 lead. On the first one, he intercepted a Tyler Sloan pass and made a nice backhand before Jose Theodore could react.

The second one was the result of a sensational pass from Evgeni Malkin. It came on the power play and seemed to come off a botched rush. Four Penguins congregated along the boards just inside the Washington blue line, but Malkin found the loose puck and whipped it to the middle of the ice. No one seemed to be there. In fact, the television camera had to pan quickly to see that Crosby was alone to the far side. He took the puck and beat Theodore with a great deke.

Tempers flared late in the period when Ovechkin was drilled into the boards by Craig Adams. Knuble instigated a fight and was tossed from the game, and Ovechkin recovered to play a key role in the game's outcome.

Ovechkin made it a one-goal game at 9:01 of the second when he broke out of his zone just as Jeff Schultz got the puck. Schultz hit him with a perfect breakaway pass, and Ovechkin made no mistake going one-on-one with Marc-Andre Fleury to score his 40th goal of the season.

Two goals by Jordan Staal in the middle of the period made it 4–1 Pittsburgh, and the visitors seemed in full control of the game. Eric Fehr, however, got one back late in the period, giving the Caps a boost heading to the dressing room after forty minutes.

A wicked snowstorm meant the Penguins had arrived in Washington only at two o'clock in the morning on that same day, and by the third period they were slowing noticeably. That's when Ovechkin went to work. Tom Poti took a point shot that hit traffic in front of the net, but Ovechkin was there to backhand the puck in, an awkward shot rather than his usual blistering wrist shot.

Just over four minutes later, Ovi tied the score. Nicklas Backstrom and Crosby lined up for a faceoff to the left of Fleury, and when the puck was dropped by the linesman the two players were a tangle of sticks and skates. Backstrom managed to kick the puck back to Ovechkin, and he drilled his patented slapshot past Fleury to tie the game.

Midway through the overtime, Brooks Orpik took a controversial high-sticking penalty on Alexander Semin, and on the ensuing power play Knuble rammed home an Ovechkin shot for the winning goal. Orpik was so furious with the call that after he came out of the penalty box he had words with the officials, leading to a game misconduct penalty.

"He's a baby," Orpik said of Semin, whom he felt embellished the incident to draw the penalty. "I don't know if it was [a high stick], but he does that all game long. I've got zero respect for the kid. Yeah, it is tough to lose on that."

Lose they did, surrendering a 4–1 lead and giving the Caps their fourteenth straight win. "It's always nice to win when you're a little bit frustrated in the first period," Ovechkin said after. "The game didn't go well for us right away."

Perhaps, but it ended well after an impressive and dominating comeback. Next up, the XXIII Olympic Winter Games.

FOR ALL THE MARBLES

FEBRUARY 24, 2010: THE OLYMPICS

NHL participation at the Olympics had one very strange result. Because of the compressed schedule, players appeared in their final NHL games on Sunday, flew to Vancouver later that night, practised Monday, and played their first Olympics games with their countries on Tuesday. After the Closing Ceremony on the final Sunday night, they flew back to their NHL cities and played Monday or Tuesday. In between, NHL teammates became national team opponents, and nowhere was this more obvious than in the case of Pittsburgh and Washington, Canada and Russia.

In fact, those two teams contributed ten players to the Olympics (five each). The Penguins sent Crosby and goalie Marc-Andre Fleury to Canada, Evgeni Malkin and Sergei Gonchar to Russia, and Brooks Orpik to the United States.

Washington sent Ovechkin, Alexander Semin, and goalie Semyon Varlamov to Russia, Tomas Fleischmann to the Czech Republic, and Nicklas Backstrom to Sweden.

Of these ten, only Fleury was not important. He was the third goalie behind Martin Brodeur and Roberto Luongo, but despite Brodeur's struggles and Luongo's frightening nervousness, Fleury did not get to make even an abbreviated appearance (though he still qualified to get his gold medal).

Without question the most important day in the four-year cycle of hockey is the quarter-finals day of the Olympics. There has never been an upset in any Olympic tournament prior to that day that has prevented the top six or seven teams from playing each other at the same time, added in with a couple of fringe countries such as Germany or Switzerland to round out the final eight teams.

Consider the quarter-finals matchups on February 24, 2010, at the Vancouver Olympics – the United States got what should have been the easy game, against the Swiss; Finland played the Czechs; Slovakia and Sweden played; and Canada and Russia met. All games were elimination. Winners advanced to the semi-finals; losers went home. End of story.

But there was no question the most compelling game was Canada-Russia. There was the history of the teams, from their first meeting, at the World Championship, in 1954, to the Summit Series in 1972 and the Canada Cup in 1987, through to the 1992 Olympic gold, all of the important junior games they played for gold – and, of course, the 2.0 version of the individual rivalries, Crosby versus Ovechkin.

They had played against each other for five years now, the first time being for gold at the World U20 in 2005, through to the many NHL regular-season games and their epic seven-game playoff battle in 2009, but this game was different. They had never played a bigger game against each other, and they never would unless they met for Olympic gold some time, perhaps in Sochi in 2014.

Prior to this quarter-finals encounter neither Crosby nor Ovechkin had been dominant players on their respective Olympics teams. Each had one glorious moment, but for the most part they played on teams with so many superstar players that even they faded a bit into the background. Both teams also had one blowout and two close games, including a loss, in the Preliminary Round, but as fate would have it Canada had to play once more, in the Qualification Round, while the Russians advanced directly to the quarters from the Preliminary Round.

Canada hammered Norway 8–0 to start the Olympics, Crosby playing well and earning three assists. Later that same day Russia hammered Latvia by an 8–2 score, Ovechkin scoring twice. Two days later, both teams were forced to a shootout, Canada winning, Russia losing. In the former, it was a game of exorcising demons from Turin. Canada had lost to Switzerland four years earlier, 2–0, both goals coming from a Canadian expat named Paul DiPietro. In 2010, the teams tied 2–2 after regulation, but in the shootout goalie Martin Brodeur was excellent and Crosby, in the highlight of his Preliminary Round, scored the winner with a quick shot under Jonas Hiller's glove.

Russia was not so fortunate. Tied with Slovakia, 1–1, after sixty-five minutes, Pavol Demitra scored the winner in the shootout for the Slovaks. Then, on the final day of the Preliminary Round, the Americans beat Canada, 5–3, to claim top spot in Group A and push Canada down to second spot, resulting in a bye for the Americans and another game for Canada. Russia beat the Czechs, 4–2, in its final game, a game that turned on an Ovechkin play that remains one of the defining moments of those Olympics.

Early in the third period, Russia holding a precarious 2–1 lead, Czech superstar Jaromir Jagr was circling and controlling the puck through centre ice, but he had his head down for a second. That's when Ovi stepped up and crushed him with an open-ice check so ferocious the collision literally echoed throughout the building. The Czechs controlled the puck off this turnover and Evgeni Malkin scored to make it a 3–1 game, a crucial goal at a crucial time, thanks to a game-defining hit. Its symbolism was also not lost on fans, who saw the passing of the torch from the old guard (Jagr was thirty-eight and seconded to the KHL by this time) to the new.

Later, Jagr spoke of how stupid he was for having had his head down. He sported a small nick on his forehead, where his helmet was pushed back into his head, producing a trickle of blood and a flood of embarrassment, but he held no animosity toward Ovechkin. Only his pride was hurt. Appropriately, Ovechkin neither gloated nor apologized. "It's just a moment," he said, downplaying the freight-train collision. "If I have a chance to hit somebody, it doesn't matter who it is."

While the Russians enjoyed three days off between this game and the quarter-finals, Canada had to do extra duty by playing the Germans. It was no contest, an easy 8–2 win, but to a man the players suggested the extra game did the team more good than harm, giving them another sixty minutes to play together, to get to know each other, and to gel. Crosby had one of the eight goals, but when Canada and Russia skated out for their quarter-finals duel, much of the talk was about how quiet the two superstars had been so far for their respective countries.

Even more surprisingly, that remained the talk after the game as neither player factored into the result. The 7–3 win by Canada was almost certainly the finest, fastest, most skilled game ever played by a Canadian team in hockey history. Passes were lightning fast, pinpoint, bullet-like. Goals were tic-tac-toe, high-speed works of imaginative art. The hitting on the small ice was intimidating and effective at moving the Russians off the ice.

Coach Mike Babcock moved Crosby onto a line with Jarome Iginla and Eric Staal, a move that wasn't always impressive against Russia but that would pay gold-medal dividends a few days later. The coach had not been pleased with the team's play in losing to the Americans, 5–3, at the end of the preliminary round robin, and he decided to shake things up.

Despite being held without a point and being limited to four shots, Crosby was much happier to admit to being a non-factor in the game than was Ovechkin, who had just three shots and was also without a point. That's the difference between winning and losing.

As it turned out, the greatest impact on the game was not 87 or 8 or any other number – it was Mike Babcock, who out-coached Slava Bykov by a wide margin. Bykov played his lines seemingly without thought, believing the players would be inspired by the moment – Olympics quarter-finals, in Canada – and would improvise on ice with commensurate brilliance.

Babcock was taking no such chances. For starters, he assigned the hulking Rick Nash to play up and down Ovechkin's wing. And, he gave Shea Weber the defence-man's assignment on the right side to contain Ovechkin if he did get by Nash. At six-foot-four and 235 pounds, Weber would give nothing to Ovechkin in the size and strength departments. Nash was as big and strong as Ovechkin, and had tons of international experience. He was not going to get creamed by Ovi in Jagr-like fashion. His job was simple. Stay between his goal and Ovechkin at all times. Weber was a defenceman's version of Nash. Bykov either didn't see just how effective Nash and Weber were in their roles, or he didn't care. Or, he thought Ovechkin could fight through the coverage. In any case, he was wrong.

Canada scored just 2:21 into the game thanks to Ryan Getzlaf, and when Rick Nash roofed a stunningly quick snap shot at 12:55 to make it 3–0, there seemed little doubt of the outcome.

"They were much faster than us. They came out like gorillas out of a cage," said Russian goalkeeper Ilya Bryzgalov, who replaced Evgeni Nabokov after the 6–1 goal.

What was most impressive was Canada's relentless intensity, which didn't subside until late in the third with the game clearly out of reach. Canada won decisively in front of a Vancouver crowd that last saw these nations play some thirty-eight years earlier, in game four of the Summit Series in 1972, an historic loss by Canada after which the team was booed off the ice and Phil Esposito delivered his famous speech to the people of Canada.

Handshakes at the end were awkward and cordial, respectful but distant, as Crosby shook the hands of Malkin and Gonchar, with whom he would again be joking and changing and making passes with in another week's time.

Crosby knew the personal rivalry was petty at this stage of the Olympics and could not fathom a discussion of such when gold was still two huge wins away and an entire nation on the edge of its collective seat in anticipation. "We won a game. It happened to be against Russia," he said with appropriate terseness.

Russia was going home, its lowly sixth-place finish already in the history books. "Everything here is perfect," Ovechkin had texted a friend when he arrived in Vancouver. After the quarter-finals, everything was anything but perfect, as he told media in the mixed zone. "Believe me, we did everything we could, but we lost. It's a pity, and all that is left is bitterness. You just feel disgusted at heart."

In another interview, for *Sovetsky Sport*'s website, Ovechkin said: "I know that now a lot of dirt is going to be thrown at us by the press and by people who don't understand anything about hockey. But for those who believe in us and love us, I want to say that we tried, and we did everything we could. There weren't any redundant players here. Nobody can say that we had a bad team. We had a great team, and everyone fought. It just turned out that way."

When he returned for his first practice with the Caps after the loss, he was more reflective but still disappointed. "I think every game against Canada is special for everybody," he explained. "Obviously, we lost and we lost pretty badly. I don't know what happened. You could see how they move, how they play, and we didn't play at all. It was a pretty bad situation for us and our country, but still, life goes on."

As bad as it was being eliminated in the quarter-finals, Ovechkin made matters infinitely worse when he was involved in two pushing-and-shoving incidents with fans. Both were captured on video, of course, for all the world to see. In the first, Ovechkin sees and seeks out a woman filming Russian players walking down a corridor after the loss. He puts his hand over the camera lens for several seconds as he walks past her, clearly not wanting to be filmed in his moment of hockey-mourning for his great personal loss. In the other, he breaks the camera of a man asking for an interview.

With this behaviour, Ovechkin just made life all the worse for himself. The criticism was universal and went something like this: How could he be so tough with fans and cameras and not so tough against Crosby and the Canadians? So, he wanted to get mad – he should have taken it out on opponents on-ice, not on vulnerable fans under the stands.

"I don't want to talk about it," he said a few days later of the altercations. "It happened. I feel sorry, but it was an emotional moment for me."

And so, interestingly enough, Crosby was 3–0 and Ovechkin 0–3 in head-to-head games of the highest importance. Yet

Crosby didn't do much to contribute directly to any of those three wins, and Ovechkin was rendered ineffective in all three losses as well – the 2005 World U20 gold-medal game, game seven of the 2009 playoffs, and now the 2010 Olympics quarter-finals.

The tournament was far from over for Canada or for Crosby, though. Two days later, the team had to play Slovakia in one semi-finals while the Americans and the Finns played in the other. It was a surreal day at Canada Hockey Place (GM Place), to be sure. The United States-Finland game started at 12 noon, and was more or less over by about 12:20 p.m.

The Americans did something no team at the Olympics had ever done before in the modern game – they scored six goals in the first 12:46 of the first period, sending a shell-shocked Miikka Kiprusoff to the bench and rendering the last 47:14 of the game more or less meaningless. Antti Miettinen scored the only other goal of the game, late in the third, to make it a 6–1 final. What had been expected to be a close and exciting game turned into the most pitiful romp in recent memory for a game of such importance.

And then into the building came Canada, playing Slovakia gratuitously given its number-seven seeding, a position reflecting its clear superiority over teams traditionally eighth, ninth, or tenth (think Germany, Latvia, Belarus, Switzerland), and its equally clear inferiority to the top six (notwithstanding their heroic gold medal at the 2002 World Championship).

So Canada was supposed to win this semi-finals, to be sure, but coming on the heels of this crazy first game, nothing could be taken for granted. Of course, the Canadians were mentally prepared for a big game, thanks to their own preparation and that of the coaching staff, and they dominated the first fifty minutes of the game, building an impressive 3–0 lead and forming an impenetrable defence around the ever-more shaky goaltending of Roberto Luongo.

Lubomir Visnovsky scored at 11:35 of the final period when he banked a shot off Luongo and in. It was a goal that gave Slovakia the hope that they had not had all game. The team kept pressing; Luongo continued to look vulnerable. And, Michal Handzus made it 3–2 at 15:07 when the goalie failed to contain another wraparound and the Slovak batted the loose puck in.

It was mayhem after that, and in the final minute, with the goalie Jaroslav Halak on the bench for a sixth skater, Slovakia poured on a full assault on the Canadian goal. Luongo then made a great save of Pavol Demitra in the dying seconds, and Canada advanced to the gold-medal game to face the United States, a rematch of the 2002 finals in Salt Lake City.

Hindsight is always a wonderful thing, but on the morning of February 28, 2010, hindsight hadn't had a chance to come into play yet. On Canada's side, the talk was about how quiet Sidney Crosby had been, about the shaky play of Luongo, about Canada's experience.

For the Americans, general manager Brian Burke had done a masterful job of protecting his young team, allowing them to play pressure-free to get to the finals. They were younger and the clear underdogs, but they were fast and fearless. What did they have to lose by going all out? No one expected them to win anyway.

They also had confidence, knowing they had beaten Canada, 5–3, during the Preliminary Round. But Canada started with relentless speed and pressure, scoring the only goal of the first period, courtesy of Jonathan Toews, and making it 2–0 early in the second, thanks to Corey Perry. Ryan Kesler got one back for the Americans before the end of the period, and both teams headed to the dressing room in good position.

If the coaches had said to Canada at the start of the tournament, "We'll be leading 2–1 after two periods in the gold-medal game," fans and players would have been happy. And if the American coaches had said, "We'll be down one goal heading into the third period of the gold-medal game," they would have been equally happy, if not happier.

Canada played a near flawless third period, containing the Americans and limiting scoring chances. With less than a minute to go, U.S. goalie Ryan Miller went to the bench with a faceoff in Canada's end. Ryan Getzlaf lost the draw and the Americans controlled play, and Zach Parise corralled a loose puck in front and slid it past a sprawling Luongo at 19:35 to send the game to overtime.

In retrospect, had Canada won the game 2–1, it would have been a great win and a terrific game, an efficient victory under tremendous pressure, to be sure, but not a win of the historic kind that would put it alongside game eight of the Summit Series or game three of the 1987 Canada Cup.

The overtime would be twenty minutes of four-on-four followed by a shootout, and any true hockey fan wanted the game to be decided by game action, not a penalty-shot contest. Canada's coach Mike Babcock again showed his shrewdness at the right time. He decided to go for the win, play his best offensive players, and count on them to control play and keep the puck away from Luongo.

About seven minutes into the overtime he sent Jarome Iginla and Crosby out as his two forwards along with offensively-gifted defencemen Scott Niedermayer and Drew Doughty. Iginla and Crosby did, indeed, control the puck in the U.S. zone. Near the end of the shift, Crosby swatted the puck along the left-wing boards into the corner, but instead of heading off on a line change he darted to the goal, surprising and eluding defenceman Brian Rafalski.

He screamed, "Iggy!" and Iginla didn't hesitate to slide a pass to the direction of the scream. Ryan Miller slid his hand up the shaft of his stick to try to poke-check Crosby as he was getting ready to control the puck, but before the goalie had a chance to do anything, Crosby snapped a quick shot that went between Miller's pads. Canada had won gold, and Crosby, who had done little most of the Olympics, now remains the one image any Canadian fan associates with the 2010 Olympics, tossing his stick and gloves in the air, screaming "Yaaaa!" as he backs into the corner boards waiting to be mobbed by his teammates.

"I watched only the overtime," Ovechkin admitted. "I think Canada deserved to win. They played better. I think both teams have good chances, but I think in overtime, Canada feel more fresher and have more opportunities to score . . . It was a big moment, an emotional moment for them."

The Closing Ceremony celebrated Canada's remarkable hosting of the Olympics and record-setting gold medal haul, but as John Furlong, the chief of the organizing committee, rightly said, "The last gold will be remembered for generations." One feature of the final event of the 2010 Olympics was a presentation of Russian culture, looking ahead to 2014 and Sochi. Among the performers were the Bolshoi Ballet, figure skaters Irina Rodnina and Evgeni Plushenko, Vladislav Tretiak, and Ovechkin, who all held hands with a group of Russian children and waved to the crowd.

Unfortunately, Canada's men's hockey team couldn't make the ceremonial farewell. Although they played practically right next door to the stadium where the Closing Ceremony took

Crosby and Ovechkin go head-to-head during the 2009 playoffs for seven thrilling games, with Sid emerging victorious and taking the Pens to the Stanley Cup.

Crosby (left) and Washington's Mike Knuble generate a little summer excitement for the outdoor game six months later, on January 1, 2011, at Heinz Field in Pittsburgh.

Top draft prospects Ovechkin (left) and Evgeni Malkin (middle) join American Al Montoya at a Canada-United States baseball game in Durham, North Carolina on June 24, 2004.

Pittsburgh's Russian star Evgeni Malkin assists compatriot, friend, and NHL adversary Ovechkin prior to an entertaining shot during the Skills Competition of the 2009 All-Star Game.

Ovechkin relishes the moment after winning the Winter Classic in Pittsburgh on January 1, 2011.

While Ovechkin enjoys victory at the Winter Classic, Crosby suffers a concussion at the end of the second period that soon forces him off the ice for the rest of the year.

Crosby and Ovi make nice at the 2007 All-Star Game.

Teammates for a day, Sid and Ovi both represent the Eastern
Conference at the 2007 All-Star Game.

Ovechkin and Crosby shake hands during the pre-game ceremony at the Winter Classic as Penguins' owner Mario Lemieux looks on.

One of the many fine moments in Crosby's career came at the 2008 outdoor game in Buffalo when he scored the winning goal in the shootout.

Probably the greatest victory in Ovechkin's career came at the 2008 IIHF World Championship when Russia beat Canada, 5-4, in overtime at Le Colisée in Quebec City to win gold.

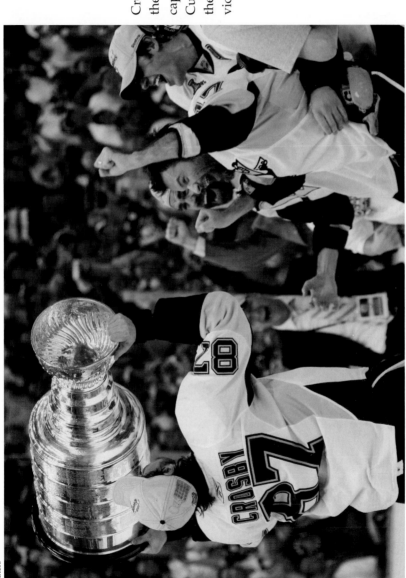

Crosby becomes the youngest captain to win the Cup when he leads the Penguins to victory in 2009.

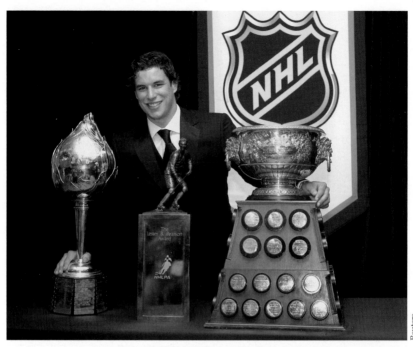

Crosby is all smiles as he poses with three great friends (l-r), namely the Hart Trophy, the Lester B. Pearson Award, and the Art Ross Trophy in 2007.

Not to be outdone, Ovechkin dominates the NHL Awards festivities in 2009 when he won the Lester B. Pearson Award, the Hart Trophy, and the Rocket Richard Trophy.

place, they were unable to navigate security and fans to get a bus from one venue to the other. No matter. They celebrated on their own, and the crowd roared with massive understanding that these games were great principally because of what Sidney Crosby had done just a couple of hours earlier.

There was Paul Henderson in 1972, Mario Lemieux in 1987, and Sidney Crosby in 2010. A hat trick of historic goals, and three pinnacles of Canadian hockey history.

OVI GETS RECKLESS

MARCH 24, 2010: PITTSBURGH 3 AT WASHINGTON 4 (SO)

It's perhaps a bit unfair to call Ovechkin's 2009–10 season anything but spectacular given that he finished with 50 goals and 109 points, but it was one marred all the same by on-ice news that was not all highlights of glorious goals. After his fantastic start, he missed two and a half weeks with an injury and then received two game misconducts in a three-game stretch, as well as a fine for a slew-footing incident.

But the final straw came on March 16, 2010, when he was suspended by the league for two games following a very dubious hit against Chicago defenceman Brian Campbell.

Campbell was being hounded by Ovechkin as Campbell tried to make a play with the puck in his own end after chasing down a loose puck. Skating towards his own end boards, Campbell dished the puck off, only to be shoulder-checked by Ovechkin at that dangerous and awkward distance from the boards. Campbell fell into the boards, suffering a broken collar bone, fractured rib, and concussion, and Ovechkin was given a five-minute boarding penalty and a game misconduct.

The additional two-game suspension cost him $232,645.40, bringing his fines this year over the $330,000 mark.

After the Kaleta incident, Ovechkin said only: "I can't do

nothing about it. I just play my game. It's not going to change. It's me."

But he wasn't taking into account his size and strength. At six-foot-two and 230 pounds, he was a physical force to be reckoned with. If he checked someone hard, that opponent felt the effects of the contact more than if, say, diminutive Martin St. Louis hit him. And for the Caps, their worry was always that the player initiating contact was just as susceptible to injury as the target.

Coach Bruce Boudreau acknowledged that he was in the awkward position of having to tell Ovechkin to tone his play down a bit, without asking him to sacrifice the intensity and competitive fire that went hand in hand with it.

"He's pretty reckless," Boudreau conceded. "It's hard telling a guy that scores 60 goals a year to change the way he plays. At the same time, I don't want to see him getting hurt. Maybe he has to pick his spots a little better. As a coach, and someone who admires him, I just don't want to see him put himself in harm's way. So, we'll see," Boudreau said. "I don't think anything said is going to change the way he plays."

Campbell missed nearly six weeks of hockey but was rewarded in the form of a Stanley Cup win with his Hawks, while the Caps were once again dispatched in the first round of the playoffs.

As for the Crosby-Ovechkin rivalry, this game was the fourth meeting between the two teams in just two months, the most condensed action between teams and players in their careers to date (excepting the 2009 playoffs, of course). And as things turned out, the intense game proved to be the third straight Washington win and the sixth loss in Pittsburgh's last eight games.

The two points also gave the Caps 108 in the standings, tying their best-ever season (set the year before), and moving them further ahead atop the Eastern Conference standings. Pittsburgh remained second with 90. Neither Crosby nor Ovechkin scored, so they both had 45 goals on the year, with ten games remaining, in the race for the Rocket Richard Trophy.

The Caps scored early in the second to take a 1–0 lead, but Pittsburgh tied the game soon after, and went ahead later in the period, thanks to a great pass from Crosby to Bill Guerin. Crosby charged in over the blue line and was driving to the net, but he lost control of the puck long enough to nullify the chance. In the blink of an eye, though, he corralled the puck with his skate and passed to the wide-open Guerin, who rifled a quick shot in the vacant side.

The third period did not start out kindly for the Pens. Crosby gave the puck away at the Caps' blue line on an early power play, and Alexander Semin walked in alone and scored to tie the game. Two minutes later, Eric Fehr put the team ahead, and only a late goal from Jordan Staal forced overtime and then a shootout.

Kris Letang and Crosby scored on their shootout attempts and Nicklas Backstrom missed. Down 2–0 in the shootout, Ovechkin was next. He needed to score – or Pittsburgh would win – and he did. Guerin then missed and Semin scored, and then in the fourth round Chris Kunitz was stopped by Theodore and Knuble beat Fleury, a rare instance of a team falling behind 2–0 in a shootout and winning.

It was the first shootout goal in Knuble's career and came about because of coach Boudreau's hunch. "I just had a gut feeling [he'd score]," he deadpanned. "And it's a big gut."

Crosby may have been on the losing side, but he wasn't about to heap too much praise on the winners. "I don't think there is any clear-cut number one," he said, despite Washington's big lead in the league's overall standings. "They've got a ton of depth and play a fast game."

SID AND OVI CHASE TROPHIES

APRIL 6, 2010: WASHINGTON 6 AT PITTSBURGH 3

I t was the final week of a long season, and one not nearly over as the playoffs were soon to be upon both Pittsburgh and Washington. The Capitals jumped into a lead and never relinquished it, winning this game 6–3, and sweeping all four games between the teams during the season in the process.

"I think playoffs are a whole new ball game," Washington coach Bruce Boudreau noted. "They are champions; they are Stanley Cup champions. It's nice that we [swept the season series], and I'm glad we did it, but I don't think it will mean a hill of beans if we see them in the playoffs."

The game had much individual meaning for both Crosby and Ovechkin. Playing before the home crowd, Crosby had a goal and two assists, giving him 100 points for the season and rousing the 17,132 fans at the Mellon Arena to a chorus of, "MVP! MVP!"

Ovechkin had two goals, the second coming into an empty net with just 0.2 seconds left in the game, giving him 48 for the season, making him tied with Crosby in the race for the Rocket Richard Trophy (Tampa Bay's Steve Stamkos was just one back). The two points also put Ovechkin into a first-place tie with Vancouver's Henrik Sedin with 106 points in the race for the Art Ross Trophy.

"All our mind in this dressing room is getting ready for the playoffs, not about personal goals and scoring leaders," Ovechkin said. "Of course, I want to win, and Sid wants to win."

The Caps took a 2–0 lead early in the second period, but Crosby cut the lead in half at 6:21 on the power play. Skating off the side boards and moving to the middle, he ripped a snap shot to the far side to make it a 2–1 game. But each of the next three Pittsburgh goals was followed by a Washington goal soon after, so a 2–1 game became 3–1, 3–2 became 4–2, and 4–3 became 5–3, the last thanks to Ovechkin. He corralled a loose puck off a faceoff in the Pittsburgh end and snapped a quick shot past the glove of Brent Johnson, who had replaced the struggling Marc-Andre Fleury when the Caps made it 3–1. The goal came just four seconds after a penalty to Bill Guerin had left the Pens short a man.

The Pens were struggling as they headed towards the playoffs, but both Crosby and Ovechkin left the building on this night with 48 goals. The goals were only the fifth and sixth for Ovechkin since coming back from the Olympics sixteen games ago.

The next week was the final one of the NHL's regular season. The Capitals finished first in the Eastern Conference with 121 points and a 54–15–13 record, the points and wins tops in the league. Their 318 goals were also tops by a country mile, the second-place team, Vancouver, having just 272. They allowed only 232 goals, and this goals differential of +82 was also the best in the league. They faced Montreal in the first round of the playoffs, a team that had qualified for the post-season only on the final day of the season and had given up more goals than it had scored.

The Penguins finished in fourth place with 101 points and faced fifth-place Ottawa. They hadn't had the same season as last year, but they also knew that there was no good to be said for going all out in the regular season to be left without energy for the playoffs. Sure enough, they handled the Senators in routine fashion after losing the first game, at home, 5–4.

Crosby had three assists in that game, and in game two, a 2–1 win, he had a goal and assist. The goal was a routine smacking-home of a loose puck. The assist was one for the ages. In basketball, it's called "posterizing," when a player does something so good at the expense of an opponent that the photo of the great play is made into a poster. Well, what Crosby did to Ottawa's Jason Spezza went on for many seconds and might be called "videoizing" or "YouTube-izing." Crosby entered a scrum in the Ottawa end and got the puck, but Spezza was on him right away. Crosby, his back to the goal the whole time, skated around behind the net, chased by Spezza the whole way. He came out the other side, stopped, turned, and went behind the net, Spezza not giving an inch but unable to get the puck as Crosby always kept his body between opponent and disc.

At this point, Crosby turned, now facing the goal as he went behind the net. Crosby got to the far corner, stopped, and went behind the net a third time, his back to the net again. He stopped more quickly, came around again and cut in front of the goal. He fell to his knees but passed back to Kris Letang at the point, and Letang's shot beat Brian Elliott in goal, who was still mesmerized by trying to follow Crosby and the puck.

This incredible play added salt to the wound, for just moments earlier Crosby had swept the puck off his own goal line with a diving poke check, saving what would have been the game-tying goal.

In game three, Crosby scored another gem when he walked out of the corner with the puck, eluded a check, outwaited

Elliott, and fired the puck into the empty side to make it 3–1. The Pens won, 4–2.

And in game four, a 7–4 Pittsburgh win, who was the first star? Crosby, with two goals and two assists. Game five: two more goals and one more assist, though the Senators won, 4–3, in triple overtime. The Pens eliminated Ottawa in game six with a 4–3 overtime win, Crosby, for once, being held off the scoresheet. Nevertheless, he managed 6 goals and 14 points in the six games of the Conference quarter-finals.

Number 87's Olympic glory and Rocket Richard Trophy–scoring were continuing through the 2010 playoffs. Not so for Ovechkin and his Capitals. Playing as if the team's incredible regular season guaranteed an automatic bye in the first round, they struggled badly against the more determined Canadiens.

It didn't start out that way. Ovechkin was invisible in game one, a surprising 3–2 overtime loss on home ice, but then he controlled the next three games, scoring four times and adding as many assists as the Capitals took a commanding 3–1 series lead. Heading home for game five, it seemed the Caps were destined to face Crosby and the Penguins again. But the Habs had other ideas. They squeaked out a 2–1 victory in that elimination game, Ovechkin getting the lone Washington goal, and then Montreal won at home in game six, by a comfortable 4–1 score.

Now the Caps were home again, for game seven, in a do-or-die battle, but they had lost their winning touch and Montreal was brimming with confidence. The Habs scored the only goal of the opening period on a late power play, and the middle period was goalless. Ovechkin scored to tie the game early in the third period, but referee Brad Watson nullified the goal immediately, ruling that Mike Knuble had interfered with goalie Jaroslav Halak on the play. The Habs scored later and Washington got a late goal to make it 2–1, but that's as close as they came. A 54-win regular season was worth only three more playoff wins before heading to a long, hot summer of doubt and depression.

Captain Ovechkin met reporters after the final game of the early playoff exit and was so uncommunicative that they gathered a stats sheet on the scrum. They summarized this: Ovechkin fielded seventeen questions. He answered seven of them with "I don't know." Three other answers consisted of one-word responses.

"We know we can win," he offered at one point, "but we don't win it. It's pretty hard. I'm in shock right now. I don't know what to say."

Despite the long season, augmented by the Olympics, Ovechkin could not have been tired. Less than a week later he was on his way to Germany to play for Russia at the World Championship, joined by teammates Alexander Semin and goalie Semyon Varlamov. They went to the gold-medal game but lost there, too, 2–1, to an unheralded Czech team led by Jaromir Jagr, Tomas Vokoun, and many Czech league stars who were clearly the underdogs to the Russian team that very much resembled its Olympic lineup.

Meanwhile, it was Crosby's turn to take on the Canadiens, and he, too, came up short in the next round of the playoffs. All looked good in game one, a comfortable 6–3 win in which Crosby had two assists and the Pens had four power-play goals. But game two saw the Habs hold Crosby off the scoresheet and skate to a 3–1 win, thanks in large measure to goalie Halak who stopped 38 of 39 shots.

The Penguins won game three, 2–0, but again Crosby was pointless. He got an early assist in game four, but the Habs evened the series with a 3–2 win. This was not going to be easy.

Game five was a 2–1 home win behind the goaltending of Marc-Andre Fleury, but the Habs managed to shut down Crosby yet again. He had a goal and an assist in game six, but the Habs won, 4–3, to force a decisive game, in Pittsburgh.

Game seven wasn't really close. The Habs took control in the first period, built a 4–0 lead midway through the game, and battened the hatches for the win. Halak was excellent; the Pens' power play didn't produce at crucial times; the energy level was simply greater on the Montreal bench than on Pittsburgh's.

Crosby could make no philosophical assessment of the loss beyond the scoreboard. "We out-chanced them two-to-one for six games," he reasoned. "I think, looking back at the series, you look back at game four, and we have the lead there, and we get a couple of bad breaks and maybe things would have been different then. But you can always look back. It's easy to be a Monday morning quarterback. It came down to execution, and it came down to one game – that's basically it. They played better and, unfortunately, we did not play well."

The disappointment was palpable, but in the last twelve months he had won the Stanley Cup and Olympic gold. He could rest well over the summer and get ready for a new season with a clear conscience.

OVI WINS HARDWARE, CROSBY GAINS MOTIVATION

JUNE 23, 2010: 2010 NHL AWARDS

I n Las Vegas for the second year of a three-year deal, the 2010 NHL Awards at the Pearl Concert Theatre inside the Palms Hotel featured a little bit of everything. For starters, the only major award already won was the Rocket Richard Trophy, awarded to the player with the most goals in the regular season. This award was shared by Crosby and Tampa Bay's Steve Stamkos, each of whom had 51 goals. Ovechkin was right behind with 50, but he wasn't able to score on the final day of the season to make it a threesome.

In fact, the trophy was decided on the final day for all concerned, and Ovi was the only player to fall short. The Caps had an afternoon home game against Boston, and Ovechkin had two huge objectives in mind. First, he and Stamkos had 50 goals, and Crosby was one behind, with 49. One or all were going to win the Richard Trophy, based on their output on this day. Second, Ovechkin was three points behind Henrik Sedin in the scoring race. A big day would have given number 8 two more individual trophies, the kinds that define a player's career. Unfortunately, he was held without a point, and lost out on both pieces of silverware.

Crosby's Pens had a 5:00 p.m. game on Long Island, and

number 87 wasted no time in notching number 50, late in the first period off a pass from Evgeni Malkin. Then, less than a minute into the second period, he scored number 51. The Penguins managed a 6–5 overtime win, and Crosby was in the lead for the Richard Trophy.

"I put a lot of hard work in," Crosby said of a season in which he set a personal best for goals. "There're a lot of guys who put in hard work, on their shot or try to shoot more and things like that. Last summer and throughout the season, I've tried to focus on it. At the end of the day, you're doing it to help yourself and help the team to make everything better. This is a nice bonus, for sure."

His father, Troy, provided a little background. "He's always been that way. Whether it was a mistake he made in a game, a shot on goal that didn't go in, or he didn't receive a pass properly, or he fanned on a shot, he would work on it after practice."

Crosby saw the extra shooting, and extra goals, as complementary facets to his passing game. Prior to this season, any defending player or goalie could pretty much assume he was going to pass when he had the puck in a dangerous position. Now, they weren't sure, making him both a more dangerous passer and a more effective shooter. "I'm not going to overpower guys all the time," he explained. "If you have a good shot, you can be effective even from areas that might not typically be great scoring areas. If you can be dangerous there, then you keep guys guessing."

While Crosby was working his magic in the northeast United States, however, Steve Stamkos was doing something similar in Florida. The Lightning had a road game against state rivals, the Panthers, a game won 3–1 by the Lightning. Unfortunately for Crosby, Stamkos scored with just thirteen seconds left in the game, into an empty net, to give him 51 as well, and a tie for the Rocket Richard Trophy. A day that began with Ovechkin seemingly in control and Crosby on the outside ended with the two young Canadians winning the goal-scoring crown and the Russian on the outside. Go figure.

As Crosby himself said, however, his scoring was the result of a determined and conscious effort to shoot the puck more. In fact, the shots on goal comparison between himself and Ovechkin over the course of their first five seasons in the league produced a staggering discrepancy. As rookies, Crosby trying to establish himself as an unselfish, pass-first player and Ovechkin working hard to be the top goalscorer, they had 278 and 425 shots, respectively, Ovechkin averaging more than five shots a game.

In year two, the differential was the same, although both players shot less often, Ovechkin with 392 to Crosby's 250. Year three was skewed by Crosby's ankle injury, which forced him to miss six weeks, but the 446–173 differential again showed Ovechkin shooting more. In 2008–09, there was no comparison. Ovi had 528 shots, more than six a game, while Crosby had a mere 238, less than three a game. The next year, this year, the numbers were the closest ever, with Crosby firing a personal best of 298 shots and Ovechkin firing a career low of 368 times.

In 2010–11, Crosby had 161 shots in 41 games, an average of nearly four a game, before he suffered a concussion and missed the second half of the season. Ovechkin's 367 shots for the full season works out to a little more than four a game, only slightly better than Crosby's average and the lowest total of Ovechkin's career. Their massive difference in styles had now practically been eliminated, although Crosby still was considered league-wide a dangerous passer, something no one would ever call Ovechkin.

The styles also presented contrasting philosophies and roles on ice. In Crosby's case, he scored more often because goalies were now less sure whether he would shoot or pass. As for Ovechkin, he subscribed to the coach's theory that no shot on goal was a bad shot. Goalies flub shots or give up rebounds all the time, and if the object is to put the puck in the net, then any attempt to get it there is a good attempt.

Ovechkin didn't leave the 2010 Awards empty-handed, though. He and Crosby were finalists, along with Vancouver's Henrik Sedin, for the Ted Lindsay Award, which honoured the best player as selected by his peers. (The trophy had been known till now as the Lester B. Pearson Award but renamed as of this year for the player who attempted to start a players' union in the late 1950s and early 1960s.) The odds favoured Sedin, in one respect, because the Art Ross Trophy winner frequently was named the best player.

Crosby, too, had a reasonable chance at the trophy, because of his outstanding season. However, Ovechkin won the award for the third year in a row, clear testament to his popularity as an entertainer and showman and the creator of many a highlight-reel play. Only Gretzky and Guy Lafleur had won the trophy three years running. "I have the most hard trophy to get – the player's award – so I'm very happy," Ovechkin said. "It's the most important thing. You play against the guys," he explained, to point out that the award was the result of votes from teammates and opponents alike.

The three were also nominated for the Hart Trophy, voted on by journalists, and in this case Sedin, more predictably, won.

Beforehand, though, the Crosby-Ovechkin dichotomy presented itself again. Asked whether he'd prefer the Lindsay or Hart, Ovechkin answered, "I'll take both."

Asked the same question, Crosby answered, "At the end of the day, that's three good seasons there and the way it ends up is the way it ends up." Never a more diplomatic answer given. No chalkboard ammo from 87, not even in June. But make no mistake. Crosby had a sensational 2009–10 season and felt more than a little disappointed he didn't win the Hart Trophy. Those who knew him knew he vowed to have an even better season next year, to leave no doubt in voters' minds about who was the best player in the game. Just as he had bounced back from a heart-breaking loss at the World Juniors to win gold, and bounced back from a loss in the Cup finals to win, he was fixing his eyes on the Hart Trophy and Lindsay Award as the best player in the game.

6

CROSBY DOES IT ALL

SID VS. OVI GETS INTO AMERICAN LIVING ROOMS

SEPTEMBER 23, 2010: HBO *24/7*

f you want mass market opinion, go to the masses. Consider this introduction to an opinion piece by John Beattie writing on www.nesn.com:

"Distinguished captain of the Pittsburgh Penguins, Sidney Crosby, is a Stanley Cup winner, Olympic gold medalist, and the face of the National Hockey League. He's clean-cut, well-groomed and happens to be one heck of a model athlete on the ice and off. Yawn."

Contrast this with his opinion of Washington's number 8: "Ovechkin is going to take the sporting world by storm for these four brilliant hours of behind-the-scenes television. Whether he's pushing triple-digits in his six-figure race car, racking up five-figure bills at clubs, or rocking out to four-figure crowds on stage, Ovi is the rock star that this sport needs to capture the hearts of the average sports fan if it wants to compete with the NFL, NBA and MLB."

This contrast is exactly what HBO hoped to capture and exploit when it announced a four-part series on the two stars – and their NHL teams – of the game leading up to the outdoor game on January 1, 2011, between Washington and Pittsburgh at Heinz Field. The exposure of the NHL on HBO was unprecedented, and despite the development of so many great young players in the game it confirmed yet again what everyone knew – numbers 87 and 8 were the names that drove the game.

In deference to the league as a team sport, HBO played up the great Pittsburgh-Washington rivalry and the timing of the four-part series immediately before and after the outdoor game. It talked about the many great players on both sides, the memorable seven-game playoff series, and all peripheral elements. But that talk could not mask what the series was really about – Sid versus Ovi, again. If Crosby had been playing for Toronto or Ovechkin for New York, then HBO never would have even known or cared about the Penguins and the Capitals, let alone have gone to such efforts to document a putative rivalry.

The big winners in this announcement were the fans. They were going to get behind-the-scenes access to numbers 87 and 8 to see them as they had never been seen before.

"The 24/7 franchise is fashioned on larger-than-life personalities, engaging storylines, and unrestricted access," said Ross Greenburg, HBO Sports president, in a statement. "With Sidney Crosby leading the Penguins and Alex Ovechkin leading the Capitals, we have all the ingredients for a dynamic show that will take viewers deep inside professional hockey and set the stage for the Winter Classic."

The 24/7 series – sort of like "a day in the life of . . ." and then some – was scheduled to include a December 23 game between the Penguins and Capitals at the Verizon Center, an appetizer, as it were, before the so-called Winter Classic on New Year's Day in Pittsburgh.

"[This series] gives us an incredible opportunity to bring our fans even deeper inside two model hockey organizations during the regular season," said John Collins, the NHL's COO. "Uniting HBO's amazing reality series with one of sport's greatest rivalries in an outdoor setting in front of 65,000 raucous fans will make this Winter Classic the most anticipated one yet."

This was the first time the HBO series had focused on pro hockey. In the past, 24/7 had gone behind the scenes with boxers Oscar De La Hoya and Floyd Mayweather and with NASCAR driver Jimmie Johnson. That alone was news, and, of course, Crosby and Ovechkin were willing participants, the former because he knew it was his duty to the game, the latter because he never met a public exposure opportunity he didn't like. Lights. Camera. Game on.

GR8 DVD VS. CROSBY DVD

NOVEMBER 16, 2010

Perhaps the greatest dissimilarity between the two giants of the game has been their off-ice personalities and how they portray themselves. Sidney Crosby seems to eat, live, breathe hockey. There is nothing about him that suggests he goes to the movies on a Friday night, picks up girls at a bar on a Saturday night, or does shots with teammates after a big win. For number 87, it's always about practice, leadership, focus, the next game. Getting better.

Not so Alex Ovechkin. He is happy to show his *joie de vivre*, happy to be seen with gorgeous women, happy to talk about a late night of drinks and partying. He plays hard and he lives hard, and if he loses a game on ice he seems to have little trouble in putting on his fun clothes, forgetting about the loss, and going out on the town. The intensity for the game and for being the best seems ingrained in Crosby, while the less serious Ovi wants to enjoy his fame not just with jumping-into-the-glass goal celebrations but with some good times far away from centre ice.

Therein lies the difference between Crosby's DVD and the one Ovechkin released, titled *GR8*. After all, if Sid had one, Ovi had to have one. As in all aspects of their careers, DVDs were no exception. *GR8* was about his life, family, and career, similar in spirit to Crosby's *On the Ice and Beyond*, released three years earlier, after 87's second season. As their subjects are on ice and off, so, too, are the DVDs different, another reflection of the players' personalities.

Crosby narrates his DVD, and the storyline is driven by events of the 2007–08 season and by comments from various hockey personalities. Important events are highlighted by headlines from various newspapers, but the thrust is hockey.

Of course, Crosby's third season is event-filled. He missed several weeks during the early part of 2008 with a serious ankle injury. The team acquired Marian Hossa at the trade deadline and then went to the Stanley Cup finals, losing on home ice to Detroit in game six. There is plenty of game action and sound bites, and several instances of Crosby swearing, which are bleeped out but nonetheless show his competitive intensity as never been seen before.

Interestingly, there are only three references to Ovechkin, and two are snapshots less than a second in duration. The third is in a Washington-Pittsburgh game, won by the Penguins, of course, but for the most part this video makes no attempt to capture or glamorize the "rivalry."

As well, there is little about Crosby's private life in the DVD. Yes, we see his father in several scenes, but it's all about hockey. Only once do we see Crosby back in Nova Scotia, fishing, and then taking shots on a net on a specially created concrete driveway down by the water. Other than that, this is a hockey video about a star player on ice and his life in the game off it.

Tellingly, the voiceover after the Penguins lose the Cup finals to the Red Wings has Crosby describing himself, ending with a speech to himself so humble it's almost embarrassing. He begins: "Sidney Crosby is someone who can be relied upon."

It finishes with: "One thing Sidney Crosby is not is a Stanley Cup champion. But hopefully one day he will be. One day."

It is a self-damning assessment post-loss, the kind of almost gratuitous criticism Ovechkin would never level against himself. Not surprisingly, it took Crosby only one year to turn his loss into a victory.

Ovechkin's DVD, on the other hand, is more like a birthday party video. Filmed in the summer of 2010 after the Capitals lost to the Canadiens in the opening round of the playoffs, it is only tangentially about hockey. It is more about a famous person and his lifestyle. There are scenes of Ovechkin driving shirtless in one of his expensive cars through the countryside outside Moscow, Russia's answer to Daniel Craig. We are introduced to his best friend who answers the front door of his apartment wearing only underwear. Most of it is shot in Russia, not Washington. Hockey fans have never seen such a home video before.

Ovechkin films several scenes himself, at the Awards show in June, for instance. He approaches Crosby, tells him he's making a DVD just as Crosby had, and asks him who will win the Hart Trophy. "You," Crosby says good-naturedly.

This DVD is not about the dedication a hockey player needs to succeed. It's not about his on-ice skill or his love of the game or his rise to the greatest heights in the NHL or Olympics. It's pure Ovechkin, who he is and what he is and how he lives.

There is one nice hockey anecdote. His father tells the story of Alex as a child. The twelve-year-old was in his last game of the season with Dynamo and was told that Pavel Bure held the record for most goals with 56. Alex had 53 but scored six goals that game. "That's when I knew he could do something special," his dad said.

And we do see Ovechkin on ice, practising at home, on one occasion. He is wearing a sweater that says "sochi.ru" on it, perhaps the most telling image in the whole DVD despite its seemingly fleeting innocence. Ovechkin has stated time and again that he will play in the 2014 Olympics, in Sochi, Russia. Whether the NHL sends its players there or not, he has declared beyond doubt he will leave the Capitals to represent his country. "How would Canadian players feel if they were told they couldn't play in Vancouver?" he asked rhetorically.

Although Ovechkin is a hockey player who has no interest in the complexities of political issues, he will not be denied this opportunity in 2014 and as such has put himself front and centre in what might become a nasty fight leading up to the negotiation of a new Collective Bargaining Agreement in September 2012, which will include a clause about competing (or not) in Sochi. For this he has to be commended and respected.

CROSBY'S
POINT STREAK CONTINUES

DECEMBER 15, 2010: HBO *24/7* SERIES, EPISODE I

Part One of the much-hyped HBO series took place at the end of a bad night for both the Penguins and Capitals, although it was far worse for the Caps. In Pittsburgh, the Penguins lost for the second straight night after winning twelve in a row, but the loss this night to the visiting New York Rangers had, as they say, a bit of an odour to it.

Pittsburgh went ahead 1–0 in the last minute of the first period thanks to a great play by Crosby and Malkin. Malkin had missed four games with a knee injury and returned to the lineup the previous night against Philadelphia. He and Crosby played on a line together for most of the game, the exception rather than the norm, and Crosby set up two power-play goals from Malkin, the only two Pittsburgh scores of the game.

Against the Rangers, Crosby got the puck at the top of the faceoff circle and faked a shot, drawing both defencemen to him. Instead of shooting, though, he dished the puck off to Malkin on the left wing, and "Geno" cut in sharply on the goal, stopped, and tucked the puck in the near side as goalie Henrik Lundqvist was sliding the other way.

The 1–0 lead held up for the next thirty minutes, but midway through the third the Rangers scored two goals just fifteen seconds apart to go ahead 2–1. They scored two late goals and won, 4–1.

The Capitals, though, lost 2–1 at home to Anaheim in overtime, their seventh straight loss. Ovechkin was held without a goal and now had just two in his last fifteen games. The team's slump was not coinciding well with HBO's lead-in to the outdoor game on New Year's Day, and Ovechkin and coach Bruce Boudreau were very much the focus of attention during the drought.

The first 24/7 episode begins with a Pittsburgh-Toronto game, a contest which seems scripted for HBO in that Crosby scored the first goal to extend his points streak to seventeen games, then scored another later. The Pens coasted to a 5–2 victory at the new Consol Energy Center, the team's eleventh win in a row.

Meanwhile, the next scene dealt with Washington's most recent game, one in which it blew a 4–1 lead at home late in the game to the same Leafs and lost in a shootout. Same opponent, markedly different results, with Crosby leading the Pens to victory, but Ovechkin all but invisible in the Washington loss.

Next up was Washington's 3–0 loss to Florida, punctuated by a tirade from Boudreau during the second intermission after the Panthers scored at 19:59 of the second to make a 1–0 score en route to victory. Another Caps loss, this time to Colorado, is followed by another Pittsburgh win, over Buffalo, the trend of teams heading in opposite directions continuing.

The episode had commentary from both coaches and general managers, and from Washington owner Ted Leonsis, but two things were clearly missing: the presence of Pittsburgh owner Mario Lemieux, and more direct coverage of Crosby and Ovechkin, who were all but invisible. Why showcase these two teams when clearly the interest was on the two players, and not on Maxime Talbot or Scott Hannan? By the end of the first hour, the only memorable moments were of Boudreau and his profanity-laced tirade, shocking more for its being televised than for its revelatory content.

SID AND OVI . . .
COME ON DOWN!

DECEMBER 20, 2010: *THE PRICE IS RIGHT*

n the half dozen or so years since Crosby and Ovechkin became a hockey item, they had taken the league out of the notoriety of a year-long lockout and into a glorious future. The marketing culmination of this might well have been the announcement of HBO's series *24/7*, which was little more than a glorified excuse to showcase the two stars of the game, but they also appeared on an episode of *The Price Is Right*, a game show with a rich history of midday success on U.S. television, to help promote the outdoor game on New Year's Day 2011.

By now, the performances of the two players were so intertwined that they needed a nickname along the lines of Brangelina or TomCat. What would be appropriate? Sidovi? Croskin? They were hockey's couple, opposites and adversaries on ice and off, but together the driving forces for the league and game.

And so it was that at 11:00 a.m. Eastern Standard Time on Monday, December 20, 2010, the pair, along with retired player Jeremy Roenick, there in person as a live buffer between the recorded players, appeared with quizmaster Dana Carvey on the game show to promote the upcoming outdoor game on January 1 at Heinz Field in Pittsburgh.

However, while Roenick was, indeed, on the actual stage of the show with Carvey, the big boys had recorded their appearances weeks earlier, talking blind to a camera hundreds of miles from each other.

Said Ovechkin in a canned hockey monotone, clearly reading from script: "You know, we've got a big game coming up with Bridgestone Winter Classic."

Said Sid in the same tone, clearly unaware of what Ovechkin had just said, though the lines were intended to sound conversational: "That's right. We're playing these guys outdoors in front of 65,000 fans, and we want you to be ready for it with this official Winter Classic gear."

After "the gear" was showcased, Alex spoke more words: "Now you have all your Winter Classic gear, it's time to put to good use."

Intoned Sid: "Pack your bags. You're coming to the Steel City to see the Bridgestone NHL Winter Classic on New Year's Day."

And so their appearance on *The Price Is Right* ended. Not exactly increased drama for the big game, but it got the word into the homes of average Americans who watch game shows in the middle of a workday Monday.

CROSBY OFF ICE

DECEMBER 22, 2010: HBO *24/7*, EPISODE 2

The democratic distribution of air time to as many members as possible of both teams continued in the second episode of the HBO series intended to promote a Pittsburgh-Washington rivalry, which would have been non-existent had Crosby and Ovechkin not played for their respective teams. And while there were many fine moments in the show, none fuelled greater interest in that rivalry beyond the desire to see more of 87 and 8.

One of the first scenes offered a succinct quote from the Pens' number 87: "Philadelphia is the definition of a road game." Cut to his hotel room, which he shared with Pascal Dupuis, as he recounted fighting Matt Niskanen earlier in the season.

Unfortunately, we see precious little of Crosby in the next 58 minutes. When we do, we are treated to another fine theme – his superstitions. Crosby doesn't go from the parking lot to the dressing room at the Consol Energy Center directly because that would require walking past the visitors' dressing room. So, he takes the long way around, alone. He also eats a peanut butter and jelly sandwich at 5:00 p.m. every game day.

Crosby explained good-naturedly how one of his superstitions was altered. He liked to be the last out onto the ice, but at the start of his second year, Evgeni Malkin's rookie season, Malkin declared *he* wanted to be last out. Crosby laughed and said, "How do you want to settle this – rock, paper, scissors?" Malkin had an answer waiting. He said because he had already played pro for three years in the KHL he had seniority, and so he should go last. Crosby couldn't think of a comeback, and a new superstition was begun.

One of the best surprises about the HBO series was that it caught the two teams heading in opposite directions. The Penguins hadn't lost in a month, and the Caps were enduring a gut-wrenching losing streak that seemed as if it would never end. The agony writ large on coach Bruce Boudreau's face was intercut with the frustrations of the players who couldn't buy a goal on ice or draw inspiration from words at turns tough and encouraging. "If it doesn't kill you, it's going to make you stronger," Boudreau philosophized.

This episode showed little of Ovechkin save a quick visit home to have a meal with his parents and pack for a weekend road trip. Perhaps his lack of face time was appropriate, given his recent scoring troubles and his inability either to contribute to the team's offence or lead the team out of the slump through words, although if such a scene had been available it would have been intriguing to watch, for sure. He looked perplexed on the bench, disconsolate on the ice, and confused every-where, as he tried to grapple with this monster losing streak.

To wit, the first scene of the episode shows his fighting Rangers' forward Brandon Dubinsky at centre ice of a disas-trous loss. As the linesmen break up the fight, Ovechkin screams at his teammates, "Fuckin' come on, for fuck's sake!" in the hopes that the fight would lead to a goal, a rally, some-thing positive. It didn't. Trailing 4–0 at the time, the Caps gave up a fifth moments later and lost, 7–0.

A fan of the game would take away from this hour just how fun winning is and how horrible losing is – and how incredibly fine is the difference between the two. As Pittsburgh coach Dan Bylsma said after his team lost to the Flyers, 3–2, despite it being their first loss in more than a month, "Losing sucks."

No one would agree more than the suffering members of the Washington Capitals.

LONG SHOOTOUT
GIVES SID ANOTHER "W"

DECEMBER 23, 2010: PITTSBURGH 3 AT WASHINGTON 2 (SO)

The first meeting between Sid and Ovi in the 2010–11 season came at almost the halfway mark, the 36th game of Pittsburgh's season, and the 37th of Washington's. What was shocking, however, was that by this point Crosby was having such a vastly superior season to his rival.

Consider their first five years in the league. Crosby took the league on his shoulders and reached the 100-point mark, but Ovechkin scored "greater" goals, more highlight-reel goals, to win the Calder Trophy. Crosby responded by having a sensational sophomore year, culminating in the end-of-season trophy distribution that saw him claim the Hart, Art Ross, and Pearson. Year three was clearly Ovechkin, as Crosby suffered a high-ankle sprain and missed almost two months of the season while Ovechkin scored a career-high 65 goals. Crosby made amends in a big way, though, by captaining the Pens to their first Stanley Cup finals since Mario Lemieux in 1992.

Year four might have gone either way, and if the Hart and Pearson had been voted on after the playoffs, when the Penguins went to game seven of the Cup finals and won, Crosby surely would have won. But, voting ended after the regular season and Ovechkin, again with some great goals rather than steady play, took the two MVP awards. The 2009–10 season, though, might well have been a tie, but voting wasn't particularly close and Ovechkin won the two trophies again. Some say Crosby was insulted and ticked off by this result and vowed not to let it happen again. Well, no player ever put his mind to something the way 87 did.

Crosby continued his torrid scoring ways in 2010–11, and so did his Rocket Richard mate Steve Stamkos in Tampa. Together, they left Ovechkin in the dust. The Pens had a bit of a slow start but picked up as Crosby took control once again. He reached a near fever pitch in November and December, going on a 25-game scoring spree that included two hat tricks in three games to tie Stamkos for the league lead, each with 21 goals. While Crosby was playing at a level that was virtually untouchable, Ovechkin was decidedly mired in a slump. Worse, he created a major controversy after a game against New Jersey on November 22, 2010, in which the Devils humbled the Caps to the tune of 5–0.

It was the third loss in a row for the Caps and extended Ovechkin's goalless slump to four games (just two goals in his past nine games). Ovechkin was demoted to the third line in the middle period and played on the second line in the final period. But all of this wasn't the trouble. While coach Bruce Boudreau was answering questions from the media after the game, Ovechkin teammate Alexander Semin, and Russian-New Jersey friend Ilya Kovalchuk stood just a few feet away sharing many a laugh, entirely inappropriate behaviour for a team captain following a humiliating loss.

Boudreau was caught glaring at the scene to his side and when asked about it, replied carefully, "I'll reserve my thoughts on that, if you don't mind."

Corey Masisak, a reporter with CSN Washington, didn't mince his words, writing, "There was something that didn't feel right about the way Ovechkin and Kovalchuk were laughing and clearly having a good time while the other players showed little emotion after the contest. It's frankly unacceptable for Ovechkin to put himself in a situation where this becomes a story."

This was the first time Ovechkin's character had been called into question. Fraternizing with an opponent after such an embarrassing defeat was so obviously inappropriate that Ovechkin shouldn't have had to been told so. As a captain and competitor, he should have been furious and upset by the loss, especially as it came at the hands of New Jersey, one of the league's worst teams at this point in the season.

And, of course, in this and all respects, a comparison to Crosby was even more damning. Crosby would never be seen fraternizing with an opponent after a game in such a public manner, let alone after a blistering loss. People might complain that Crosby was too boring in quotes, but it was absolutely understood he would never cheapen the meaning of a loss as had Ovechkin.

Meanwhile, on the same night, in Florida, Crosby had a goal and an assist in the first eleven minutes of the game to lead the Pens to a 3–2 win over the Panthers. The contrast could not have been more stark, but it was only typical of what had been happening all season long. Ovechkin was stuck at 10 goals on the year to Crosby's 21, and none of those 10 were of the highlight variety that would push the Hart Trophy in his direction.

The timing couldn't have been worse for Ovechkin, either. He had just released his DVD *GR8*, and HBO was in the middle of filming the four-part special featuring the two teams and the two players.

As game day approached, things continued on in opposite directions. The Pens had won 14 of their last 16 games, and Crosby had surpassed Stamkos for goals and points by a wide margin, to be far and away the dominant force in the league.

The Capitals hit rock bottom on December 12, a 7–0 loss to the Rangers at Madison Square Garden. The game was marked by Ovechkin's first real fight in his career, with Brandon Dubinsky at centre ice in the second period with New York ahead, 4–0, a fight that had little positive effect. It was an ugly loss that demanded leadership from the team captain.

"We have to group together," Ovechkin said after the game. "We don't have to say this guy played bad or made mistakes. We all make mistakes. It's a lot of mistakes. We have to keep together as a team and as a group. We haven't had this kind of situation in a long time. It's something new for us. Good teams find wins."

Wayne Gretzky chimed in again on Crosby during an appearance on TSN on December 9. "He scores big goals when you need to score big goals for your team," he told Gord Miller. "He's a winner. He's won a Stanley Cup and a gold medal. He's a special player. We all know how talented he is and how good he is, but to me it's his work ethic," Gretzky went on. "He's the hardest working guy in the league, and that's why he's the best player in the game. He's got the right guy – Mario – in Pittsburgh. He's got a tremendous leader right in front of him. He gets better every game, and I think he's going to be better next year than he is this year. Right now he's playing the best hockey I've seen him play."

This Washington-Pittsburgh game lived up to the pre-game hype, which was a daunting task, to say the least. It was the first meeting of the year between the teams. HBO had just broadcast its second installment of its 24/7 feature on the teams. The Caps had snapped a dreadful eight-game losing streak by winning its previous two games, while the Penguins had won 4 of its last 6. Crosby entered the game on a career-best, league-best, 22-game-points-scoring streak. And the New Year's Day outdoor game was only nine days away.

The hype started in the stands two days earlier during a Caps home game when they manhandled the then hapless New Jersey Devils, 5–1, to make up for their 5–0 loss to the same team a month earlier. Fans started chanting, "We want Pittsburgh!" both mocking the opponents that night and trash-talking the Penguins for a game that wouldn't take place for another forty-eight hours.

"The crowd wants us to play against those guys [the Penguins], and we want to play against them, too," Ovechkin admitted. "It's going to be a big matchup, a pretty exciting game for everybody."

"You talk about the hype and the buildup and the rivalry and then the puck drops and it is exactly what the buildup is," Pittsburgh coach Dan Bylsma said after the game this night. "You think sometimes these games are overbilled, but this was a playoff-type game. The building was rocking and [there were] a lot of ups and downs in that game and a lot of emotion not to disappoint the fans."

In the warmup, Ovechkin wore a toque as a nod to the upcoming outdoor game, and on his first shift of the game he drilled Evgeni Malkin with a devastating hit to set the tone. On the next shift, Malkin drew a penalty for a hit on Ovechkin, but as soon as the Penguins killed that off they struck for the opening goal.

Kris Letang spotted Crosby to the side of Michal Neuvirth's

goal and drilled a hard shot that Crosby deflected beautifully into the net at 3:21 for an early 1–0 Pittsburgh lead. That extended his point streak to 23 games, the longest since 1992–93 when Mats Sundin recorded a point or more in 30 straight games. It was a goal marked by Crosby's inventiveness.

While most players like to deflect the puck from directly in front of the goal or to their backhand side, Crosby, a left-hand shot, liked to stand to the left of the goalie and redirect the puck off his forehand, a more difficult angle, to be sure, but one the goalie has little chance to react to or get his body in front of.

Not much happened the rest of the period, but Ovechkin got off several shots only to have many of them blocked. When they got through, goalie Marc-Andre Fleury was excellent.

Malkin earned a penalty shot early in the second period when he was hooked on a partial breakaway, but Neuvirth stopped him on the freebie to keep it a 1–0 game. Just a few minutes later, on a similar play, Crosby was hooked, but no penalty shot was called, and he was also stopped by the Caps goalie on the play. The Caps were the better team in the period and tied the game on their second five-on-three advantage, defenceman Mike Green ripping a wrist shot over Fleury's glove from the slot for the tying score.

Crosby, however, was not done. Early in the third he drove in on goal and was checked off the puck, but he managed to push it out front where Chris Kunitz knocked it in for a 2–1 Pittsburgh lead with the ice still wet.

The Caps persevered, though, and Mike Knuble tied the game at 14:31 with a great short-handed effort, beating Fleury while being hooked on the play. The rest of regulation time and overtime was tense and exciting, but without a goal, leaving the game to be decided by a shootout.

Ovechkin had been stoned all game by Fleury, but as the first shooter he beat Fleury with a backhand. Letang, though, scored on the next shot, and then the next eleven shooters, including Crosby, failed to score. It took Pascal Dupuis, in the seventh round of shots, to win it for the visitors.

"I think we played great," Ovechkin said. "I think all four lines did [a] great job. We don't make mistakes, [we] finish checks, get [pucks] deep, have lots of shots. I know Fleury played unbelievable today. They are great players. They have a chance [and] they use it. We have to use our chances."

Crosby, meanwhile, pointed to his goalie as the difference in the game. "He came up big. Without him and his play, that is a much different outcome. At the start, at the end, all the way through, he was a big part of us finding a way to win tonight. It is too bad we couldn't capitalize on one of those power plays in the third. That would have been big for us to get the next one, but he did a great job of keeping us in there."

CAPTURING THE SLUMPING CAPS

DECEMBER 29, 2010: HBO *24/7*, EPISODE 3

What was becoming patently clear as the HBO series progressed was that this noble effort to capture something of the spirit of the game through an inside view would fail only because of the extreme ambition of the endeavour. In truth, HBO had bitten off more than it could chew.

To wit, this was the first such documentary attempt to capture the game in such a day-to-day way, so it was breaking new ground. But the full title for the series, *Penguins-Capitals: Road to the NHL Winter Classic*, suggested a focus that was artificial, that the four hours of coverage had as its focal point an outdoor game that was, in truth, noteworthy only because it was played outside. Furthermore, by concentrating on the two teams – their players, coaches, executives, staffs, perhaps seventy or eighty people in all – it had too much ground to cover to do any one portion of it extremely well. More to the point, Crosby and Ovechkin were given short shrift in the series' attempt to distribute the attention.

Recall Wayne Gretzky's famous remark after the fantastic two-game series against the Soviets in Rendez-vous '87 when he said, "Let's face it. No one wants two games. And no one wants to watch Canada play West Germany. Everyone wants Canada and Russia in eight games."

So, too, can one apply that to the true heart of the HBO series and the outdoor game itself. Honestly – no one wanted to see Pascal Dupuis in his living room or Nicklas Backstrom at Christmas dinner. Fans wanted Crosby and Ovechkin. Period.

Ignoring this simple truth, the series gave us a story on Mike Knuble's broken jaw and Bylsma playing hockey with his son in the family basement and several other bits and pieces that made up this hastily stitched quilt, but it flared to life when the two teams faced off in a thrilling game just before Christmas, with Crosby and Ovechkin front and centre.

After beating Florida, 5–2, on December 22, Bylsma told his team, "We've got another game tomorrow. I think you know who we play."

The HBO writing then reached its zenith as it not only pitted players against each other, it showed this Caps-Pens game firstly as a battle of ideas and strategies set out by its coaches. Scenes shifted back and forth showing Boudreau speaking, then Bylsma in the dressing room, talking to their players about what to do and what not to do.

Boudreau: "I don't think Crosby cares whether you hit him or leave him alone, but Malkin does. If we hit him, get him off his game, he will take penalties. And then we capitalize on the power play."

Bylsma: "Be aware where 8 is," not even bothering to call Ovechkin by name.

The game was close, the cameras ice-level at the boards to capture the speed, the movement, the ferocity, the excitement. Crosby was fouled on a clear break but wasn't given a penalty shot, resulting in a potty-mouthed tirade at the referee. He scored the opening goal on a sensational deflection.

Ovechkin also tossed around the f-bomb with aplomb, notably near the end of the game when he was given a tripping penalty, a marginal call, to be sure. The game went to a shootout, and Ovi scored while Crosby missed, but the game wasn't decided until the seventh round when Pascal Dupuis buried the winner and sent the Pens to Christmas break with a 3–2 win.

What was clear with this HBO series was what's clear in hockey. Players were most personable and most mesmerizing when they were doing what they do best – playing hockey. There were storylines for every member of every team, but the most compelling storyline was the one involving the best players playing their best, on ice, their pride and reputation on the line every shift.

That's hockey.

7

THE RIVALRY DAMAGED

RIVALRY CRASHES HEADFIRST

JANUARY 1, 2011: WASHINGTON 3 AT PITTSBURGH 1
(WINTER CLASSIC)

The so-called rivalry between Pittsburgh and Washington was the reason the NHL had awarded the 2011 outdoor game to Pittsburgh. Promoting the game through the fiercely competitive nature of the Crosby-Ovechkin storyline, the league was building excitement for the game months prior to its being played on January 1, 2011.

What had started as an intense battle between two number-one draft choices who'd entered the league at the same time had morphed into an ongoing competition with offshoot mini-wars, to enhance the flavour of the rivalry. There was the Malkin-Ovechkin war, and later the "I don't see anything special" comments by Alexander Semin about Crosby. Then, on July 27, 2010, Pittsburgh's Maxime Talbot added an ounce or two of fuel to the fire with comments about Ovechkin during an interview with a Pittsburgh radio station.

Said the player to The Z 105.9 about Washington's number 8: "I just hate the guy. I can't lie. Sorry. Even more so for a guy like Ovechkin. Like, seriously, okay . . . yeah. I don't like him."

He went on to elaborate: "You hear a lot of stories about a guy, but sometimes they're not true. You hear of guys who are not good guys, and you're like, 'Yeah, okay, I'll give the guy a shot.' The first time I met him, let's say he didn't give the best impression to me, so better reason to hate him even more.

"I was actually at the NHL Awards last summer [2009] with Malkin, and we brought the Stanley Cup over there after the season," Talbot explained to The Z. "Malkin knew Ovechkin, and introduced me to him, and the first impression wasn't great. I'm not really gonna say what happened, but I'm like, 'Okay, this guy is a real douche.'"

Thinking of an opponent as a "douche" isn't quite the same as Toronto playing Montreal fourteen times a season for decades to create a rivalry, but if this was what the NHL had to work with, so be it.

The outdoor game got a boost from a pre-Christmas game between the teams that went to a shootout, the Penguins prevailing, as well as from three episodes of the HBO series documenting the lives of the players in the weeks leading up to the New Year's Day game.

But the January 1 game itself, while setting records for TV viewers in the United States, will be remembered for all the wrong reasons – namely bad weather, a dull performance from Ovechkin, and, worst of all, a serious concussion to Crosby, which the NHL didn't just ignore but actively swept under the rug entirely, as if it had never happened.

The weather was a topic of conversation fully a week before the game because the forecast every day that week was for rain, and it showed no sign of changing before the opening faceoff. NHL commissioner Gary Bettman, as was his way with everything, steadfastly refused to alter the starting time of the game – Saturday, 1:00 p.m. – but the league did have contingency plans.

First, the game could be rescheduled for Saturday evening. Second, it could be played the next day, Sunday. Third, it could be cancelled and moved indoors later in the season, in which case all tickets for the Heinz Field game would have to be refunded at the point of purchase, an option only slightly more palatable than, say, waterboarding for the NHL.

Even on December 30, John Collins, the NHL's chief operating officer, was confident: "We're planning to play at one o'clock," he maintained.

The next day, December 31, was special, because the two teams played an alumni game under perfect conditions. Penguins owner Mario Lemieux skated for the first time since retiring, and he was joined by Paul Coffey, Ron Francis, and Bryan Trottier, among many other former stars. The game was a huge success and ended 5–5 before 10,000 fans. Caps players included Peter Bondra, Paul Mulvey, and Mark Lofthouse. The most unique participant was certainly Rod Buskas, who was a pilot for Hawaiian Airlines in his post-NHL life. "I go to paradise when I go to work every day," he joked.

After a flood, the current Penguins and then the Caps practised on the outdoor ice for the first time.

Later that day, though, less than twenty-four hours before the opening faceoff, the league finally decided to postpone the game to 8:00 p.m. Saturday night, hoping the inevitable rain would come and go and that ice czar Dan Craig and his crew would have time to whip the ice into a playable state. It was the only solution given the downpour that Pittsburgh experienced Saturday during the day, but weather was still a factor at night.

"I don't see anything wrong with playing underneath the lights," Crosby said with the political correctness of the league's playing-spokesman. "I think that would be pretty nice. Whatever the scenario, I think we've got a pretty open mind to whatever happens, and we should all be enjoying ourselves."

Ovechkin agreed. "For me, it's better if it's going to be evening because it's like we have a game almost every time. So, if it's going to be at eight, it's going to be okay because you can sleep, you can eat normal food, and take a nap before the game. If it's going to be at eight," he ended with a mischievous smile, "you can celebrate New Year's, too."

By the time of the opening faceoff, the ice was in barely passable shape. Crews had removed an incredible 3,000 gallons of water from the ice surface and tried to get it firm enough to play. Small puddles dotted each end, and bad bounces made the puck look like a tennis ball all too often, rendering the "skill players" ineffective. As Bruce Boudreau said after the game in typical humour, "That ice was melting faster than Frosty the Snowman."

This was too bad as both teams had been playing well in the time leading up to the game. Pittsburgh was a staggering 16–3–1 in its last twenty games while the Caps, after snapping an HBO-inspired eight-game losing streak, were 4–0–1 in their last five games. The Penguins' previous game was a disappointing 2–1 loss to the New York Islanders in a shootout, a loss made worse because Isles' goalie Rick DiPietro shut down Crosby, ending 87's 25-game point-scoring streak.

"It's always easy to look back," Crosby said afterwards, not as disappointed about the streak as about the loss. "There are times when I got points over the span of that streak when I didn't have as many chances as I did tonight, but I put one in, or someone else put one in . . . There were chances to be had [tonight], and they didn't go in."

The New Year's Day game was the first of the season for Jordan Staal; the previously resilient forward had missed the entire season to date with hand and wrist injuries. The two coaches presented polar opposite pictures behind the bench.

Dan Bylsma went for the Original Six look, sporting a fedora, while Boudreau, bald as a billiard ball, sported only his bare dome for the chilly evening game.

Bylsma started Crosby and Malkin on the same line, a rare occurrence outside of the power play or final minute of a period, and goalie Marc-Andre Fleury had trouble seeing the puck at his end of the ice. The two star attractions each had one nice moment in the opening period.

Ovechkin bore down on defenceman Zbynek Michalek behind the Pittsburgh net and thundered him into the boards, dislodging the glass and delaying the game. Later in the period, Crosby made a great play at the Capitals blue line. He took a pass by chipping the puck past defenceman Mike Green, who moved up to check him, and raced past him. Green flat-footed, turned, and hauled Crosby to the ice, earning a two-minute penalty that could have easily been called a penalty shot.

The first period was intense, the best of the game, with plenty of hitting, one fight, and a good atmosphere that epitomized what playing outdoors was all about. Not so the second period. It started to drizzle during the first intermission, and the drizzle got more intense to the point that by the midway mark of the game it was adversely affecting play.

Ovechkin had a breakaway early in the second but was stopped by Fleury, and moments later the two had another showdown, Fleury stopping Ovi point-blank to keep the game scoreless. The first goal came thanks to Malkin, who scored between Semyon Varlamov's pads on a clear break.

The Capitals got two goals later in the period, though. They tied the game on a scramble in the crease, and a few minutes later Fleury mishandled the puck behind his own net. Eric Fehr got it in the slot and snapped it into the open goal. Action went back and forth but there were few quality scoring chances because of ice and weather conditions.

And then it happened. The play that changed Sidney Crosby's career.

In the dying moments of the second period, he skated into the Washington end as the Caps had control of the puck. He was simply doing a little light forechecking, and the Caps made a pass up ice. The puck went by Crosby's leg, and he turned to see where it was going. He curled to skate back down ice. As he did, David Steckel skated by him and drilled the unsuspecting Crosby directly in the head with his right shoulder.

The camera angle from above and behind the Caps net showed an unflattering view of Steckel running Crosby over, almost oblivious to the player directly in his path. Crosby twirled in mid-air, fell to the ice on his side, slowly turned and got to his knees, and spat out his mouthguard. He skated slowly to the bench as time expired. No penalty was called on the play, although it was clearly a foul that could be penalized as (a) a direct head shot, (b) elbowing, (c) interference, (d) roughing, (e) unsportsmanlike conduct, or (f) all of the above.

Not only did Crosby come out for the third period, however, he played more in the final period than either of the first two, skating for 9:28, nearly half the period. He had 7:31 of ice time in the first and 7:57 in the second. He wasn't particularly effective, though, which was unusual because he always seemed to rise to the occasion, and with his team down a goal, at home before 68,111 fans, this was clearly "an occasion." But given that he had had his proverbial bell rung, his ineffectiveness was hardly surprising.

Fehr got the only goal of the third period, snapping a shot over Fleury's glove on a partial breakaway, and Ovechkin scored another that was disallowed because he interfered with the goalie. But when the game ended, Ovechkin celebrated like he had won the Stanley Cup, his exaggerated jubilation not quite matching the only moderate importance of the game.

At a press conference after the game, Crosby was diplomatic but clearly affected by the Steckel hit. "I couldn't even tell you what happened," he began. "I think the puck was going the other way, and I turned, and the next thing I know, I'm down. I can't really comment on it. I think it's pretty far behind the play, so maybe the refs didn't even see it. A lot of people didn't, but . . . I don't even know, honestly, I don't. He got my head, that's for sure, but . . . I don't even know how it developed."

Steckel had a different explanation: "I was backing up," he said, although he was clearly skating forward on the play. "The puck was going the other way. I was looking the other way. I guess he hit me. I haven't seen it yet. Obviously, it wasn't intentional."

For only the second time in their careers, neither Crosby nor Ovechkin registered a point in a game they played against each other. Incredibly, though, they both had exactly the same career points totals, 571, before (and after) the game.

Indeed, the Winter Classic was a tale of two opposites. While Ovechkin basked in the HBO glory of victory, Crosby slumped in the dark of what was to become a lengthy and horrific bout of post-concussion syndrome.

WHAT A CONCUSSION
SOUNDS LIKE

JANUARY 5, 2011: HBO *24/7*, EPISODE 4

The fourth and final episode of the HBO series focused, of course, on the New Year's Day outdoor game, played before 68,111 fans at Heinz Field in Pittsburgh. Unfortunately, it made not even passing reference to the alumni game on New Year's Eve, played before a capacity crowd of 10,000, in which Mario Lemieux participated.

As for the outdoor game itself, Washington's Brooks Laich noted beforehand, "It's a great game only if you win it."

Ovechkin had one comment as he came to the stadium for the game: "Fuck this Shitsburgh."

What HBO provided, which was lacking from the television broadcast, was a frank assessment of the ice, namely its poor condition. Caps coach Bruce Boudreau stressed that the soft and sticky ice required hard passes and shots, not pretty plays. Shoot when you get the chance, was his strategy.

HBO also provided what might turn out to be unique and valuable footage of Crosby just moments after he suffered his concussion. As the second period ended, he skated to the bench in a daze and then went to the dressing room with his teammates. As he sat at his stall, he was clearly still reeling, wiping his brow with a gesture that suggested ongoing discomfort. As cameras picked things up, a teammate continued a conversation with him by saying, "You don't remember what happened?"

Crosby answered, "I turned and just got hit. I don't know. I didn't have the puck or anything."

He played the third period and the next game four days later, and then missed the rest of the season because of post-concussion syndrome. That hit cost Crosby the Rocket Richard Trophy, the Art Ross Trophy, and almost certainly the Ted Lindsay Award as well. It cost David Steckel not so much as a two-minute minor penalty, a one-game suspension, or a $500 fine. Indeed, it was almost certainly one of the "accidental" concussions (i.e., unpunished) to which NHL commissioner Gary Bettman referred to at the All-Star Game in trying to explain the increase in concussions this season.

And so, the HBO series ended. After a month of following the players of both teams around, after covering the outdoor game until the winners went home happy and the losers miserable, viewers learned that hockey people swear a lot and are tough as nails. They learned that a team is like a family of brothers; that losing is unendurable agony, and winning, its joyous counterpoint; but did they learn more about Crosby and Ovechkin, how they tick, why they're great? Probably not.

OVI ENTERTAINS WHILE
CROSBY REMAINS IN THE DARK

JANUARY 30, 2011: THE 58TH NHL ALL-STAR GAME

O n November 10, 2010, the NHL attempted to add another chapter in the Crosby-Ovechkin file through a press conference regarding the NHL All-Star Game to be hosted by the Carolina Hurricanes on January 30, 2011. The NHL and the NHLPA jointly announced a new setup for the glitter game in which two captains would choose the players for their respective teams *à la* road hockey, where two kids call out names alternately to build their teams. The new format was the brainchild of Brendan Shanahan, the vice president of hockey and business development for the league.

The format was simple. First, fans would choose the starting six players, as they have done in recent years. The NHL's Hockey Operations would then choose the next 36 players for a total of 42 – two teams of 21 players: 3 goalies, 6 defencemen, and 12 forwards. On top of this group of players, Hockey Operations would add another 12 rookies for the skills competition (doing away with the Young Stars game in the process), so that a total of 54 players would participate in the All-Star Weekend. Those 54 players would then choose two captains, any two players from among their number.

Of course, the ideal scenario would have had Crosby and Ovechkin named as the two captains, but this was rendered impossible for two reasons. First, and most significantly, Crosby was still suffering from post-concussion syndrome and had to withdraw from the All-Star Game. Second, Ovechkin was having a very un-Ovi-like season to date and didn't deserve to be one of the captains, especially without Crosby as his counterpart. As a result, the players selected the forty-year-old future Hall of Famer, Nicklas Lidstrom, as one captain and Eric Staal, captain of the host city Carolina's Hurricanes, as the other.

The weekend of events kicked off on Friday, January 28, with a draft conducted by Lidstrom and Staal. They filled out their team's rosters by alternating selections, and then each captain took another six rookies for the skills contest. The ignominy of being the final selection went to Phil Kessel of the Leafs, further embarrassment to the team, which had had another poor season despite being the hockey capital of the world.

Ovechkin was chosen by Staal's assistant captain and Washington teammate Mike Green third overall. Both Green and Ovechkin barely arrived in time for the ceremony, having missed their early flight from Raleigh. "We were at the bar," Ovechkin jokingly explained of their late arrival.

The format change was the most radical in NHL All-Star Game history, which had its first incarnation in 1947, a showdown between the Stanley Cup champion and a "best of the rest" all-star team. What had used to be a fiercely competitive battle of pride and loyalty had turned into a dull game in recent decades, one with no hitting, no competitive spirit, and little entertainment.

In the last twenty years, low points included high scores with little excitement; Brett Hull playing without a helmet to prove the game's lack of animosity; formats like North America vs. the World that were politically correct and equally dull; a weekend that catered only to the NHL's corporate sponsors with few tickets available for fans. This new format was exciting and generated immediate buzz. It could not but succeed, if only for its novelty, and both the NHL and the players' association deserved full marks for trying to revive interest in the game.

The draft on January 28, 2011, did just that. The game two days later did not.

But in between there was the skills competition, and Ovechkin did his part to entertain the crowd. He won the breakaway contest when he skated in over the blue line while holding the puck down with the butt end of his stick and then flipping the stick properly and beating a prone Marc-Andre Fleury with a simple deke. In an earlier attempt, he bounced the puck off the blade of his stick several times while skating in on goal before swatting at it. Fleury made the save that time.

Ovechkin received 38.5 per cent of the text votes submitted following the competition, a result that shocked even him, given Corey Perry's highly entertaining lacrosse-style move in which Perry handled the puck on the blade of his stick extended high above his head. He then ripped a shot off the crossbar, likely his undoing because the fans wanted goals.

Ovechkin attributed his win to his "magic hands" but admitted, "It's pretty hard to create something when you see these guys make some sick moves like Perry did." Perry finished with just 12.2 per cent of the votes.

It was the third straight time Ovechkin won the breakaway contest, having won in 2008 and 2009 (the 2010 festivities had been postponed because of the Olympics).

Ovechkin also took part in the hardest-shot contest, but he was well behind the top guns of Zdeno Chara (Boston) and

Shea Weber (Nashville). He broke one stick on the breakaway event, and after clocking 98.2 mph on another, he broke his only other stick, so that he had to borrow a twig from Kris Letang of the dreaded Penguins. "I didn't think I was going to need three sticks for the skills competition," he joked.

As for the game itself on Sunday afternoon, Ovechkin scored the opening goal in the first minute of play, his shot from the side boards at a bad angle bouncing off the skate of Duncan Keith and past Marc-Andre Fleury for a 1–0 Team Staal lead.

Ovechkin deliberately had a hand in All-Star Game history midway through the game. While Team Lidstrom's Matt Duchene went in on a breakaway in a 7–7 game, Ovechkin playfully and purposefully threw his stick to try to distract Duchene. This resulted in a penalty shot, the first ever in the game's history.

"Why not? It's fun," Ovechkin theorized. "I think fans love it. It's a good moment. He didn't score, right? I want to be in history, so now I'm in history."

Ovechkin and Team Staal had an early 4–0 lead in the game but lost 11–10. Still, everyone had some fun. "I like it," Ovechkin said. "Lots of offense with no defense." He went home with one prized souvenir anyway, a sweater signed by all his teammates.

Meanwhile, that same day, Crosby was cleared by doctors to begin light skating. It looked like a sign of progress in his battle with post-concussion syndrome. It wasn't.

THE CONCUSSION
AND THE SLUMP

FEBRUARY 5, 2011

The concern over the concussion Pittsburgh's 87 had suffered as a result of the Steckel hit soon developed into a far greater worry. On January 5, Crosby played in the team's next game, a home date against Tampa Bay, and again an incident in the second period proved worrisome.

Crosby was checked into the end boards by Victor Hedman. It was a tough hit but not particularly vicious, and Crosby dropped to the ice hard after hitting his head against the glass. Hedman got a boarding minor, but the damage done was much greater than the penalty suggested, the significant residual effect from the Steckel hit now compounded by this new hit to the head, leaving Crosby dazed.

Still, he played on, finishing with more than nineteen minutes of ice time in the game but feeling unwell afterwards. The team – including Crosby – travelled overnight to Montreal for a game against the Canadiens on the 6th, but Crosby was not in the lineup.

In the end, he would miss the rest of the regular season – and all of the playoffs; 48 games in total – recovering from a concussion. In discussing the Steckel hit with TSN, Crosby was as opinionated as he has ever been in his career, voicing displeasure at the league for ignoring the two head hits and for not punishing either Steckel or Hedman.

"It's really tough to decide if he meant to or didn't mean to [hit me]," Crosby said of the play with Steckel during the outdoor game. "I feel he could have gotten out of the way and avoided me. Whether he tried to hurt me, only he knows. We'll never know that, but you still have to be responsible out there. I don't see anything; he sees me there. He sees the whole ice, and he doesn't avoid me. I don't think that's responsible on his part. He's got to be the one to try to avoid me in that situation."

Crosby expanded: "You talk about headshots and dealing with them; that's something that's been a pretty big point of interest from GMs and players. When I look at those two hits and we talk about [blindsiding] – that's a big word – [an] unsuspecting player, there was no puck there on both of them. It was a direct hit to the head on both of them. If you go through the criteria, I think they fit all those.

"I know it's a fast game; I've been hit a thousand times. When you get hit like that, there's nothing you can do. There's no way to protect yourself. Those are things that hopefully they pay more attention to. It's easy saying that being in this situation, but those are two hits I can't say I should have done something different or had my head down. I wouldn't change anything."

His emotion came from the nature of the injury, for which the treatment is far less certain or tangible than for any injury he'd previously experienced. "It's a little bit different than a shoulder or things like that," he said. "That, you can play through in the course of the season." As for a head injury? "It's pretty serious," he said, sounding very much concerned.

"Who knows when I actually got it," he said of the concussion. "Wednesday throughout the [Tampa] game, I just didn't feel right. Does that mean that I had all these huge symptoms? No. There are just times when you play, and you feel there's a difference. I would compare it to when you're sick; you just feel a little off. That's when I went to the doctor after the game and told them that things felt a little off.

"At that point, my head was starting to hurt me a little bit more. But leading up to that, it was a lot more neck than head. And that was to be expected considering what happened [with the Steckel hit]. You're hit a lot in hockey, and you have neck soreness; that's pretty typical. Wednesday, when it started to get more in my head and I felt a little off, that's when I saw the red flag."

Several vital questions about the league's operations come into play. First, consider the timeline. January 1, Crosby suffered a concussion that he felt at first was nothing more than a stiff neck. The game was played in Pittsburgh, and the Penguins didn't play again until the 5th, also at home. During this game, Crosby suffered further head damage as a result of a much less intense hit, a clear indicator that the Steckel hit had softened the brain for further damage. The team, with Crosby, flew that night to Montreal for a game the next night, and it was during that day, January 6, that Crosby finally felt something was wrong enough that he couldn't play that night. At that point, he flew back to Pittsburgh.

The injury "is not connected" to the Steckel hit, coach Dan Bylsma said in Montreal that night, adding, "When he woke up this morning, we decided he was not going to play in the game, and he'd be evaluated back in Pittsburgh." Fortunately, Matt Cooke had chartered a plane to Pittsburgh that day because of a family illness, so Crosby joined him. When he was evaluated, doctors discovered a marked difference from his baseline testing done while healthy during training camp. The change clearly indicated a concussion.

During the summer of 2010, the NHL insisted on a stronger rule 48 that included new wording for a hit to the head – "a lateral or blindside hit to an opponent where the head is targeted." Crosby had had no clue Steckel was about to run him down (i.e., it was a blindside hit), and he was hit squarely in the head. Incredibly, the league didn't suspend Steckel after reviewing the play and GM Ray Shero didn't express a particularly strong opinion about the hit.

More incredibly, Crosby still lived at home with owner Mario Lemieux. Wouldn't the owner have been furious about the hit? Wouldn't he have insisted in the ensuing four days between games that Crosby be thoroughly checked by doctors, just to be absolutely, perfectly certain that the injury was as minor as Crosby, not a doctor, had suggested? Watching a replay of the hit, Crosby spinning in mid-air, spitting his mouthguard out in clear discomfort, should have been enough to justify having him, at the very least, evaluated.

And after the second hit, by Hedman, which had Crosby again clearly reeling, how could the team not have taken him from the game and had him undergo every test in the books to determine his health? The Penguins weren't at fault for the hits, of course, but considering Crosby was their prime asset and the league's most dynamic player, shouldn't they have been more cautious?

As for the date of his return, the league's marquee player and leading scorer could only guess. "I think it's kind of a process," he said, by now a month off the ice. "You just go based on your symptoms. Hopefully, soon I'll be symptom-free and be able to start doing exercises. If I can get through that, I will go to the next step and start skating. Hopefully it will be sooner rather than later."

But Crosby sounded a note of caution as well. "You have to rely on the doctors and what they say. It's important to let them know your symptoms and everything going on. There will be a lot of communication that way. There has to be no symptoms [before starting exercise again]."

A week later, it was clear Crosby was nowhere near ready to resume skating and coach Dan Bylsma was getting tired of the same questions about his star centre every day. So, he issued a polite but firm edict to reporters: "We're not going to give daily updates on Sidney Crosby. As we've stated, he needs to be symptom-free to move forward. When there's an update, we'll give that to you."

A day later, he did offer a tidbit to keep the press happy. "Physical activity is not something that he's involved in right now, but he's been around the rink an awful lot talking hockey, thinking about the power play, doing things to try to stay motivated and be involved."

Ironically, Crosby was finally cleared by doctors for light skating on Friday, January 28, just as players were arriving for the NHL's All-Star Game Weekend. But light skating was a very conservative term that involved nothing more than putting on a pair of sweat pants and taking a spin around the ice. Three days later, Bylsma offered a somewhat more meaningful update.

"He's been on the ice, but, literally, it's in track pants up and down the ice, not in a workout-type mode. Light rehab is very light exercise," he stressed. "Moderate, very moderate biking activity. It's very light activity, and that's part of what the doctors have prescribed as his functional rehab at this point. Again, progressing to the next level means he has to get better in certain areas, and he's going through that process right now."

By the time the Penguins and Capitals hooked up for a matinee on Super Bowl Sunday, their first meeting since the Steckel hit, Crosby was still far from being healthy enough to play again. In fact, he had returned to Nova Scotia to spend several days with his parents, his light skating producing nothing positive to report and his return far from impending.

"If you had seen Sid around the rink, he's still thinking about hockey, maybe even more now," Bylsma explained. "This was an opportunity to kind of take a step back from that and get some rest and relaxation for the mind and the body, try and take his mind off hockey a little bit."

As for the other half of the Sid vs. Ovi rivalry, questions persisted about Alex Ovechkin, and those questions revolved around one theme – what was wrong with *him*? Ovechkin entered the game with just 20 goals and 55 points in 53 games on the season. He was ninth place in the league's scoring race. These were stats that another player would have enjoyed, but for Ovi he was on pace for the *fewest* goals and points in his career, and by a long margin at that. Furthermore, this marked the fourth straight season his production decreased and at a stage in his career when fans and followers would have assumed his numbers would have increased as he matured and gained experience.

The usual answer to this central and recurring question was that Ovechkin was saving himself for the playoffs. He had too often gone all out in the regular season only to have a disappointing run in the playoffs, and now he hoped to ease his foot off the gas during the 82-game marathon that was the regular season and save the afterburners for the playoffs.

If this were indeed the case, it was a risky game he was playing. Players can't just stop and start producing offence like that, and saving energy over a long season offers no guarantees or promises of greater things to come in the play-offs, when action is more intense anyway.

Furthermore, Ovechkin continued to do what he did best – shoot the puck. He was still leading the league in shots on goal, with 249, but obviously he just wasn't scoring as much. This was in part due to goalies bearing down more on him, but also reflected that he wasn't getting shots of the same quality.

"The reason is all about me," he admitted. "I've had chances to score goals and I haven't, so now people will say, you know, 'he's no good any more,' and then I'll have a ten-, fifteen-game scoring streak, and that will all go away. I'm not worried about it."

Much of the blame for decline can go to the Caps' new team play, which emphasized a defence-first system, as Eric Fehr admitted. "It's a pretty big change. We're really limiting teams' opportunities to gain speed in the neutral zone . . . We're sitting back a little more, which is different for this team."

Brooks Laich noted that what you practise in the regular season is what you preach when it counts, during the play-offs. "We haven't had the success we've wanted," he admitted. "We've had great regular season success. Ultimately, we lost one-goal games in the playoffs that sent us home in April."

As important, teams were starting to key on Ovechkin like never before – and he had failed to find another gear to let him continue scoring in the face of the additional attention. "If I have a puck, I have two guys around me all the time," he acknowledged. "And the third guy comes down behind me, slash me, or do something like that."

Teams were playing smarter defensively against him. They weren't allowing him to cut to the middle, in the slot, to let rip a shot. They weren't giving him the space between their legs where he loved to shoot. They were keeping him to the outside, closer to the boards, where his wicked shot was rendered ineffective. He simply wasn't adjusting.

"Time will move forward, and we are going to find a way to play against this strategy," he vowed.

Coach Bruce Boudreau blamed the poor performance with the extra man. "I think his scoring touch will come when our power play starts to click the way it's supposed to," he explained. "This time last year, we had about twenty-five power-play goals, and he must have had about twelve of those. Now, he has two. As the unit improves, his numbers will come right back up to what he's used to."

Regardless, a Pittsburgh-Washington game in February at an important time of the season lacked much of the usual drama because the game's greatest player was injured and its second-greatest was mired in a lengthy scoring slump (for whatever reason one might choose to believe). The two players who were the talk of the town for saving the game in the post-lockout era were now the talk of the town for all the wrong reasons.

A DULL AFFAIR

FEBRUARY 6, 2011: PITTSBURGH 0 AT WASHINGTON 3

Fans who bought tickets to this game at the beginning of the year hoping for another chapter in the Sid vs. Ovi rivalry were disappointed by the time they got to the Verizon Center on this night, for Crosby was still recovering from the concussion he'd suffered during the outdoor game on New Year's Day. This was only the second time in thirty NHL meetings between the two teams that one of the players did not play.

Making the game even more of a letdown was the absence of Evgeni Malkin, who had missed the previous five games with a left knee injury. He had returned to the lineup two nights earlier, against Buffalo, but was hit by hulking defenceman Tyler Myers along the boards and now suffered a serious injury to his other knee. The right knee's ACL and MCL were torn, requiring season-ending surgery for "Geno."

Nonetheless, a game that lacked the usual Crosby-Ovechkin drama was crazily significant because of those two players.

The first period was uneventful to the point of dull, with few scoring chances going either way and without even a power play to enliven matters. As the period ended, though, Washington defenceman Mike Green was hit in the ear by a slapshot. He fell to the ice, creating a pool of blood, and he didn't return to action because of dizziness.

The Caps got the only goal within the opening twenty minutes when Brooks Laich scooped home a rebound, and they made it 2–0 early in the second period on a short-handed goal from Marcus Johansson.

The third period was where the action was. Midway through, Tim Wallace, playing his first game of the season for the Penguins, challenged Steckel to a fight, retribution for the hit on Crosby on New Year's Day. Then, near the end of the game, Matt Cooke delivered another in a series of dirty hits that went unpunished by the league. He clipped Ovechkin just below the knee, and number 8 fell to the ice in pain. He stayed down for just a moment, but for any Caps fan that moment was very scary.

"It's Matt Cooke, okay? Need we say more?" Washington coach Bruce Boudreau later asked rhetorically. "It's not like it's his first rodeo. He's done it to everybody and then he goes to the ref and says, 'What did I do?' He knows darn well what he did. There's no doubt in my mind that he's good at it and he knows how to do it. He knows how to pick this stuff."

More contemptuous and dismissive, Ovechkin said only, "That's his game. He plays like that."

Ovechkin could say that; he had been lucky. He had narrowly missed a serious injury like the ones Crosby and Malkin hadn't been fortunate enough to avoid.

Mike Knuble scored an empty-netter to round out the scoring, but Ovechkin was ineffective all game and the Pens continued to miss Crosby. Although they were 8–4 without him, they couldn't keep winning forever without their captain.

LOW POINT IN THE RIVALRY

FEBRUARY 21, 2011: WASHINGTON 1 AT PITTSBURGH 0

The last regular-season meeting between the Caps and the Pens occurred too early in the season for it to have any post-season meaning, but by this time playoff fever was in the air. Crosby's season was in serious jeopardy, but Ovechkin was playing a bit better, and the Caps were clearly headed to the Cup chase again.

Was there any doubt already that Ovechkin was the greatest hockey player ever produced by the Soviet Union or Russia? He was as great a skater as any of his countrymen; his shot was without compare; his scoring ability was sensational. He was captain of his team and had played for his country each and every opportunity he had been given.

The list of great Russians in the NHL is not long. Think Pavel Bure. Perhaps a greater skater than Ovi but he never had the game-breaker ability as a scorer. What about Alexander Mogilny? Pure scorer as well, but with not an ounce of the physical presence of Ovechkin. Sergei Fedorov? As a member of the Red Wings dynasty, he was an exceptional two-way player, but his role was always second fiddle to Steve Yzerman or Slava Fetisov. Alexei Yashin? Huge contract, to be sure, but a disastrously selfish player who disappeared when times were tough or games important. Ilya Kovalchuk? Tremendous shot and an international resumé of excellent quality, but again not a game breaker, and he had played for his entire NHL career with non-playoff teams.

There was but one thing missing on Ovechkin's resumé, and that was victory at the highest level. He had a World Championship gold medal, which was a start, but he hadn't taken the Caps anywhere close to the Stanley Cup. When he came closest, in game seven of the Conference finals against Pittsburgh in 2009, he was overwhelmed by Crosby.

At the 2006 and 2010 Olympics, the team fell noticeably short both times. Ovechkin's skills were unquestioned and his individual accomplishments irrefutable, but he had yet to win that huge game that defined the greatest of the great athletes.

Although this was a game that was supposed to be the grand finale in a season-long rivalry, there was more than a little that was anticlimactic about the last regular-season meeting between the teams. In part, it was Ovechkin's seemingly endless scoring slump – or, scoring mediocrity – but in larger part it was Crosby's prolonged absence from the game.

On February 10, five weeks after the hit and without having played again, Crosby talked about the possibility of missing the rest of the season. "It could happen," he told a scrum of reporters gathered at the Consol Energy Center for an update. "But am I sitting here packing it in? No. I hope I'm back, and, geez, I hope I play this year. But that's the thing with these things – you don't know. There's no time frame. I'm expecting to play this year."

The nature of the injury was not something to be trifled with, as he was learning quickly. "It's a little different when you're talking about your brain. It's scary. But, to a certain extent, there's nothing you can do except give yourself a chance to heal and hope that it happens sooner rather than later. The progression is improving, but it's at a slower rate than I'd want it to be."

And so it was that as players from both teams, Ovechkin included, skated out for the fourth meeting of the season between the Pens and the Caps, Crosby was sitting at home working the remote.

In fact, the Penguins dominated the game, but Ovechkin got its only goal. He was stoned by Marc-Andre Fleury on a first-period breakaway after getting a perfect outlet pass from Nicklas Backstrom, but the Pens were dominant all night. They lost only because of a lack of finish and to the great play of Caps' goalie Michal Neuvirth, who stopped all 39 shots he faced, including Jordan Staal on a breakaway only moments before the only goal of the game.

Ovechkin's 24th goal of the season came late in the second period on a blast from the point on the power play, one of the hardest shots he's ever unleashed. "That is what he does, and this is what he wasn't doing in the first 45–50 games," Capitals coach Bruce Boudreau said of Ovechkin, who scored his third goal in four games. "He wasn't getting his shot off. I didn't even see it [the goal] in the replay at all. He has been playing like that for the last two weeks and being a real leader."

The Pens were now 10–8–2 without Crosby, and the Caps were now 10–0–2 against the Penguins in their last twelve regular-season games dating back to the start of the 2008–09 season. They'd also won the last seven games played in Pittsburgh.

The only question now was whether the teams would face each other in the playoffs, or whether Crosby and Ovechkin would next meet at the NHL Awards ceremony in June.

EPILOGUE

SID AND OVI MISS OUT
AT NHL AWARDS

JUNE 22, 2011

A season that was so widely anticipated in training camp by the hockey world for the Crosby-Ovechkin rivalry ended in such disappointment that neither player was even a factor at the NHL Awards Ceremony in June in Las Vegas, at which one or both had been central figures in each of the last five seasons.

Crosby might well have won the Art Ross Trophy, Hart Memorial Trophy, Rocket Richard Trophy, and Ted Lindsay Award based on his play over the first half of the season, but on this night he was at home, his career uncertain, trying to eliminate post-concussion syndrome from his life.

Even two months later, David Steckel was still trying to maintain his innocence on the play that altered the life and career of Crosby. "It was completely unintentional," Steckel reiterated in early March. "I didn't mean to hit him at all. I tried to get out of the way. It's unfortunate because I feel really bad that he's been out for so long."

Steckel explained that he had talked to Penguins player David Engelland, a teammate with Steckel when they were in Hershey in the AHL, after the New Year's Day game, and asked him to tell Crosby he was sorry.

Breaking news occurred on March 14, 2011, when Crosby was cleared by doctors to skate for the first time. He skated for fifteen minutes in full equipment after being symptom-free for a week, the first step on the road back to the team. He skated again the next day, a clear indication that he was symptom-free after his first skate. After taking a day off, he skated again for a third time in four days, but he tempered any optimism with strong caution.

"I don't want symptoms, and I obviously don't want to rush anything," Crosby explained. "It's something you can't rush. It's going to take time."

A week later, Crosby was skating with teammates, another great sign. At the end of the month, he went on a road trip with the team to Florida, continuing to skate with other injured players, notably Nick Johnson, Matt Cooke, and Eric Tangradi. On March 31, he even skated with the team on the game-day skate for an hour in non-contact drills.

Fans got one last look at Crosby after the last home game of the regular season, when players gave away their sweaters. Called "Shirts Off Our Back" night, that night Crosby stepped out to the ice wearing a nice suit, holding an 87 sweater in his hand. Of course, attention to his condition intensified further with the playoffs at hand, but given his injury and lack of conditioning, rushing Crosby back for one playoff run in a career that will hopefully include another fifteen such runs would have been ludicrous.

But Crosby was not idle as the Penguins readied themselves for the first round of the playoffs, a best-of-seven series against Tampa Bay. He became an ad hoc assistant coach for the team, watching games from a private box and wearing a headset that connected him to Tony Granato, assistant coach behind the bench.

This contribution paled, of course, to what he could do on ice, evidenced by the team's shocking loss to the Lightning in seven games. Pittsburgh was leading the series 3–1, only to lose the last three games and face a longer-than-expected summer. The team scored only fourteen goals in the series, further indication that it badly needed Crosby's offence. Although the Pens' record without him in the lineup was impressive, its goal production had dropped.

Even worse, the team revealed that Crosby had had setbacks in his skating regimen and hadn't skated for a week. Doing the math, Tampa Bay eliminated Pittsburgh on April 27, so he hadn't skated since April 20. Since his return to the ice on March 31 was well publicized, this meant that after three weeks of skating, Crosby was now back to square one, unable to work up a sweat without experiencing post-concussion symptoms. At no time had he participated in contact drills.

"I've got to wait until I feel better before I can really start doing anything," Crosby said. "Hopefully, it's not too long, but as long as it takes to feel better and, hopefully, start training for next year. The progression was going well, but I still wasn't ready," he admitted. "Hopefully, the next step doesn't have any hurdles, and I can get ready for next season, as usual."

The words were chilling. What started out as a "minor concussion" now seemed like a career-threatening injury. Out since January 5 with no end in sight – and a nebulous structure of recovery called "simply rest" his only guidance – there seemed no guarantee whatsoever that he would be ready even for training camp in September.

His season was over and so was his team's, and the NHL Awards were the furthest thing from the minds of all concerned. Indeed, the only good news was that after attending the Cannes film festival in early May with some teammates, he was cleared to resume his off-ice summer training.

A similarly disappointing scenario played out in Washington. Ovechkin scored just 18 goals after the New Year's Day game, and three came in one game against Toronto at the Air Canada Centre. He finished the regular season with 32 goals and 85 points, his lowest totals, but the team had had a great season playing a more defensive system, finishing in top spot in the Eastern Conference with 48 wins and 107 points. As a result, Ovechkin had the chance to redeem himself in the playoffs.

That never happened.

The Caps disposed of the New York Rangers in five games but were then embarrassed in a four-game sweep by Tampa Bay. The highlight of the Rangers' series came in game four, which went to double overtime. New York's Marian Gaborik made a huge gaffe in front of his own goal, allowing Jason Chimera to poke the puck in and giving the Caps a commanding 3–1 series lead. They finished the Blueshirts off in the next game.

Against the Lightning, the Caps were inferior in every area of the game, from star power to coaching and goal-tending. Ovechkin had ten points in nine playoff games overall, but he wasn't sensational in any game, and didn't lead his team to greater heights or raise the level of his play by any substantive amount. True, two games in the Tampa Bay series were decided by one goal and two by two goals, but at the end of the day a loss is a loss. That was playoff hockey. Nothing special.

Making matters worse, the most visible face of the team after defeat was owner Ted Leonsis. An avid blogger who speaks to fans directly, he admitted the sweep by Tampa Bay was crushing. "Their role players outplayed our highest paid players," he admitted. Tampa's players "adhered to their coaches' system better than we adhered to our coaches' system. The wheels fell off for us. No doubt about that."

He continued: "In times like these, people are emotional, angry, and demand change. I understand. The best course of action for us, though, is to let a few days pass, be very analytic about what needs to be improved, articulate that plan, and then execute upon it."

Almost immediately after being eliminated, Ovechkin accepted an invitation to join Russia at the World Championship, a decision that perhaps reveals more than it should. The World Championship always runs concurrently with the first couple of rounds of the playoffs. Ovechkin has played for his country at the Worlds and various junior events every year since 2002 except 2009 (when the Caps went to the Conference finals). It seems that his spiritual and emotional attachment to playing for his country is greater than his physical willingness to get the job done in the Stanley Cup playoffs.

The 2011 World Championship was played in Slovakia, and Ovechkin arrived in Bratislava on May 7, ready to help his team try to win another gold medal. In seven previous Worlds, he had won a gold, a silver, and two bronze medals. This year, however, he was shockingly ineffective. In five games, he registered not a single point to go with two minor penalties. He was guilty of several turnovers, and his play had a direct effect on the team's play. Russia had only one win in those five games (a 2–1 quarter-finals gem against Canada) and finished in fourth place after losing the bronze-medal game to the Czechs by a 7–4 score. To say Ovechkin's play was uninspired is being kind.

And that was the end of the hockey season for Crosby and Ovechkin, the former having to spend the summer worrying about his career, the latter worried about his place in the game's pantheon, seemingly unable to lead his team to Stanley Cup glory and finishing on a low note at the World Championship. The 2010–11 season started with the Sid-Ovi rivalry as the centre of the hockey universe, but the season ended with questions marks which made the 2011–12 season intriguing, to say the least, for the two great stars.

LOOKING AHEAD TO SOCHI

FEBRUARY 7–23, 2014: OLYMPIC REMATCH

n addition to the usual assortment of minor penalties Crosby and Ovechkin have earned during their careers, they have picked up a few major penalties along the way. But even in this category they are different.

Ovechkin was first to draw a major penalty when, on September 28, 2006, he got into a fight with Philadelphia captain Mike Richards during a scrum in a pre-season game. Ovechkin rarely has looked so incensed, but Richards wrestled him to the ice before many punches were thrown. Two and a half months later, though, Ovechkin got into another incident in a regular-season game with Paul Gaustad of Buffalo, on December 2, 2006.

Ovechkin nailed Daniel Brière with a vicious blindside hit as Brière was heading off on a line change. Brière fell headfirst into the boards, and Gaustad came to his team-mate's defence immediately, drawing an instigator penalty, fighting major, and game misconduct. Ovechkin never dropped his gloves but received five minutes for fighting anyway, as well as a five-minute boarding penalty and game misconduct, though he drew no supplementary discipline over and above a $1,000 fine levied by Colin Campbell, NHL vice president.

"I just want to hit him," Ovechkin said of the play against Brière, "but he was turning and I don't have time to do something . . . I hope Brière is okay."

This was the only fight that he had been involved in prior to the 2010–11 season, but he has received three other game misconducts, all in the 2009–10 season, all because of dirty hits. And, Ovechkin also received a game misconduct during the 2007 World Championship in his hometown of Moscow, for a hit to the head of Swiss player Valentin Wirz. The penalty also resulted in an automatic one-game suspension. In December 2010, he got into his only real fight when he dropped the gloves to take on Brandon Dubinsky of the New York Rangers during a one-sided New York victory.

Although he wasn't kicked out of the game, Ovechkin's nastiest moment came in a game on January 1, 2009. He ended the career of former Caps teammate Jamie Heward, slamming his head into the glass as he chased Heward from behind. Heward was vulnerable on the play, but Ovi took full advantage knowing the glass was there. Heward was taken off on a stretcher.

Ovechkin's reaction to Heward's injury, while contrite, was of little consolation. Echoing his words after the Brière hit, he said, "I didn't want to hit him hard. He was turned. It was an accident, and I'm really sorry. I never hurt somebody, especially my old teammate."

Heward never played another game, retiring a year and a half later after it was clear the head injury was too severe to overcome.

Crosby has never been suspended or been given a game misconduct for a dirty hit, but he has been involved in six fights in his career, most notably during the calendar year 2009 spread over two seasons. What's interesting is that all of his fights, except the first, were attempts by him to rally his team.

Crosby's first fight occurred on December 20, 2007, against Andrew Ference of Boston. The two were chasing down a loose puck in the corner, jostling for position, and wound up dropping their gloves. Crosby had a goal and an assist in the first period and a fight in the second period to complete his "Gordie Howe hat trick," and the Pens won the game in a shootout. "It's not something I'm going to make a habit of, by any means," he said after losing his fistic virginity midway through his third NHL season. "You don't really plan it."

Ference was more lighthearted about the set-to. "I'm glad I could help him out with the assist, goal, and the fight," he offered. "I think we're probably about the same calibre of fighter. He probably picked a good partner for his first one."

Indeed, it was more than a year before he fought again. On January 3, 2009, in a game against Florida, the Panthers were dominating by late in the second period, leading 4–1 and in control. Crosby and Brett McLean fought off a faceoff, but Crosby was the instigator and got a double minor, a major, and a misconduct penalty. The Panthers extended their lead on the ensuing power play and won, 6–1. Crosby's actions drew praise and scorn both, players realizing he was trying to kick-start his team, others not so sure it was a smart strategy or McLean a willing combatant.

"Everybody can kind of understand what he's doing for his team there," McLean said. "He's their leader."

Florida's Nick Boynton wasn't convinced, though. "You don't jump a guy while his head's down taking a faceoff," he said. "That's pretty immature and childish."

Crosby fought in a Florida game again just three months later, this time in defence of Evgeni Malkin. Keith Ballard hit Malkin with a low check, which Crosby objected to, and he went right for Ballard after the hit, earning the instigator penalty again but in the name of defending one of the team's star players. Rare are the times, though, when the superstar captain of the team has to come to the defence of a teammate; usually it is the fourth-liner who does the dirty work. The game was tied 1–1 at the time and the Penguins eventually lost, 4–2, but Crosby stood up for his mate.

Crosby got into his fourth fight on Hallowe'en night 2009 against Minnesota's Marek Zidlicky. Late in the second period of a 2–1 Wild win, the players slashed at each other and then went one step further, dropping the gloves and duking it out in a veritable wrestling match. Both players received seven minutes in penalties, two for the initial slashing and five for fighting.

Crosby also tangled with Matt Niskanen on November 3, 2010, in a rough game that Dallas was leading comfortably at the time. "I never saw that coming," Niskanen said. "We were up 4–1, he was trying to get the team going a little bit, he asked me to go, and we went."

Of course, both players are physical in a physical game, but Ovechkin has a much bigger fight on his mind as the world looks to the next Olympic Winter Games, in Sochi, Russia, in 2014. His fight is to ensure NHL participation in those Olympics, a fight by no means close to being won.

NHL commissioner Gary Bettman has time and again refused to be lured into committing beyond Vancouver. On the one hand, he was making clear this would be a bargaining chip during the NHL-NHLPA negotiations leading to a new Collective Bargaining Agreement, the old one set to expire

September 15, 2012, but he was also trying to position the league in a place of power with the International Olympic Committee (IOC). Olympic participation was a windfall for the IOC but the NHL received no money – or, in Bettman's view, respect – for loaning the world's best hockey players to showcase the Olympics.

Bettman was trying to make sure NHL participation would be tied in with money, seemingly unaware of or unwilling to comprehend the concept of national pride, amateur participation, or loyalty to anything other than the dollar. Virtually every NHL player who might be expected to participate in the Olympics strongly recommended continued Olympic participation, leaving Bettman alone with his mantra of "There are good reasons to go to the Olympics, and good reasons not to go."

Ovechkin was defiant in stating categorically he would leave the Capitals in mid-season to play in Sochi, if that's what he had to do to play. He will surely be true to his word, but whether Crosby goes as well depends on the NHL.

APPENDIX

THE NUMBERS GAMES

NHL REGULAR SEASON

SIDNEY CROSBY

	GP	G	A	P	PIM
2005–06 PIT	81	39	63	102	110
2006–07 PIT	79	36	84	120	60
2007–08 PIT	53	24	48	72	39
2008–09 PIT	77	33	70	103	76
2009–10 PIT	81	51	58	109	71
2010–11 PIT	41	32	34	66	31
TOTALS	412	215	357	572	387

ALEX OVECHKIN

	GP	G	A	P	PIM
2005–06 WAS	81	52	54	106	52
2006–07 WAS	82	46	46	92	52
2007–08 WAS	82	65	47	112	40
2008–09 WAS	79	56	54	110	72
2009–10 WAS	72	50	59	109	89
2010–11 WAS	79	32	53	85	41
TOTALS	475	301	313	614	346

NHL PLAYOFFS

SIDNEY CROSBY

	GP	G	A	P	PIM
2005–06 PIT			DNQ		
2006–07 PIT	5	3	2	5	4
2007–08 PIT	20	6	21	27	12
2008–09 PIT	24	15	16	31	14
2009–10 PIT	13	6	13	19	6
2010–11 PIT			DNP		
TOTALS	62	30	52	82	36

ALEX OVECHKIN

	GP	G	A	P	PIM
2005–06 WAS			DNQ		
2006–07 WAS			DNQ		
2007–08 WAS	7	4	5	9	0
2008–09 WAS	14	11	10	21	8
2009–10 WAS	7	5	5	10	0
2010–11 WAS	9	5	5	10	10
TOTALS	37	25	25	50	18

NHL AWARDS

SIDNEY CROSBY

2007	HART TROPHY
2007	LESTER B. PEARSON AWARD
2007	ART ROSS TROPHY
2010	ROCKET RICHARD TROPHY (WITH STEVE STAMKOS)

ALEX OVECHKIN

2006	CALDER TROPHY
2008	ART ROSS TROPHY
2008	HART TROPHY
2008	LESTER B. PEARSON AWARD
2008	ROCKET RICHARD TROPHY
2009	HART TROPHY
2009	LESTER B. PEARSON AWARD
2009	ROCKET RICHARD TROPHY
2010	TED LINDSAY AWARD

INTERNATIONAL

SIDNEY CROSBY

		GP	G	A	P	PIM	FINISH
2004 WM20	CAN	6	2	3	5	4	S
2005 WM20	CAN	6	6	3	9	4	G
2006 WM	CAN	9	8	8	16	10	4TH
2010 OG	CAN	7	4	3	7	4	G
TOTALS	WM20	12	8	6	14	8	G,S

~IIHF DIRECTORATE WORLD CHAMPIONSHIP BEST FORWARD (2006), WORLD CHAMPIONSHIP ALL-STAR TEAM/FORWARD (2006)

ALEX OVECHKIN

		GP	G	A	P	PIM	FINISH
2002 U18-M	RUS	8	14	4	18	0	S
2003 U18-M	RUS	6	9	4	13	6	B
2003 U20	RUS	6	6	1	7	4	G
2004 U20	RUS	6	5	2	7	25	5TH
2005 U20	RUS	6	7	4	11	4	S
2004 WM	RUS	6	1	1	2	0	10TH

ALEX OVECHKIN (CONT'D)

		GP	G	A	P	PIM	FINISH
2004 WCH	RUS	2	1	0	1	0	6TH
2005 WM	RUS	8	5	3	8	4	B
2006 OG	RUS	8	5	0	5	8	4TH
2006 WM	RUS	7	6	3	9	6	5TH
2007 WM	RUS	8	1	2	3	29	B
2008 WM	RUS	9	6	6	12	8	G
2010 OG	RUS	4	2	2	4	2	6TH
2010 WM	RUS	9	5	1	6	4	S
2011 WM	RUS	5	0	0	0	4	4TH
TOTALS U18-M		14	23	8	31	6	S,B
TOTALS U20		18	18	7	25	33	G,S
TOTALS WM		52	24	16	40	55	G,S,2B
TOTALS OG		12	7	2	9	10	–

~WORLD CHAMPIONSHIP ALL-STAR TEAM/FORWARD (2006, 2008)

HEAD-TO-HEAD RESULTS

NHL REGULAR SEASON

		CROSBY			OVECHKIN		
DATE	**SCORE**	G	A	P	G	A	P
NOV. 22, 2005	WAS 4 AT **PIT 5**	1	1	2	0	1	1
JAN. 25, 2006	WAS 1 AT **PIT 8**	1	3	4	1	0	1
FEB. 11, 2006	**PIT 6** AT WAS 3	1	1	2	1	0	1
MAR. 8, 2006	PIT 3 AT **WAS 6**	0	1	1	1	2	3
DEC. 11, 2006	**PIT 5** AT WAS 4 (SO)	1	1	2	0	2	2 (1)
FEB. 3, 2007	WAS 0 AT **PIT 2**	0	0	0	0	0	0
FEB. 18, 2007	WAS 2 AT **PIT 3**	0	1	1	0	0	0
MAR. 27, 2007	**PIT 4** AT WAS 3	1	1	2	0	1	1
OCT. 20, 2007	**PIT 2** AT WAS 1	0	1	1	0	0	0
DEC. 27, 2007	WAS 3 AT **PIT 4** (OT)	0	2	2	1	0	1

NHL REGULAR SEASON (CONT'D)

DATE	SCORE	CROSBY			OVECHKIN		
		G	A	P	G	A	P
JAN. 21, 2008	**WAS 6** AT PIT 5 (SO)		DNP		2	1	3 (2)
MAR. 9, 2008	**PIT 4** AT WAS 2	2	0	2	0	2	2
OCT. 16, 2008	**WAS 4** AT PIT 3	0	2	2	0	0	0
JAN. 14, 2009	**WAS 6** AT PIT 3	0	2	2	2	1	3
FEB. 22, 2009	PITS 2 AT **WAS 5**	0	1	1	1	1	2
MAR. 8, 2009	**PIT 4** AT WAS 3 (SO)	1	1	2	1	0	1 (3)
JAN. 21, 2010	**WAS 6** AT PIT 3	1	0	1	2	1	3
FEB. 7, 2010	PIT 4 AT **WAS 5** (OT)	2	0	2	3	1	4
MAR. 24, 2010	PIT 3 AT **WAS 4** (SO)	0	1	1	0	1	1 (4)
APR. 6, 2010	**WAS 6** AT PIT 3	1	2	3	2	0	2
DEC. 23, 2010	**PIT 3** AT WAS 2 (SO)	1	1	2	0	0	0 (5)
JAN. 1, 2011	**WAS 3** AT PIT 1	0	0	0	0	0	0
FEB. 6, 2011	PIT 0 AT **WAS 3**		DNP		0	0	0
FEB. 21, 2011	**WAS 1** AT PIT 0		DNP		1	0	1

(1)—Crosby 0–1, Ovechkin 1–1 in shootout

(2)—Ovechkin 1–1 in shootout

(3)—Crosby 1–1, Ovechkin 0–1 in shootout

(4)—Crosby 1–1, Ovechkin 1–1 in shootout

(5)—Crosby 0–1, Ovechkin 1–1 in shootout

PLAYOFFS

DATE	SCORE	CROSBY G	CROSBY A	CROSBY P	OVECHKIN G	OVECHKIN A	OVECHKIN P
MAY 2, 2009	PIT 2 AT **WAS 3**	1	0	1	1	0	1
MAY 4, 2009	PIT 3 AT **WAS 4**	3	0	3	3	0	3
MAY 6, 2009	WAS 2 AT **PIT 3** (OT)	0	2	2	1	1	2
MAY 8, 2009	WAS 3 AT **PIT 5**	1	1	2	0	1	1
MAY 9, 2009	**PIT 4** AT WAS 3 (OT)	0	0	0	2	1	3
MAY 11, 2009	**WAS 5** AT PIT 4 (OT)	1	1	2	0	3	3
MAY 13, 2009	**PIT 6** AT WAS 2	2	1	3	1	0	1

INTERNATIONAL

DATE	EVENT	SCORE	CROSBY G	CROSBY A	CROSBY P	OVECHKIN G	OVECHKIN A	OVECHKIN P
JAN. 4, 2005	WM20	**CAN 6**–RUS 2	0	1	1	0	0	0
FEB. 24, 2010	OG	**CAN 7**–RUS 3	0	0	0	0	0	0

ALL-STAR GAMES

DATE	HOST	SCORE	CROSBY G	CROSBY A	CROSBY P	OVECHKIN G	OVECHKIN A	OVECHKIN P
JAN. 24, 2007	DALLAS	**WEST 12**– EAST 9	0	0	0	1	0	1*
JAN. 27, 2008	ATLANTA	**EAST 8**– WEST 7	DNP			2	0	2*
JAN. 25, 2009	MONTREAL	**EAST 12**– WEST 11	DNP			1	2	3*
JAN. 30, 2011	RALEIGH	**LIDSTROM** 11– STAAL 10	DNP			1	1	2**

*BOTH PLAYERS IN EAST

**OVECHKIN PLAYED FOR TEAM STAAL

ALL-STAR VOTING

	CROSBY	**OVECHKIN**
2007	825,783	475,297
2008	507,274	177,574
2009	1,713,021	470,276
2011	635,509	245,180
TOTAL	3,681,587	1,368,327

ACKNOWLEDGEMENTS

The author would like to thank the many people involved in supporting and producing the book, starting with M&S president and publisher Doug Pepper for his enthusiasm and support. Also to the team at M&S, namely Liz Kribs, Ruta Liormonas, Val Capuani, and Andrew Roberts. To the helpful staff at the Hillman Library, University of Pittsburgh, and the Library of Congress in Washington, D.C. To my agent, Dean Cooke, and his excellent assistant, Mary Hu, for sorting out the business side of the publishing process. And finally to those who are no rivals, namely Liz, Ian, Zac, Emily, my dear sweet mom, and lastly to the multi-dimensional Mary Jane Podnieks for her keen interest in my every book project.

Mary Jane Podnieks

ANDREW PODNIEKS is the author of more than sixty books on hockey. In addition, he has covered three Olympics and nine World Championships for the International Ice Hockey Federation (IIHF) and is the creator and editor of the *IIHF Media Guide & Record Book*.

Please visit **www.andrewpodnieks.com**.